BELIEVING *INTO* CHRIST

BELIEVING *INTO* CHRIST

Relational Faith and Human Flourishing

Natalya A. Cherry

BAYLOR UNIVERSITY PRESS

Cover and book design by Kasey McBeath
Cover image: Jason Gubbiotti, *One ON One* (for NS), 2021, acrylic on wood, 9 x 6 inches, courtesy of the artist and Civilian Art Projects

The Library of Congress has cataloged this book under ISBN 978-1-4813-1543-2.

Library of Congress Control Number: 2021939821

Printed in the United States of America on acid-free paper with a minimum of thirty percent recycled content.

In memory of Father Scott Pilarz, SJ, PhD, a colleague in the calling without whom I would be neither Reverend nor Doctor.

CONTENTS

ACKNOWLEDGMENTS

When the seed of this book was an incomplete dissertation proposal, I already was practicing bold surrender, thanks to a tornado that destroyed our home and most of its contents while we were away for Christmas. My gratitude to all of the following people begins with my spouse, Paul, for risking life and limb to rescue from the wreckage my laptop with the proposal on it.

Enduring the "death by a thousand cuts" of recovery was eased by the patient support of my SMU directors and committee, Beka Miles, Billy Abraham, Jim Lee, Natalia Marandiuc, and Kendall Soulen. Ted Campbell and I enjoyed helpful early conversations about classical literature and *credere* considerations.

Various units of AAR and SWCRS deemed my work worth presenting, and participants' feedback helped propel the project forward.

At Brite Divinity School, Joretta Marshall granted course release that made publication preparation possible. My administrators and fellow faculty, including Michael Miller and Newell Williams, inspire me daily. Early encouragement came from Ed Waggoner, Bryce Rich, Russ Dalton, Lance Pape, Jeff Williams, Wil Gafney, Bar McClure, and Tim Robinson.

At Baylor—the press where David Aycock twice has made me feel at home: first when I'd lost my own as a customer, and now as an author—Cade Jarrell has been a champion of my work with humor and serendipity. The generous responses of anonymous readers he found amid pandemic transformed this manuscript. The unanimity of the press committee's decision was a boon while revising with limited library access and teaching remotely. Upon final submission of my manuscript, Jenny Hunt and Bethany Dickerson devoted careful attention to its care and reading. Creative Kasey McBeath generously embraced the gifts of my longtime friend Jason Gubbiotti, whose inimitable artwork graces the cover.

Writing accountability partners Tomi Oredein, Grace Vargas Avella, Lisa Hancock, and Courtney Lacy (thanks for the nudge!), your friendship and feedback are treasures to me always. The journey began with the solidarity of dear friends and co-finishers Leslie Fuller (still solving bibliographic mysteries) and Julie Mavity Maddalena.

I've had great student assistants: Dani Musselman got me started, Chad Ewing kept me going, and puck glass saw me through rewrites and revisions, going above and beyond.

My episcopal leaders, clergysiblings, and members of every church and community I served sent me to this task. Tina and others trusted me with their heartfelt questions that started me on this research road.

The road has been longest for my family. Susan Adler, David Adler, and Beth Hufnagel expanded my childhood's concept of possibility with their PhDs. My splendid siblings, cousins, and in-laws offered constant care. Paul, you have salvaged much more than just my laptop, and there is no one with whom I'd rather take this road trip. Last of all, my firstborn, Gregory: I know this work has taken me half your life, but seeing you grow into the comical, compassionate young adult you are becoming fills me with a joy that makes me believe that flourishing is possible and believe into Christ all the more.

ABBREVIATIONS

BEM	World Council of Churches, *Baptism, Eucharist and Ministry*
DDC	Augustine, *Teaching Christianity (De Doctrina Christiana)*
Enarrat. Ps.	Augustine, *Enarrationes in Psalmos*
Tract. Ev. Jo.	Augustine, *Sancti Aurelii Augustini In Iohannis Evangelium tractatus CXXIV*
In Septem	Bede, *In Epistolas Septem Catholicas*
Scriptum	Thomas Aquinas, *Scriptum super Sententiis, liber III a distinctione XXIII ad distinctionem XXV*
Serm.	Augustine, *Sermones*

INTRODUCTION

For years, members of churches, communities, and classes I have served have asked me time and again how individuals could call themselves Christians but spend so much energy on self-centeredness, harming others, or any number of negative actions and attitudes that seem so unlike the Jesus described in the Gospels. "Because sin exists" was simply not a satisfying answer for me to offer, let alone for them to hear. I began turning to thoughts I had entertained in seminary, sparked by an unnumbered footnote to an ecumenical document: the World Council of Churches Faith and Order Commission, *Confessing the One Faith: An Ecumenical Explication of the Apostolic Faith as It Is Confessed in the Nicene-Constantinopolitan Creed (381).*[1] The note (marked only by a modest asterisk) gave a very brief commentary on the creed's opening phrase, "We believe in one God. . . ." It vaguely began, "In the West, Augustine pointed to three aspects of the act of believing."[2] I remember thinking it was the most nonspecific reference I could imagine, citing not one of Augustine's writings. Certainly, I could not have gotten away with submitting such vagueness to my professors! It felt like the equivalent of citations such as "The Bible says . . ." or "Shakespeare wrote . . . ," which tend to be less than helpful for understanding context. Nevertheless, even without the context, I knew enough Latin to notice something very unusual in one of the phrases describing the act of believing, the third one: *credere in Deum*. Though the WCC had translated it simply as "believing in God," its unusual grammar technically translated into English as

---

[1]   World Council of Churches, *Confessing the One Faith: An Ecumenical Explication of the Apostolic Faith as It Is Confessed in the Nicene-Constantinopolitan Creed (381)* (Geneva: WCC Publications, 1991).
[2]   World Council of Churches, *Confessing the One Faith*, 16.

"believing *into* God." It would be more than a decade before I would begin to discover just where Augustine "pointed to three aspects of the act of believing," which appeared in his preaching and commentaries, scattered across multiple works. Numerous theologians had systematized these aspects before, finally, they got lost in translation.

Meanwhile, without access to other sources that could help me learn more about the curious phrase "believing into God" (which I would learn also existed as "believing into Christ"), I was left to explain it as best I could to folks who asked me how harmful people could call themselves Christians. I would start the same very general way the footnote had—that "in the West" a theologian-pastor-bishop named Augustine had noted that it's one thing to believe God exists, another to believe God's promises come true, and still a whole other thing to do what translates as "believing into God." Inevitably, my conversation partner would note the awkwardness of that phrase, which I readily acknowledged. I would then give my best guess at what it seemed to mean, using metaphors like "putting all our eggs into God's basket" and "living and loving only as Jesus lives and loves." Noting the three different aspects of belief, I'd suggest that when it comes to calling oneself a Christian, there's a difference between a bobbleheaded nod of assent to propositions or tenets *about* God on the one hand and clinging in relationship to God through Jesus Christ by the Holy Spirit in a way that transforms every other relationship in care for others on the other. It was the best I could do with what little I had to go on, but it always resonated with my conversation partner. Regardless of their educational level, socioeconomic status, race, sexual orientation, nationality, or even religion (or lack thereof), this explanation seemed to make sense. Some of those who identified as Christian would ask me, "Why haven't I heard this before?" Others who were only mildly acquainted with Christianity would declare, "If I'd learned this when my friend dragged me to Sunday School as a child, I might have stuck around."

So, as you can see, my concern for where Christian theology lost this key element of its contribution to human flourishing arose rather organically. My journey to discover what has been missing in Christianity and the Christian life—the tale of it becoming lost and ideas of how we can restore it—has been twenty years in the making. Why had I had to learn it out of sheer curiosity over an obscure footnote, I wondered along the way? Where "in the West" did Augustine point to it? If "believe into God" is in the first phrase of major Christian creeds, how much does it define what Christianity is (or is intended to be)? Depending on the answers, I began to suspect that a key element to stopping harm, such as my questioners had experienced, and finding, instead, flourishing was out there. What I discovered in my research exceeded my expectations.

The Structure of This Book

The narrative arc of this book will chart a journey that begins with an explanation and exploration of this key component of the Christian life. The path then leads along the historical trajectory of its loss in translation in order to arrive at the constructive place where we consider how we might restore it and give rise to greater human flourishing.

Chapter 1, "Faith and Flourishing," defines terminology essential to the framework of the book, such as "flourishing," "relational," and "deification." It briefly describes the three distinct parts of the three-part *credere* formula and prepares the reader for deeper exploration of its establishment and implications in the next chapter.

Chapter 2, "The Formula in Augustine: Exegeted and Established," explores the establishment of the formula, from its roots in Scripture (both Greek and Latin) to its discovery and elaboration in preaching by Augustine in his African context of robust connections between belief and practice within the Roman Empire among everyday churchgoers. Here we develop the connection between "believing into Christ," deification, and flourishing more fully, in conversation with Augustine scholars, for broad application to doctrines and traditions and the practices that make for human flourishing.

Chapter 3, "The Formula after Augustine: Systematized, Reduced, Faded," traces the formula through its systematization in the early days of the English language's formation, through the Venerable Bede and Peter Lombard to Thomas Aquinas,[3] who strips it of its bodily, active qualities. It then moves along the historical trajectory of its loss

---

[3]   Bede was an influential English Benedictine monk of the seventh to eighth centuries, known for his *History of the English-Speaking Peoples* but at least as prolific in his writings on faith. Peter Lombard was an influential Italian scholastic theologian of the twelfth century who became bishop of Paris and wrote the seminal theological textbook *The Sentences*. Aquinas was an enormously influential Dominican friar of the thirteenth century, most famous for his massive work *Summa Theologiae*, upon which much of Roman Catholic doctrine and law is based.

in translation, noting cultural influences and resulting bifurcations of belief and praxis. Identification of what is lost in theological translation prepares readers to consider what restoration may involve and make possible.

Chapter 4, "Restoring the Relational Sense," recalls the communal reception of doctrine and liturgy of the early church and recognizes the reflection of what has been lost in the current state of the contemporary church. In dialogue with contemporary theologians of flourishing, it also brings together theory and praxis to offer concrete examples of what it means to restore the formula and the relational sense of belief.

Chapter 5, "Flourishing Praxis: Sacraments, Creeds, Catechesis," draws out implications of restoration for specific practices that undergird human flourishing. It offers clear steps for transforming catechesis and sacramental practices, depicting flourishing by believing-into as overcoming oppression and social barriers in contemporary ecclesial communities and the world they inhabit today.

Finally, the conclusion reviews the previous chapters' concepts and incorporates ecumenical Christian hopes for flourishing in the form of more dynamic witness in word and deed. It brings everything full circle while pointing ahead to future applications.

The appendix offers a chart comparing the different kinds of belief, by listing major scriptural passages on belief in English, Koine Greek, and Latin for those interested in deeper study of grammatical and translation elements.

Throughout my research, I have come to believe that this relational sense of believing-into is constitutive of the Christian faith. If embraced and used as a lens on teachings, sacraments, and life together, believing-into just might mitigate the bitter invective polluting public discourse and contribute to the flourishing that God intends for all.

Faith and Flourishing

Flourishing by Believing-into

What does it mean to flourish? Briefly, it is more than merely "living the good life." It is our enjoying the wholeness of existence as people connected in life-giving relationship with one another.[1] In a world where a scarcity mindset often dominates the discourse, the world's religions aid in this flourishing by helping us to see these life-giving relationships as sourced in something inexhaustible, something beyond ourselves yet fully available, strengthening our connections.

How does Christianity contribute to such flourishing? Ideally, Christianity offers access to this inexhaustible source through intimate relationship to the divine, in the person and after the pattern of Jesus of Nazareth, exhibited in a faith working through love of neighbor as self, including (and especially) love of enemies. Such a statement requires further unpacking, as it actually represents a number of distinct relationships that Christianity invigorates: relationship to the divine, relationship to self, relationship to neighbors, relationship to fellow worshiping bodies (in multiple senses of that ultimate word). This ideal looks like constant contact with the divine that nothing can come between, leading to assurance, confidence, and growth in love

[1]   Ideally, flourishing also encompasses vital relationship to the planet and its nonhuman inhabitants, as well. Lamentably, while the field of ecotheology is itself flourishing, attending in depth to planetary and nonhuman creaturely flourishing is beyond the scope of the present volume. I mention here the planet and nonhuman inhabitants thereof to reflect my desire to avoid funding a destructively anthropocentric concept of flourishing (i.e., at the expense of the planet and nonhuman creatures). For the present work, this desire must be satisfied by the presence and engagement of ecotheologian Sallie McFague, as well as by extended implications of believing into and experiencing deification toward the One whose creating care extends to the planet and its nonhuman inhabitants, suitable for exploration in greater detail in a future work.

of the loving One. As this love grows, it encourages understanding of self as humble yet confident, secure in connection to the divine and therefore safe to take relational risks with fellow humans. It makes not only possible but desirable the effort to seek active, loving connection with unknown neighbors and deepening of connections with known neighbors, including fellow believers, primarily for the purpose of growth in love that extends to the as-yet unknown neighbor. If this ideal does not square with reality, why not?

In reality, this ideal is something that first must be retrieved, having been largely lost in translation by Christians themselves. This faith working through love is in essence what it is to be Christian; what has been lost in translation is "believing *into* Christ." The beginning phrase of major Christian creeds when rendered in Latin, *Credimus in Deum*, literally means "We believe into God." What this admittedly awkward construction conveys is the relational sense of active, moving, and living belief. This relational sense is fit for the flourishing of human agents who relate with a living and active God on the move who moves us to act in life-giving ways. In order to contribute to the flourishing of all, this element must be foundational to the most basic practice of Christian faith by every believer, not just a nice aspiration for the upper echelon of super saints and deepest disciples.

This foundational phrase, "believe into God," was lost in translation, despite the fact that the great figure of Western Christianity, Augustine, bishop of Hippo, described this *credere in Deum*, "to believe into God," as the culmination of Christian faith, distinct from *credere Deo*, "to believe God,"[2] and from *credere Deum*,[3] "to believe that God exists." More surprising still is the fact that, despite the resulting formula's having been further systematized by later theologians as (a) believing in God, (b) believing God, and (c) believing into God, this nuanced

---

[2]   Augustine, *In Iohannis Evangelium tractatus* XXIX (CCSL 36:33ff.) (translation mine; hereafter abbreviated *Tract. Ev. Jo.* XXIX). This occurrence is believed to be Augustine's first treatment of the matter, in which he contrasts the ideal believing into Christ only with believing him. Throughout this work, my English translations are deliberately literal and may appear somewhat rigid, as opposed to translation for flow, but this choice has been made to maximize clarity and insight into the theological concepts in play for readers (especially nonreaders of Latin).

[3]   Augustine, *Serm.* CXLIV (PL 38:135) (translation mine). In this occurrence, he contrasts believing into him with believing in his existence/identity only. In a sermon to be addressed later here, he addresses both believing him and believing in his existence/identity in drawing contrast between them and believing into him.

understanding of belief that culminates in the relational sense has been replaced by a predominant understanding of Christian belief that is largely propositional and excludes most anything other than propositional evidence as central to what it means to be Christian. The cumulative effect of the loss of this curious, yet vital, element at the heart of Christian faith is evident in modern philosophical and systematic theology, which has tended to place a sharp divide between belief (as assent) and praxis. This divide, in turn, has led to a practice of Christianity in which love is not always evident, and harm is often present. In short, instead of seeing a witness to a living and active God of love, neighbors notice only disconnect between word and deed, such as what used to prompt many to ask me, then a local pastor, how people call themselves Christians but do awful things.[4]

"Belief into Christ," by contrast, brings about an element of bold surrender in the Christian faith that entails the *practice* of that faith as integral to the definition of what it means to be Christian. Moreover, believing-into entails a participation in Christ's own life with a result known as deification, divinization, or *theosis*, the process by which the Holy Spirit unites human life fully into the life of God. Flourishing from this perspective is precisely a participation in divine life and becoming not "holier than thou" but more *wholly Christlike*. I believe that this element may be Christianity's greatest contribution to universal concepts of flourishing.

Before fleshing out this reality in preparation for the chapters ahead, it is appropriate to clarify precisely what is at stake and the terminology involved. The word "relational" throughout this work describes belief that is aimed at union with God and participation in God through Jesus Christ by the sanctifying power of the Holy Spirit. Thus "believing into Christ" is "believing so as to be united vitally with Christ."[5] The treatment of the relational sense, then, as constitutive of the Christian faith, involves evaluating every tenet, every doctrine, every decision, and every action in light of whether and how it is moving the "believer-into" into more vital unity with Christ. It also acknowledges that the more completely one entrusts one's life into Christ's keeping, the more "vital" is the

---

[4] See first paragraph of the introduction above.
[5] Edward H. Sugden, ed., *The Standard Sermons of John Wesley* (London: Epworth, 1921), 1:162. Sugden was one of few twentieth-century scholars to take note of "believing into" but focused on the Greek, not Augustine's Latin.

"unity"—recalling biblical language expecting love of God with all one's heart, soul, mind, and strength (in various combinations thereof, from Deut 6:5 throughout the Hebrew Bible, and including Christ's identification of the greatest commandment in Matt 22:37). The result is a shift from philosophical discourse in the marketplace to relationship with fellow human beings as the primary means of spreading the Christian message.[6] What remains to be clarified, then, is what precisely is meant by the phrase used above in connection to the usefulness of the relational sense, "the flourishing of human agents who relate with a living and active God," and what makes such flourishing a desirable end.

In recent years, there has been a surge of interest in what makes for human flourishing. While this interest transcends disciplines, with research centers arising in multiple schools and universities and including various interdisciplinary efforts,[7] Christian theologians of several subfields have taken it up in earnest. Womanist theologian Eboni Marshall Turman notes that womanist scholars in subfields and specialties ranging from ethics to homiletics advance Black women's God-talk and flourishing as the source of theological discourse, considering how the commitment of Black women to overcome their oppression and thrive enhances the flourishing of all people.[8] Ecotheologians like Sallie McFague note that human flourishing is intimately bound up in care for all of

---

[6]   E. P. Sanders, *Paul: A Very Short Introduction* (New York: Oxford University Press, 1991), 24. Sanders suggests that Paul, not known as an eloquent speaker, likely did not rely principally upon public address, but rather "was probably most effective . . . one-to-one, or in small groups."

[7]   The Wellbeing at Work research team at the University of Notre Dame is an example of interdisciplinary interest in flourishing. Initially the effort was housed in the university's Mendoza School of Business. Its projects carry titles such as "Flourishing in Ministry" and "Called to Flourish," investigating job-force thriving in the humanistic services sector (educators, clergy, humanitarian workers). See https://workwellresearch.org/ and Matthew Bloom, *Flourishing in Ministry: How to Cultivate Clergy Wellbeing* (Lanham, Md.: Rowman & Littlefield, 2019).

[8]   Eboni Marshall Turman, "Black Women's Wisdom," *Christian Century* 136, no. 6 (March 13, 2019): 30–31, 33–34. (The digital version is entitled "Black Women's Faith, Black Women's Flourishing.") This article chronicles the blossoming and imagines the future of womanist theological scholarship since its seeds were planted in the late 1980s and early 1990s by ethicists Katie Geneva Cannon and Emilie Townes, theologians Delores Williams and Jacquelyn Grant, and biblical scholar Renita J. Weems.

creation, imagining the very planet as God's body.[9] Pastoral theologian Barbara McClure offers an extensive study of the role of emotions in human flourishing.[10]

One of the most prominent and prolific scholarly treatments of flourishing has been led by theologian Miroslav Volf, founding director of the Yale Center for Faith and Culture at Yale Divinity School. In *Flourishing: Why We Need Religion in a Globalized World*, Volf positions the relational as intrinsic to flourishing, as he considers "God's relation to human beings and human beings' relation to God to be the condition of possibility for human life and flourishing in all dimensions."[11] Volf introduces flourishing as "the life that is lived well, goes well, and feels good,"[12] and he examines these "three formal components" of flourishing in some detail, giving examples of the different ways that various world religions conceive of each component and its relationship to the others.[13]

He presses beyond a simple definition, however, taking as his major thesis the words of Moses (Deut 8:3) echoed by Jesus in the Gospels (Matt 4:4; Luke 4:4), that "One cannot live by bread alone, but by every word that comes from the mouth of the Lord."[14] Volf

---

[9]   Ecofeminist theologian Sallie McFague wove this theme throughout her oeuvre in books such as *The Body of God: An Ecological Theology* (Minneapolis: Fortress, 1993) and *Life Abundant: Rethinking Theology for a Planet in Peril* (Minneapolis: Fortress, 2001).

[10]   Barbara J. McClure, *Emotions: Problems and Promise for Human Flourishing* (Waco: Baylor University Press, 2019).

[11]   Miroslav Volf, *Flourishing: Why We Need Religion in a Globalized World* (New Haven, Conn.: Yale University Press, 2015), 9.

[12]   Volf, *Flourishing*, ix.

[13]   Volf, *Flourishing*, 75. While references to the components arise throughout his book, here Volf expands upon Nicholas Wolterstorff's *Justice: Rights and Wrongs* (Princeton, N.J.: Princeton University Press, 2008) to identify "*life being led well* (in Jesus' teaching, loving God and neighbor; in Job's case, fearing God and being righteous), *life going well* (in Jesus' practice, healing the sick, feeding the hungry; in Job's case, health, abundant possessions, many children), and *life feeling good* (in Jesus' teaching, joy; in Job's case, feasting)." Other world religions have something similar, Volf contends, though they may differ in "how they conceive the nature of life lived well ('love of God and neighbor,' 'submission to God,' 'extinction of desire,' to name some), in how they imagine a life that is going well (for example, the difference in the importance of progeny in Judaism and Christianity), in what positive emotion they highlight in life that feels good ('fun' in contemporary Western cultures or 'joy' in Buddhism, Confucianism, Christianity, and Judaism), and in how precisely they see the relation among the three." According to Volf, leading life well has primacy over and in fact sustains the other two components in all world religions.

[14]   Volf, *Flourishing*, 22.

depicts at the heart of human flourishing the Word as "the bread of life" that "gives abundant life," without which "we shrivel even when we are in overdrive, we fight and destroy, we perish."[15] While world religions—over and against a reputation for being escapist—are promoters of ordinary goodness very much in the here-and-now of common human experience, they prioritize transcendent goodness in a way that infuses that ordinary goodness with abundant life. It is after this life that humans yearn.

The yearning that Volf describes exceeds the confused requests of Jesus' hearers, whether those hearing his invitation to living water at a well or those hearing his bread of life sermon, who I suggest misplace their focus on the ordinary and ephemeral while Jesus, by means of ordinary things, points to the transcendent and eternal. Consider, for example, the Samaritan woman at the well, who responds to Jesus' description of the living water that becomes a spring in the drinker and gushes to eternal life, "Sir, give me this water, so that I may never be thirsty or have to keep coming here to draw water" (John 4:15).[16] Nevertheless, Jesus persists not with exasperation but persistent conversation, until she lifts her gaze to the mountains and hears plainly his self-identification and accepts his invitation.

Volf recalls the often-quoted line from *Confessions* in which Augustine addresses God: "'You move us to delight in praising you; you have formed us for yourself, and our hearts are restless till they find rest in you.'"[17] Thus, Volf insists, "when we come to love God and surrender to God in faith, to formulate the matter in Christian terms—the relation to the divine becomes the axis of our lives."[18] For Volf there is no other axis around which life can turn well. "Relationship to God . . . belongs to the very makeup

---

[15]   Volf, *Flourishing*, 22 (see John 6:35).

[16]   Another example that is even more germane to Volf's focus here, from the same chapter of John's Gospel that is a major focus in Augustine's formulation, is that of the crowd that follows Jesus to Capernaum after the feeding of the five thousand; hearing of the life-giving bread of God that comes down from heaven they respond, "Sir, give us this bread always," but soon make it clear that what they are requesting is food for the stomach, and not Christ himself, when he identifies himself as the bread to which he refers (John 6:34).

[17]   Volf, *Flourishing*, 81; he quotes *Confessions* 1.1.1, trans. J. G. Pilkington, in *A Select Library of the Nicene and Post-Nicene Fathers*, First Series, vol. 1., ed. Philip Schaff (Buffalo, N.Y.: Christian Literature, 1887).

[18]   Volf, *Flourishing*, 81.

of human beings,"[19] he concludes, having claimed from the start that world religions "articulate visions of flourishing, at whose center is the ultimate attachment to the divine."[20] This attachment echoes Augustine's description of *credere in eum*, believing into him (Jesus).

Within Volf's argument about world religions, he calls expressly for reformation and renewal of the Christian faith, even as he has cited John 6:35 for the vision of abundant life described above: "Jesus said to them, 'I am the bread of life. Whoever comes to me will never be hungry, and whoever believes in me will never be thirsty.'" Volf's call hearkens to Augustine's emphasis on the need to embrace the relational sense of Christian belief as constitutive of Christian faith that leads to human flourishing. In fact, much of his preaching mentioned above, in which he appeals to that grammatical structure unique to Christian literature, *credere in eum*, arises as he exegetes the same gospel, and in more than one instance even the same chapter, that Volf would cite centuries later. Yet Augustine's contributions along these lines appear to have been inaccessible or unavailable to Volf, like so many before him. He wouldn't be the first great thinker in pursuit of the role belief can play in human flourishing to miss the formula and its unique, relational "belief-into" that could perfectly encapsulate the whole point, had it not been lost, in translation and otherwise. The relational aspect of belief as a key component of human flourishing has eluded even the brightest philosophical minds to have influenced theology in the last hundred years. Analytic philosophy of religion, which arose with particular strength in Great Britain amid a twentieth-century atheism particularly prominent after the atrocities of World War II, produced several thinkers who assiduously studied and debated the subject of "belief."

Great Minds Thinking Alike but Missing a Link

Imagine four formidable figures—no, not the writers of the four Gospels, but writers nonetheless. The four gentlemen in this imaginary conversation are four great analytic philosophers, H. H. Price,[21] Robert

---

19   Volf, *Flourishing*, 202.
20   Volf, *Flourishing*, 24.
21   Henry Habberley Price (1899–1984) was a Welsh-born British philosopher and Wykeham professor of logic at New College, Oxford, who wrote on thinking, perception, and philosophy of religion.

Audi,[22] Louis Pojman,[23] and Basil Mitchell,[24] all of whom at various points throughout the twentieth century took up the weighty matter of belief. Deep and wide-ranging as their studies and arguments were, they nevertheless were unable to uncover the relational sense of belief inherent in "believing into God." In our mind's eye, we can see them sitting in an imaginary study, the walls lined with shelves upon shelves of books, though none of them contains Augustine's sermons. After all, even theologians rarely read Augustine's sermons, as his more scholarly tomes such as *Confessions* and *City of God* have garnered fame and dominated the attention of scholars for centuries. We can well imagine that this oversight would not sit well with Augustine, whom we now picture standing at the door to the study where the scholars sit (our imaginations not limited by over 1500 years' distance from his life to theirs). His knock might even be said to be startling, if the tea-drinking gentlemen whose conversation it interrupts were capable of being startled. These four are not given to such trivialities as amazement, however. They are lovers of wisdom (the meaning of "philosophers"), and as such they have amassed much of it, fond of startling or amazing *others* with their pronouncements, perhaps, but far too secure in their knowledge to be startled by anything, except doubt.

Doubt is, in fact, the very topic about which one of them, Pojman, has been going on at length. Deeply concerned about many religious people, who simply cannot force themselves to believe propositions like the doctrine of the Trinity, that God is three-in-one, Pojman is focusing on the existence of God as shorthand for all doctrines.[25] Isn't it enough, he asks his conversation partners, for faith to be understood

---

[22] Robert Audi (b. 1941) is an American philosopher who is O'Brien Professor of Philosophy at the University of Notre Dame whose career has spanned ethics and political philosophy, epistemology, philosophy of mind and action, and philosophy of religion.

[23] Louis P. Pojman (1935–2005) was an American philosopher who taught at the University of Mississippi and the U.S. Military Academy at West Point, whose work focused on applied ethics and philosophy of religion.

[24] Basil George Mitchell, F.B.A. (1917–2011) was an English philosopher and one-time Nolloth Professor of the Philosophy of the Christian Religion at the University of Oxford who famously debated atheists and developed a cumulative-case argument for the rationality of religious belief.

[25] Louis P. Pojman, *Religious Belief and the Will* (London: Routledge & Kegan Paul, 1986), 212–14.

as hoping something is true, instead of definitely believing that it is, in order for someone to obtain the benefits of religious belief?[26]

Pojman cannot be blamed for thinking this way, when Christianity has been boiled down even by its adherents to little more than assenting to a list of propositions about God contained in traditional creeds. He tips his hat to Price, whose landmark publication is entitled *Belief*, based on not one but two separate series of Gifford Lectures.[27] Price had been speaking of various degrees of belief, from surmising to conviction (some of which he might have been able to map onto believing that God exists and believing that God's promises are true, had he been aware of the formula, but he apparently is not).[28] His fascinating explanation that belief that is like knowledge by acquaintance is stronger than belief that is like knowledge only by someone else's description—like the distinction between "belief that" and "belief in"—is interesting but still doesn't reach the depths of believing-into.[29]

Mitchell, among the four, is the one who most explicitly identifies himself as a Christian theist, and of the four imagined conversation partners, he has come closest to describing something like the relational sense of belief that is fit for human flourishing. With his explanation of a difference between faith understood as *fides* versus faith understood as *fiducia*, Mitchell suggests that what his three fellow philosophers have been missing is that belief is a guide to living, not a matter of proving or disproving God's existence.[30] Propositional beliefs, assent to which he calls mere faith or *fides*, are not the entirety of Christian faith for Mitchell, who insists upon *fiducia*, an unconditional reliance on God.[31]

We can imagine, as this conversation continues, that Augustine's knocking is growing louder. Audi has begun arguing that Mitchell is

---

[26]   Pojman, *Religious Belief and the Will*, 217–19. The "benefits" to which Pojman refers include salvation (without indicating salvation *from what*, per se).

[27]   H. H. Price, *Belief* (New York: Humanities Press, 1969). The Gifford Lectures are annual lectures that respected philosophers historically have been invited to deliver at one of the four major universities of Scotland on any topic they choose that deals with the knowledge of God.

[28]   Price, *Belief*, 81.

[29]   Price, *Belief*, 76–77.

[30]   Basil Mitchell, *The Justification of Religious Belief*, Philosophy of Religion Series (New York: Seabury, 1974), 39.

[31]   Mitchell, *Justification of Religious Belief*, 139.

not being sufficiently rational in his approach to religious belief and needs to examine the seven different kinds of everyday ways of speaking of faith that Audi offers in his work.[32] Curiously, not one of these seven involves believing *into* God, not even the one that mentions trust.

In our mind's eye, it is this last bit that Augustine's loudest knocking interrupts. As Pojman rises from his wingback chair, he sets down his teacup and now turns the doorknob. We can well imagine the color draining from Pojman's face as he pulls the door open and instantly recognizes the rich, dark tones of the voice and face revealed on the other side of the door. After all, Pojman would be most likely to recognize the ancient North African bishop of Hippo, having offered the first sustained philosophical analysis of faith in the works of Augustine![33]

"*Do* you want to understand belief?" Augustine asks with a rhetorical gesture as he strides confidently into the room, episcopal robes billowing behind him. "Then begin by believing! That's right, *Believe*. Otherwise you cannot understand that believing into the one whom God has sent is the thing that you all crave yet all have been missing. Why don't you wise ones read the words I preached to ordinary people who had bothered showing up to worship?!" The saint is incensed, demanding to know how it can be that they don't know what he so explicitly laid out in his sermons!

The philosophers, eyebrows raised, shrug their shoulders and murmur that sermons are not of interest to philosophers, a vocation Augustine would not understand to be separate from that of theologians. This reasoning does not meet with the saint's approval. He nevertheless follows their line of thinking, asking why don't their theological friends enlighten them as to the content of his sermons? Upon learning that theologians don't read them much, either, Augustine, in exasperated response, delivers a long lecture and criticism of the philosophers for flattening all doctrines into "the existence of God." Augustine has given his original hearers, as well as anyone who reads his sermons, rich, bodily imagery, with which he describes belief as going into Christ and

---

[32]   Robert Audi, *Rationality and Religious Commitment* (New York: Oxford University Press, 2011), 53–65. He lists "propositional faith," "attitudinal faith," "creedal faith," "global faith," "doxastic faith," "acceptant faith," and "allegiant faith." The last comes closest to a relational sense, but then Audi dismisses this aspect from the common sense of "faith" (65).

[33]   Pojman, *Religious Belief and the Will*, ix.

being incorporated in his limbs, yet the philosophers' propositional focus on existence of God has rendered belief purely intellectual and utterly bodiless.

Deification as Union with Love Incarnate

It is no accident that Augustine's language is itself so rooted in movement and body, as the believer-into comes to think of every body as precious, and every believer's body equally united into Christ's body. It may seem counter to the popular characterization of Augustine to emphasize bodily language and a transformation that affects not only soul but body. Augustine is routinely blamed for Western Christianity's dualistic opposition between the spiritual (generally considered capable of being good with divine assistance) and the bodily (generally understood to be depraved). More recent scholarship on Augustine, however, suggests that this charge is actually the fault of scholars who have chosen to interpret Augustine in purely Platonic philosophical terms.[34] As will become evident in the next chapter, the more Augustine spent time in ministry in the real world among everyday people, the more readily he saw and taught about the connections, rather than bifurcations, between the visible church in action on earth and the invisible church as spiritual reality in heaven, as well as between the body and soul, and between the believer and God.

This book therefore joins the efforts of Augustine scholars like Margaret Miles, James Lee, and David Meconi, who have attempted to recover the tangible aspects of Augustine's theology. Deification, understood as "transformative union"—in other words, the taking up of human life fully into the life of God through the redemptive power of Christ by the Holy Spirit—is spread throughout Augustine's work in many ways, often without using the actual word, *deificare*, according to Meconi (though his work does not include attention to the *credere* formula).[35] Simply put, as God is love, the believer into God becomes love.

Furthermore, the transformation this union effects goes beyond the individual. Deification in this way insists that Christian faith as believing into Christ is not simply about individual believers

---

[34]   James K. Lee, *Augustine and the Mystery of the Church* (Minneapolis: Fortress, 2017), xvi.

[35]   David Meconi, *The One Christ: St. Augustine's Theology of Deification* (Washington, D.C.: Catholic University of America Press, 2013), xi–xii, xvi.

obtaining their own benefits from faith—contrary to what the philosophers' approaches suggested. Rather, it is about living so united to
Christ that we are glued to him, so our limbs stretch in the direction
Christ's always have, toward anyone we may perceive to be "other"
or who has been "othered" by another. It is communitarian without
being normative, as all whose bodies are thus adhered to Christ also
recognize themselves as equally adhered to one another. Another's
flesh—whether it looks like, moves like, and loves like mine or not—is
as valuable to me as is my own, and I will protect and cherish it,
because all together we are fused into Christ's flesh. Sacraments play
a key role in furthering and sustaining this relationship, of course, yet
are themselves amplified as we imagine what peace and nonviolent
action become possible when we understand one another's bodies
and lives as connected to our own in this way.

This relational, body and soul, understanding of Christianity can
provide a corrective to the colonialist notions often bound up in
Christianity. The bifurcation between bodies and souls has undergirded a history of conquest, conversion by force, and even blessing
of slavery as divinely ordained. An understanding of transformative
union of bodies and souls with Christ's can expose and subvert domination, control, and commodification of human bodies, as every decision is filtered through the lens of relationship with Christ, each other,
and others. The relational sense of believing into Christ and the deification it entails thus contribute to flourishing because they have the
power to transform how humans view power itself, even the power to
help one another. Believers into Christ who have any kind of power
in church and society become eager to relinquish it to those who have
less power, not out of pity but from a deep sense of interconnected
love. The potential for a broad appeal of the resulting witness may
be seen in the words of Lilla Watson, Aboriginal elder, activist, and
educator from Queensland, Australia: "If you have come to help me,
you are wasting your time. If you have come because your liberation
is bound up with mine, then let us work together."[36]

While presenting possibilities for restoring "believing into Christ"
and transforming Christian faith and its contribution to flourishing, it is important to acknowledge some limitations on the scope of
this book. Though dealing with deification, a key concept of Eastern

[36] "Lilla: International Women's Network," 2007, https://lillanetwork.wordpress
.com/about/.

Orthodoxy, there is not space to dive deeply into the resources of that tradition. The argument for "believing into" presented here obviously relies on translation from Augustine's Latin into English, and further work is necessary to understand how this distinction is best conveyed in languages other than English. The book gestures toward but must leave to future works the possibilities for training "believing into Christ" as a lens on specific doctrines, as well as case studies of significant figures whose flourishing demonstrates believing into Christ, even if the concept is not explicitly articulated in their works. The next chapter is an exploration of the establishment of the formula, from its roots in Scripture (both Greek and Latin) to its discovery and elaboration in preaching by Augustine in his African context of robust connection between belief and practice within the Roman Empire among everyday churchgoers.

2

The Formula in Augustine

Exegeted and Established

Just a Preposition?

The unusual nature of the construction *credere in eum*, "believing into him," comes from its preposition, "into." Thus, a brief explanation of the use in Koine Greek of prepositions with πιστεύω (*pisteuō*) and more extensive exploration of the use in Augustine's Latin of prepositions with *credere* will be necessary.

Before we turn to that grammatical discussion, however, it is worth asking: What is the big deal about a little word? Why emphasize awkwardness that relates to a little preposition? One thing Augustine understood, not only as an exacting instructor of rhetoric, but also of Christianity and its texts, is that little things mean a lot. Starting with Jesus himself, the infinitely uncontainable God, come as a tiny being of frail flesh, there's the difference between "Jesus who is God" and "Jesus who is *from* God" in the way an angel is sent *from* God. Here we see how the presence or absence—or both—of a preposition can be so important. Once fully grown, Jesus delivers teachings laden with small details that make a big difference. Consider the vast reign of God that is like a minuscule mustard seed! Once Jesus is pointed toward the cross, the point of little prepositions becomes even more poignant: Consider the Gospel account of Jesus' stopping to wash the disciples' feet, "knowing that the Father had given all things into his hands, and that he had come from God and was going to God" (John 13:3, NRSV). Such "coming from" and "going to" are highly significant markers of Trinitarian identity, to say the least. With the preposition in question here, "in," the grammatical case of the word that follows it governs its meaning in a way that makes this construction entirely unique to Christian Latin literature, a point Augustine repeatedly seizes on, as any good homiletician-theologian should.

In fact, much of Christian theology, famously dubbed in the West "footnotes to Augustine," requires noting subtle distinctions that make a huge difference in the life of the church and world.[1] Consider *filioque*, the controversy that divided the East from the West over the addition of "and the Son" in describing the Spirit's procession in the Nicene Creed. The Protestant Reformation hinged largely on the word *sola*, whether describing salvation *sola fide*, by faith alone, or *sola gratia*, by grace alone. A few tiny letters separate pantheism from panentheism but make a big difference in whether everything is God or God is in everything. All of these examples follow the one at the heart of this book, originated by the theologian who defended the use of rhetoric in religion. So when Augustine happened upon a turn of phrase that hinged on a little preposition and the way its object was declined (the process by which a different ending added at the end of a word's root changes the word's grammatical function in the sentence and even the meaning of words around it), he recognized the opportunity to define the uniqueness of a full-bodied Christianity that is more than recognition, or reflection, or reverence alone but is, in addition, rigorously relational.

In order to understand the turn of phrase "believing into" as Augustine plays upon it in Latin, a brief background on the biblical Greek is helpful.

The Greek behind Augustine's Latin

Augustine scholar Peter Brown laments that, though he was the great rhetor of Milan and bishop of Hippo, Augustine was a "casualty" of late Roman pedagogy, in which Greek lessons bored him even as Latin classics fascinated him. Brown dubbed him "the only Latin philosopher in antiquity to be virtually ignorant of Greek."[2] Thus examining the original Greek at all may seem superfluous. The grammatical rules of the Koine Greek and of the Latin into which it was translated in the *Vetus Latina* and the Vulgate are not identical. It is from the uniqueness of the grammatical structure in Latin that Augustine draws a play on words to make a point, in his case to emphasize the relational

---

[1]   Jaroslav Pelikan, *The Christian Tradition: A History of the Development of Doctrine*, vol. 1, *The Emergence of the Catholic Tradition (100–600)* (Chicago: University of Chicago Press, 1971), 330.

[2]   Peter Brown, *Augustine of Hippo: A Biography*, rev. ed. (Berkeley: University of California Press, 2000), 24.

sense of belief. Many medieval preacher-scholars who followed him likewise worked in Latin, not Greek. Then why seek to give attention to the Greek foundation now?

What may seem to be an esoteric excursus in fact serves two straightforward purposes: (1) it foregrounds the discussion of a grammatical-structure-turned-theological-tool by showing the way that roots of linguistic evolutions make Christian innovations with language possible, and (2) it aids in understanding one of many reasons the formula may have been lost in translation, as modern philosophers were more likely to study ancient Greek, which predates the Koine Greek of early Christian literature. Attention to the first, linguistic innovation, especially undergirds the constructive proposals in this book.

The Greek preposition εἰς (*eis*) is followed exclusively by words in the accusative case, which is mainly the case of the direct object.[3] It is important to remember, for speakers primarily or solely of English, that in both Greek and Latin, like many languages, verbs and pronouns consist of a root that carries primary meaning with a changeable ending. The change to the ending of a noun, adjective (which must match the noun it modifies), or verb determines its function and reference point. Other parts of speech, such as prepositions and adverbs, do not have changeable endings, but their meaning can be governed by their use with the changeable words they describe. The ending of a noun in the accusative case on its own tells a reader that this word is the direct object of the verb in this sentence. When it is preceded by a preposition, then it is part of a prepositional phrase. The primary meaning of εἰς (*eis*) is "into."[4] It most often appears with verbs of motion, as in John 1:9. There the famous verse "The true light, which enlightens everyone, was coming **into the world**"[5] ends with a verb of motion (coming—in Greek ἐρχόμενον/*erchomenon*), followed by a phrase employing the word

---

[3] There are adverbial applications for the accusative case as well, for example, those denoting "extent to which."

[4] Wesley J. Perschbacher, ed., *The New Analytical Greek Lexicon* (Peabody, Mass.: Hendrickson, 1990), 120. See also Timothy Friberg, Barbara Friberg, and Neva F. Miller, *Analytical Lexicon of the Greek New Testament* (Grand Rapids: Baker, 2000), 132.

[5] Here I agree with the New Revised Standard Version, though I could choose the literal "all humanity" in place of "everyone."

for "into" with an object and its article in the accusative case, εἰς τὸν κόσμον (*eis ton kosmon*).[6]

Another preposition, ἐν (*en*), can be used interchangeably with *eis*. Unlike the way that *eis* is used exclusively with nouns with accusative case endings, *en* takes the dative case, the case serving primarily as that of the indirect object.[7] This preposition, *en*, can mean either "in," "within," or "into," and sometimes it can even mean "on," depending upon context. Even with this variability in meaning, its primary sense is not motion, but static location, "within."[8] This preposition is the obvious cognate for the Latin preposition "in," which ends up doing the work of both *eis* and *en*. One result of this etymological evolution is that the case of the noun that is paired with (i.e., follows) the preposition has a much more distinct impact on the meaning of the preposition than it did in the Greek.

The verb πιστεύω (*pisteuō*), "I believe,"[9] can mean either "believe something or someone is true or truthful," as in the case of believing someone's testimony, or—as became the case in Koine versus classical Greek—to trust someone or entrust something to someone. In classical Greek, *pisteuō* had been used mainly in a propositional sense, followed by ὅτι (*hoti*, "that"), and it did not take a preposition at all, nor the accusative for its object.[10] It is also possible to infer that the influence of Hebraic structures informed the change in meaning and structure (from not using prepositions to doing so, for example) in the transition from classical Greek to Koine Greek.[11] While this

---

[6]   Barbara Aland, Kurt Aland, Johannes Karavidopoulos, Carlo M. Martini, and Bruce M. Metzger, eds., *The Greek New Testament*, 4th rev. ed. (Stuttgart: Deutsche Bibelgesellschaft, 1998). The full sentence is ἦν τὸ φῶς τὸ ἀληθινὸν ὃ φωτίζει πάντα ἄνθρωπον, **ἐρχόμενον εἰς τὸν κόσμον** (*Ēn to phōs to alēthinon, ho phōtizei panta anthrōpon, **erchomenon eis ton kosmon**).

[7]   Perschbacher, *New Analytical Greek Lexicon*, 121.

[8]   Friberg, Friberg, and Miller, *Analytical Lexicon*, 147.

[9]   English lacks, as did Latin before it, a verb for "to faith in." "Trust" doesn't quite convey it.

[10]   Thomas Camelot, "*Credere Deo, Credere Deum, Credere in Deum*: Pour l'histoire d'une formule traditionnelle," *Revue des Sciences Philosophiques et Théologiques* 30, no. 1 (1941–1942): 149. Camelot does indicate that occasionally the neuter adverbial accusative (used to express the extent of an action, for example) could be used with πιστεύω.

[11]   Camelot, "*Credere Deo*." Camelot infers that this change in structure (to using prepositions, etc.) and meaning emerges from the influence of Hebraic structures and is related to tendencies in modern Greek generally to replace ἐν + dative with εἰς + accusative.

propositional sense with *hoti* continues to be used in Koine Greek, *pisteuō* also may be followed by prepositions throughout the New Testament,[12] including both *eis* and *en*. The result appears to be a growing sense of *pisteuō* as more than merely cognitive or intellectual assent. Though one source lists its first definition as being related to intellectual activity, a second definition that emerged in the transition from classical to Koine Greek is "primarily a religious commitment, especially with God or Christ as the object of faith."[13]

It is not uncommon to see both πιστεύω ἐν (*pisteuō en*) and πιστεύω εἰς (*pisteuō eis*) in close proximity in the New Testament as this sense seems to have continued to develop. One salient example includes the biblical passage most often quoted by Christians and sports fans the world over, the pericope describing the night visit to Jesus by Nicodemus. John 3:15 uses the verb *pisteuō* as Jesus describes the one who believes as having life ἐν αὐτῷ (*en autō*, "in him," that is, in Christ).[14] In the ensuing famous verse 3:16, πιστεύων εἰς αὐτὸν (*pisteuōn eis auton*), "believing into him" (to translate that preposition and case literally), applies to the one who does not perish but has eternal life. It is intriguing that the far less frequently quoted ensuing verse, 3:17, includes the same "into the world" concept and construction as in John 1:9, discussed above. This time, the phrase appears in the mouth of Jesus, as he assures Nicodemus that not condemnation but salvation δι' αὐτοῦ (*di autou*), through him, is the reason ἀπέστειλεν ὁ θεὸς τὸν υἱὸν εἰς τὸν κόσμον (*apesteilen ho Theos ton huion eis ton kosmon*), God sent the Son into the world.

Augustine's Latin: A Unique Turn of Phrase Takes a Theological Turn

Augustine worked throughout most of his life with the collection of Latin translations of the Bible known as the *Vetus Latina*.[15] Only slowly

---

[12]   In koine, πιστεύω may also be followed by ἐπί (*epi*, "on/upon"), which also takes an object in the accusative.

[13]   Friberg, Friberg, and Miller, *Analytical Lexicon*, 314.

[14]   While the sense of "within" works perfectly well here, it is worth noting that Aland et al. footnote variations in other manuscripts, including the appearance instead of *eis auton*, potential evidence that the distinctions in meaning of prepositions really were still in the process of developing as koine evolved. What led the dominant manuscripts to include the two different prepositions remains unnoted.

[15]   James J. O'Donnell, "Bible," in *Augustine through the Ages: An Encyclopedia*, ed. Allan Fitzgerald and John C. Cavadini (Grand Rapids: Eerdmans, 1999), 101. With reference to Anne-Marie La Bonnadiere's *Biblia Augustiniana* (Paris:

did he come to use the translation that Jerome completed during his life-time, which has come to be known as the Vulgate. It is likely that Augus-tine worked with numerous versions of Scripture (as the exact makeup of the *Vetus Latina* remains a mystery), and Augustine is known to have resisted Jerome's project at the outset.[16] Augustine expresses awareness of the difficulties and dangers of not having access to the biblical texts in their original language in a work to which we shall give more atten-tion momentarily, *De Doctrina Christiana* (*Teaching Christianity*).[17] There he states:

> But the proper meaning of a passage, which several translators attempt to express . . . can only be definitely ascertained from an examination of it in the language they are translating from; and translators frequently deviate from the author's meaning, if they are not particularly learned. So one should aim either at a knowledge of those languages from which the scriptures have come to their Latin . . . versions, or else get hold of translations which have been the most strictly literal, word for word, renderings of the original, not because they are sufficient in themselves, but because they can help one to control the freedom, or even the mistakes, of those translators who have preferred to follow the meanings rather than the words of the authors. (II.13.19)

Clearly precision matters to Augustine. So attention to the basic rules of Latin grammar will assist us in understanding how Augustine's attention to those rules helps him make a strong theological point as he interprets the Gospel of John to his congregation.

In Latin, the functions of the Greek *eis* and *en* are covered by a single preposition, *in*, and the difference in meaning is, in Latin, gov-erned entirely by the case of its object (signified by the ending of the word following the preposition). This arrangement is unusual, even within Latin. In Latin, most prepositions consistently take for their objects a word in *either* the accusative (the case that, on its own, is used for the direct object, recall) *or* the ablative (the case that, on its

---

Études Augustiniennes, 1965–1970) and her *Saint Augustin et la Bible* (Paris: Beauchesne, 1986).

[16]   James J. O'Donnell, *Augustine: A New Biography* (New York: Harper Peren-nial, 2006), 92–93.

[17]   Augustine, *Teaching Christianity*, trans. Edmund Hill, The Works of Saint Augustine: A Translation for the 21st Century 1/11 (Hyde Park, N.Y.: New City Press, 1996), 138.

own, is used to describe manner or means), but rarely does a single preposition take both. *Sub* ("under") and *in* are the only prepositions used with both the accusative and the ablative, and with both *sub* and *in*, the ablative is used to signify location or resting on the part of the subject, while the accusative is used to signify motion.[18] *In* with a noun in the ablative case carries the same simple meaning as its English cognate, "in." *In* with the accusative case becomes "into."

Now we turn our attention to the verb in the phrase that captured Augustine's attention, *credere*, "to believe," and its unusual usage with *in* + an object in the accusative.[19] Complicating matters is the way in which Latin, having already two ways of using this verb without prepositions (with the accusative or with the dative case that is usually assigned to indirect objects), also takes on additional usages inherited from biblical Greek constructions that involved *pisteuō*. As noted by Christine Mohrmann, one of the few twentieth-century scholars to address Augustine's use of the *credere* formula, these usages are two more pairings of *credere*: one with the preposition *in* and an object of the preposition in the ablative (referring to rest or static location) and one with the preposition *in* and an object of the preposition in the accusative (referring to motion).[20] How nonsensical to think of motion or location in conjunction with a verb of intellectual assent! Isn't intellectual assent what it means to believe? Why would one combine it with phrases referring to location and motion?

This last construction, *credere in* + accusative, is unique to biblical and Christian literature; it does not occur in classical secular literature written in Latin. In fact, though the construction is believed to be rooted in the εἰς Θεόν (*eis Theon*) of the Septuagint and New Testament, that phrase in Greek paired with *pisteuō* was itself unique to the New Testament, as its appearances in the Septuagint are not

[18] Charles E. Bennett, *New Latin Grammar* (Boston: Allyn and Bacon, 1918), 108.

[19] A predictor of the difficulties and loss in translation that will be the later focus of this book arises here, as the word supplanting the Koine Greek's *pisteuō* is the non-cognate *credo*, "I believe." Discussion of loss in translation and of doctrinal impact thereof in later chapters will address the ongoing complications of etymology regarding this verb.

[20] Christine Mohrmann, "Credere in Deum: Sur l'interpretation theologique d'un fait de langue," in *Mélanges Joseph de Ghellinck, S.J.* (Gembloux: J. Duculot, 1951), 278.

associated with belief.[21] Whereas Latin literature had long used the construction *credere deos* (*credere* + accusative without preposition) in reference to believing in gods (i.e., that they exist),[22] the new *credere in* + accusative construction brought in the awkward equivalent of a construction of physical movement into some place or thing with what had traditionally been a verb of intellectual assent (*credere*, "to believe"), the equivalent in English of "believing into God."

Initially the *credere in* + accusative and *credere in* + ablative constructions seem to have been used side by side, but gradually a tendency to distinguish among the various expressions describing the act of faith arose, between the prepositional constructions (of which *credere in* + accusative overtook *credere in* + ablative in frequency) and the use of *credere* alone with the dative, such as *credere deo*, "to believe God" (i.e., believe God's words are true, consider God credible).[23] While in the time of Cyprian these distinctions had not yet been fully established,[24] Augustine seized upon this uniqueness, drawing contrasts between the constructions, in order to identify a distinction in the Christian faith, in his preaching.

In light of the distinctions' not yet being fully established in Cyprian, it is worthy of note that Augustine delivered the sermons in which he addresses the differences during the period between the suspension and continuation of his work that is frequently treated as the foundational Christian preaching manual, *De Doctrina Christiana* (*Teaching Christianity*; henceforth abbreviated *DDC*).[25] For it is

---

[21]   Eugene TeSelle, "Faith," in Fitzgerald and Cavadini, *Augustine through the Ages*, 349. A thorough consultation of the occurrences of this phrase throughout the Septuagint confirms that it is nowhere paired with *pisteuō*, most frequently occurring in multiple prophetic utterances in which God looks forward to Israel being God's people and God being their God, as in Jeremiah 24:7 (καὶ ἐγὼ ἔσομαι αὐτοῖς εἰς θεόν, *kai egō esomai autois eis theon*). The nonsense of a literal translation here exceeds the awkwardness of the "believing into God" we are uncovering in the Latin: "and I will be to them into God."

[22]   Mohrmann, "Credere in Deum," 277. Examples Mohrmann offers include Seneca and Pliny.

[23]   Mohrmann, "Credere in Deum," 278. Note that some occurrences of *credere in* + ablative remain in the Vulgate, including some that do not appear to agree with the contstruction of the sentence in Koine Greek—see appendix.

[24]   Mohrmann, "Credere in Deum," 279.

[25]   James J. Murphy, "The Debate about Augustine and a Distinctly Christian Rhetoric," in *The Rhetoric of St. Augustine of Hippo*: De Doctrina Christiana *and the Search for a Distinctly Christian Rhetoric*, ed. Richard Leo Enos and Roger Thompson, Studies in Rhetoric and Religion (Waco: Baylor University Press, 2008), 206.

in *DDC* that Augustine responds to a reluctance on the part of pre-decessors such as Cyprian to employ rhetoric in the service of the gospel.[26] In all of the sermons in which Augustine focuses on the distinctiveness of *credere in* + accusative, the pulpit serves as labora-tory for Augustine's ongoing experiment with rhetoric as an effective means of moving hearers likely to be unfamiliar with Scripture into an understanding of its good news, resulting in a formula for entering into relationship with God through Christ.

Augustine's Formula: Believing in Christ, Believing Christ, Believing into Christ

In Johannis Evangelium tractatus XXIX (29th Tractate [or Homily] on the Gospel of John, henceforth abbreviated *Tract. Ev. Jo.* XXIX), he preached most likely at Hippo, of which he had become bishop sev-eral years earlier in 395/396.[27] Its ostensible text is John 7:14-18, which is logical, as Augustine has preached on John 7:1-13 the day before. Over the course of several years, the theologian/homiletician/teacher had been working his way through a continuous series of messages on the Gospel of John by preaching—sometimes daily—over the course of five months. He began the current series with John's fifth chapter, where he had left off during a series many years earlier.

Here we are hearing from the mature Augustine, who has many other irons in the fire, works that will receive much more attention as history and theology move forward than will the seemingly mun-dane task of preaching. For example, he is otherwise busy working on the early chapters of *De Civitate Dei* (*The City of God*), the mas-terpiece that will give rise to just war theory, among many other concepts foundational not only to the Western church but also the medieval world and beyond. In addition, Augustine is busily writing and preaching against the Donatists, whose movement is waning

---

[26] Amy K. Hermanson, Drew M. Loewe, Kristi Schwertfeger Serrano, Lisa Michelle Thomas, and Sarah L. Yoder, "Saint Augustine and the Creation of a Distinctly Christian Rhetoric," in Enos and Thompson, *Rhetoric of St. Augustine of Hippo*, 4. The authors name Cyprian in a list of "Christian leaders" who consid-ered rhetoric a dangerous pagan practice to be avoided by Christian preachers, including Titian, Gregory of Naziensus [*sic*], and Basil of Caesarea.

[27] Augustine, *Tract. Ev. Jo.* XXIX.6 (CCSL 36:286–87). In this edition, a superscription reads *Habitus Dom. XII post Pentec., die 17 Augusti 413*. The actual composition and/or preaching date is, like most of the *Tractatus*, a matter of debate.

but whose influence remains strong on the church in North Africa (the place where Christians first spoke Latin and where translation of the Bible into Latin began),[28] emphasizing the rejection of lapsed Christians (the usual designation of those priests and members who had handed over Holy Scriptures or refused to endure martyrdom in the face of persecution).[29] The difficulty on the one hand of recognizing the dangers in state-sanctioned religion (which can lead to state-sanctioned violence against dissenters) and on the other of recognizing the mercy of God and source of sacramental efficacy in God rather than in the holy or lapsed priest is one that occupies much of Augustine's attention.[30] Archaeological evidence of liturgical rites such as Eucharist and burial from this period demonstrate commitment, particularly on the part of Augustine's Catholic (or Caecilianist) church, to effacing distinctions of social class with a grace equally available to all.[31] Most recently he has begun to write against Pelagius, who passed through Hippo teaching of original good will and humans' ability to choose good and God on their own apart from grace, shortly after the fall of Rome to the Goths only a few years earlier.[32]

Yet, busy as he may be writing in his capacity as theologian, the bishop remembers that the prologue of John's Gospel was once pivotal in his own recognition of the Christian Scriptures as superior to Neoplatonist doctrine. Thus he remains determined to fulfill his pastoral intention to preach in depth upon the entire gospel.[33] Several years into that effort, he preaches this sermon within a week of the previous three sermons, a relevant detail, as the passage from which the *credere* formula begins to emerge is actually one outside the present pericope, to which he refers back in greater depth to undergird a present point.

---

[28]   J. Patout Burns and Robin M. Jensen, *Christianity in Roman Africa: The Development of Its Practices and Beliefs* (Grand Rapids: Eerdmans, 2014), 38.

[29]   David E. Wilhite, *Ancient African Christianity: An Introduction to a Unique Context and Tradition* (New York: Routledge, 2017), 20–21, 226.

[30]   Brown, *Augustine of Hippo*, 208.

[31]   Burns and Jensen, *Christianity in Roman Africa*, 236, 410.

[32]   Brown, *Augustine of Hippo*, 208.

[33]   Allan D. Fitzgerald, introduction to *Homilies on the Gospel of John* (1–40), ed. Allan D. Fitzgerald, trans. Edmund Hill, The Works of Saint Augustine: A Translation for the 21st Century 3/12 (Hyde Park, N.Y.: New City Press, 2009), 15–16.

The tone Augustine uses in all the *Tractatus* continues here, evincing clear concern for his hearers/readers to gain a genuine understanding of the words of Jesus in John's Gospel. He wants them to recognize the transcendent plane on which Jesus operates, rather than miss it for lack of ability to look beyond the ordinary, which is the fixation of Jesus' hearers within the text. Augustine tries to offer as an alternative to the ordinary the only axis around which Christian life can turn well: relation to God (to borrow Volf's turn of phrase). Pausing to acknowledge that his unpredictable audience may be confused by Christ's statements in John 7:16, "My teaching is not mine, but is his who sent me," he asks, *Intellegere vis? Crede.*[34] Augustine is blunt: "Do you wish to understand? Believe."

He emphasizes this point thoroughly, raising Isaiah 7:9 from the Septuagint ("Unless you have believed, you will not understand") and connects his advice to the next verse of the Gospel, in which Christ continues, "If anyone wishes to do his will, he will learn concerning the teaching, whether it be from God, or whether I am speaking on my own" (John 7:17). Augustine asks what the first phrase means and, anticipating (or perhaps seeing with his own eyes) his congregation's confusion, he reminds them: *Si non intellixisti, inquam, crede. Intellectus enim merces est fidei.* "'If you have not understood,' I said, 'believe. For understanding is the wages of faith.'"[35]

Language of wages raises the idea of work, which takes him back to a previous day's passage and encourages his listeners toward more than only intellectual understanding. He has connected "he will learn" with understanding and made it the result of "do(ing) his will," which he links to believing. Jesus himself has explained the fact that doing God's will means doing God's work, in a portion of the previous chapter of the Gospel, which Augustine has exegeted in *Tractatus* XXV (Homily 25) and now examines in greater depth.

> *Ipse autem Dominus aperte alio loco dicit*: Hoc est opus Dei, ut credatis in eum quem ille misit. *Ut credatis in eum; non, ut credatis ei. Sed si creditis in eum, creditis ei: non autem continuo qui credit ei, credit in eum.*[36]

[34] Augustine, *Tract. Ev. Jo.* XXIX.6 (CCSL 36:287). All ensuing translations mine, unless otherwise indicated.
[35] Augustine, *Tract. Ev. Jo.* XXIX.6 (CCSL 36:287).
[36] Augustine, *Tract. Ev. Jo.* XXIX.6 (CCSL 36:287). Unless otherwise indicated, ensuing block quotations are from this section of *Tract. Ev. Jo.* XXIX.

Indeed the Lord himself openly said in another place: "This is the work of God, that you believe <u>into him</u> whom he has sent."[37] "That you believe <u>into him</u>," not "that you believe him." But if you believe <u>into him</u>, you believe him; however, not everyone who believes him also believes <u>into him</u>. (emphasis added)

Augustine explains that doing the work that God requires amounts to *ut credatis in eum quem ille misit*, literally "that you believe into him whom that one has sent." He wants to be sure that his listeners note Christ's choice of words. What Jesus describes is apparently more than just affirming the truth of his words as ambassador of the One (*ille*, "that One," indicating a distance) who sent him. Affirming the truth of his words is part of what Augustine describes, yes, but the reverse is not automatically true—believing Jesus does not equate to believing into Jesus. He offers an example:

Nam et daemones credebant ei, et non credebant <u>in eum</u>. Rursus etiam de Apostolis ipsius possumus dicere, Credimus Paulo; sed non, Credimus <u>in Paulum</u>: Credimus Petro; sed non, Credimus <u>in Petrum</u>. Credenti enim <u>in eum</u> qui iustificat impium, deputatur fides eius ad iustitiam.

For the demons also believed him, and yet they did not believe <u>into him</u>. Again also, of his own apostles we are able to say, "We believe Paul" but not "We believe <u>into Paul</u>"; "We believe Peter" but not "We believe <u>into Peter</u>." *For whoever believes <u>into him</u> who justifies the wicked, their faith is reckoned as justice.*[38]

Even demons believed Jesus, but that's as far as the relationship went between them and him. Augustine employs the example of demons' belief to illustrate the limit on *credere* + dative (*ei/Christo*) elsewhere in his writings, including when he is preaching on Psalm 130, going into far greater detail about the demons to demonstrate the contrast

---

[37]   Translator's note: I am deliberately keeping the awkward construction to highlight its uniqueness, to distinguish it from the use of "believe in God" to mean "to believe that God exists" (or "believe in Christ" as in "to believe that Christ is divine") or any other construal of that phrase, and to make it easier to distinguish in translation from the other part of the formula that arises from the next sermon to be considered here.

[38]   Literally, the faith of the "believing" or "believing ones" (*credenti*) is reckoned "toward" (*ad*) justice (in the sense of justification).

between their belief and "ours."[39] In *Tract. Ev. Jo.* XXIX, however, he quickly proceeds to a holier example than demons, that of belief as it regards the apostles. We (Augustine and his listeners) may talk about believing the apostles. The testimonies of Paul and Peter are accepted as true, but no one talks about believing *into* Paul and Peter. What Jesus is calling for his hearers to do, "believe into the One whom God has sent," is bolder than just believing God. Augustine then recalls Romans 4:5, in which believing into him who justifies the wicked is "reckoned as justice." Augustine lingers here to raise the question, "What is it, 'to believe into him?'" What is Jesus talking about? Augustine's answer will echo for centuries, before eventually dying out:

> *Quid est ergo credere in eum? Credendo amare, credendo diligere, credendo in eum ire, et eius membris incorporari.*

> What is it, therefore, "to believe into him?" By believing to love, by believing to hold dear, by believing to go into him, and to be incorporated in his members.

The *Credendo* Crescendo: From Feeling to Flesh

The phrase builds from the ethereal to the concrete, and it bears examination, part by part. In this section, we will consider carefully what theological points Augustine is making by means of rhetorical flourish. I have come to call this portion of his sermon the "*credendo* crescendo," because Augustine repeats the word *credendo*, "by believing," to open each of a short series of phrases describing what "believing into God" entails, which grows in intensity with each phrase. It is important to note, in light of the heavy traditional emphasis on Augustine's preference for the ethereal and eschatological over the visible and earthly, that we are here dealing with the mature Augustine in his more mundane ministry setting. As recent scholarship on Augustine suggests, there is a fleshing out of the spiritual and practical dimensions of Augustine's theological system that becomes possible by understanding the balance struck in his later years between the invisible and visible work of God.

Augustine's ecclesiology is rife with bodily language that encompasses both. Far from the bifurcation of visible and invisible, earth and

---

[39]   Augustine, *Ennarat. Ps.* CXXX (CCSL 40:1898).

heaven, or body and spirit with which Augustine is routinely charged, the mature Augustine finds in the incarnation of Christ a model for the church as mysterious union of visible and invisible.[40] The identity of the bodies assembled as the church—the body of Christ—relies on a shared experience of humanity, both human nature and human flesh.[41] One can imagine hundreds of the faithful, perhaps literally rubbing elbows or shoulder-to-shoulder, as they stand together in the nave and aisles of the cathedral church, attention turned toward the apse and the raised chancel area to see and be seen by Bishop Augustine and hear his words describing what it means and what difference it makes "to believe into Christ."[42]

Credendo amare, "by believing to love"

This opening phrase seems simple enough. *Amare* is the quintessential first conjugation verb that remains Latin students' first grammar lesson. The classifications of love in Greek are not directly mappable onto Latin terminology for love. Nevertheless, *amare* can be understood as a simple form of love, judging by Jerome's choice for the Vulgate's John 21:15 of *amo* as the translation of φιλῶ (*philō*), "I love," the expression of friendly affection with which Peter answers Jesus, who had asked if Peter loved him (albeit using the verb denoting stronger, pure Godly love, *agape*).

Credendo diligere, "by believing to hold dear"

This phrase is as complex as *amare* is simple. One Oxford Latin-English dictionary offers two choices of definition for *diligere*, "esteem

---

[40]   James K. Lee, *Augustine and the Mystery of the Church* (Minneapolis: Fortress, 2017), 42.

[41]   Lee, *Augustine and the Mystery*, 42.

[42]   Burns and Jensen, *Christianity in Roman Africa*, 159–60. Excavation of the *Basilica Pacis* (*Basilica Maior*) in Hippo, considered likely to have been Augustine's cathedral church, has revealed that the "apse was elevated and accessed by a short flight of steps, corresponding to Augustine's reference to steps leading up into the presbyterium" (158). Burns and Jensen describe the likely placement of the bishop's throne or chair (*cathedra*) in the center of the curved bench (*synthronon*) that would have him seated among the presbyters, though elsewhere he does describe preaching from pulpits. The dimensions of this church fit Augustine's own descriptions of his "large church," and Burns and Jensen go on to describe possibilities of how worshipers may have been grouped and located as they stood (widows and virgins near the apse, catechumens and penitents in aisles toward the back, etc.), before concluding that "the church would have had a nave and aisle area of about 564 square meters (6,070 square feet). With everyone standing, as was the custom, this church could have accommodated more than 2,000 people for festivals" (159).

highly" or "hold dear,"[43] but every dictionary offers different choices, ranging from "select" (in the University of Notre Dame's online Latin-English *William Whitaker's Words*)[44] to "cherish" (the choice of The Works of St. Augustine translator Edmund P. Hill).[45] Despite numerous options, English translations of the Vulgate and other Latin Christian literature default to "love." In fact, throughout the Vulgate, the most famous passages on love from all four Gospels use the verb *diligere*, not *amare*.[46] Indeed, as Augustine further develops the concept of *credere in eum/Christum*, he will frequently use *diligere*. Peter Brown noted that its noun form, *dilectio*, is an important concept for understanding Augustine's view of religion and society: the motivations of people groups—which can be assessed by the quality of the loves they share for good or ill—could be explained by *dilectio*,

[43] "Diligo, exi, ectum," in *Oxford Latin Desk Dictionary*, ed. James Morwood (New York: Oxford University Press, 2005), 58.

[44] "Diligere," in *William Whitaker's Words*, University of Notre Dame, http://archives.nd.edu/cgi-bin/wordz.pl?keyword=diligere. "Select" as the primary meaning is followed by alternatives "pick, single out; love, value, esteem; approve, aspire to, appreciate."

[45] Augustine, *Homilies on the Gospel of John* (1–40), trans. Hill, 493. While taking more poetic license in translation, Hill nevertheless takes pains to indicate the distinction of Augustine's choices here by noting in parentheses the original Latin words "by believing to love (*amare*) him, by believing to cherish (*diligere*) him." Hill further notes, "The distinction between the two Latin words, *amare* and *diligere*, is delicate. *Amare* refers to love in general terms; *diligere* means having a high regard or valuing someone. But Augustine does not always make a distinction, occasionally using these two words as synonymous, or switching their meanings." Thus it is difficult to pin down a translation, but it is fairly clear from context that Augustine is moving from general to specific, particularly to the specific person of Christ.

[46] For example, in all three Synoptic Gospels, as here in Matt 22, the famous "Golden Rule" appears with *diligere* as the verb:

> [37] "**Diliges** Dominum Deum tuum in toto corde tuo et in tota anima tua et in tota mente tua: [38] hoc est magnum et primum mandatum. [39] Secundum autem simile est huic: **Diliges** proximum tuum sicut teipsum."

It could just as easily be translated:

> "You shall hold the Lord your God dear in all your heart, and in all your soul, and in all your mind: this is the greatest and first commandment. The second is similar: You shall hold your neighbor as dear as yourself."

The Vulgate is freely accessible on The Vatican's website: http://www.vatican.va/archive/bible/nova_vulgata/documents/nova-vulgata_nt_evang-matthaeum_lt.html#22.

The same *diligere* is present in John 3:16 ("For God so loved the world") and 1 John 4:8 ("God is love").

"which, for Augustine, stands for the orientation of the entire personality, its deepest wishes and its basic capacity to love."[47] The point for now is that, in going from *credendo amare* to *credendo diligere*, Augustine takes his hearers/readers a step closer to the One who has descended from heaven and drawn near to humanity in the flesh.

Credendo in eum ire, "by believing to go into him"

This phrase plays upon the uniqueness of the grammatical construction that interests us here, *in eum*, which we have noted emphasizes *motion*, to conjure concrete, intimate images of bodily union. It also evokes the movement of catechumens into the baptismal waters, in which persons die with Christ and rise to newness of life and a new body of believers. Later chapters here will explore—in even greater, full-bodied depth than the waters in which the baptized would be immersed—the far-reaching implications of these movements for Augustine's hearers and for us today who seek to restore the relational sense. Going into Christ makes believers-into one with Christ in tangible ways that are represented in the sacramental elements whenever such believers go into gatherings of the body of Christ that is the church. The matter encountered in these rites matters for uniting the visible with the invisible (much as Augustine is charged with bifurcating the two, here he employs images that unite them). As we shall see from other instances of his preaching thus, it matters not only for baptismal waters but also for the eucharistic table.

A Kind of Coda: *et eius membris incorporari*, "and to be incorporated in his members"

This phrase may sound to the modern mind like a simple reference to being received or "incorporated" into local church membership, but the language, to original listeners in the church at Hippo, would also carry connotations every bit as concrete as the previous phrase, with which it already has in common baptismal implications. *Membrum*, the neuter (i.e., neither feminine nor masculine gender) noun Augustine uses here, means "limb" and especially refers (according to

---

[47]   Peter Brown, *Religion and Society in the Age of St. Augustine* (New York: Harper & Row, 1972), 42.

both Oxford and Notre Dame) to the "male genital member."[48] The plural here most likely encourages the listener to take the simpler meaning
of "limbs." It permits listeners to consider their hands and feet as intri-
cately bound up with those of Christ, moving in love and reaching out
to those whom Jesus touches: the poor, sick, and powerless. Nevertheless, the choice of a word that also has such intimate reference is likely
designed by Augustine to capture his hearers' attention and communi-
cate the intimacy of the incorporation that *credere in eum* entails.[49] His
use of the word *membrum* elsewhere has come to light in a relatively
recently discovered and authenticated, extended version of a previously
translated and published sermon on the martyrs Perpetua and Felicity
(*Serm.* CCLXXXII, Sermon 282). There Augustine uses the language
of "member" to suggest that Perpetua was able to withstand the devil
despite the weakness of her sex by supernatural intervention that converted her into a man, complete with being awarded a "very special
member" so that she was lacking in manhood in no way ("manhood"
construed classically, that is—contemporary understandings of gender
would problematize the assumption that manhood requires the genital
member in question).

Problems of attention span among Augustine's listeners in the
sanctuary at Hippo are considered a reason for his sprinkling sermons with "words that seek to revive the attention of his listeners,"
and there is little doubt that *membra* would be such a word.[50] His
listeners' appreciation of such efforts has been the topic of reflection

---

48   "Membrum, I," in *Oxford Latin Desk Dictionary*, 114; "membra," in *William Whitaker's Words*, University of Notre Dame, accessed online at http://archives .nd.edu/cgi-bin/wordz.pl?keyword=membra. This entry includes several additional meanings that depend largely on context, such as "member, limb, organ; (esp.) male genital member; apartment, room; section."

49   I am grateful to Dr. Meg Cotter-Lynch, who brought the "new" sermon to my attention in response to my presentation on *Tract. Ev. Jo.* XXIX. See Isabella Schiller, Dorothea Weber, and Clemens Weidmann, "Sechs neue Augustinuspre-
digten: Teil 1 mit Edition dreier Sermones," *Wiener Studien* 121 (2008): 263–64. It is likely mere coincidence that *membra* is also the name of a rhetorical device, the usage of which in the Pauline epistles Augustine identifies in *DDC* as evidence of the presence of oratory and rhetoric even where not deliberately intended. Those *membra*, carefully intertwined with another device known as *caesa*, he cites more than once in defense of eloquence as a tool for the spread of the gospel, in repu-
diation of his fideist contemporaries' opposition to what they perceive to be the pagan (read: Sophist) tool of rhetoric (*DDC* IV.7.11 on Rom 5:3-5; IV.20.40 on Rom 13:6-8).

50   Fitzgerald, introduction to *Homilies on the Gospel of John* (1–40), 26–27.

by more than one scholar of Augustine. Brown noted that, even when North Africa, the first place Christians spoke Latin, was suffering neglect from imperial administrators and its inhabitants lived in denial of its own decline, they still "delighted in the sheer play of words, in puns, rhymes and riddles," such that "as a bishop, Augustine will be hugely admired by his congregation, for being superbly able to provide a display of verbal fireworks."[51] Mohrmann noted that in the process of baptizing everyday words for Christian use, his puns, in particular, struck the fancy of these early Christians and even resulted in spontaneous applause.[52] Nevertheless, he would use such attention-getters not for the praise of his own glory, but out of love for those who trusted Christ for salvation,[53] to drive these listeners' attention toward the truth, in this case, the truth that union with Christ exceeds the fulfillment even of sexual union. The relationship resulting from believing into Christ is marked by a *caritas* intimacy of a quality that is unimaginable except by raising the imagery of *cupiditas* intimacy (in the sense of *concupiscentia*, concupiscence, or *libido*, lust, with which it is negatively linked) in order to associate it with the all-consuming nature thereof. As Augustine deems God the ultimate object of desire and the only one who satisfies every desire, so too he holds that humanity's baser appetites could be transformed into holier affections by grace guiding the human will properly.[54]

The Intimate Incorporation of Faith Working through Love

It is worth noting here that this incorporation in limbs/members accurately describes "the ultimate attachment to the divine" that lies at the center of Volf's definition of flourishing. It reveals Christianity's particular way of carrying out world religions' "crucial and abiding role in a globalized world," which is to "attend to the structural

---

[51]   Brown, *Religion and Society*, 10.

[52]   Mohrmann, "Le latin comun et le latin des Chretiens," in *Vigiliae Christianae* 1, no. 1 (1947): 6–7.

[53]   Fitzgerald, introduction to *Homilies on the Gospel of John* (1–40), 25.

[54]   Barbara J. McClure, *Emotions: Problems and Promise for Human Flourishing* (Waco: Baylor University Press, 2019), 50, 54. One of the most recent scholarly treatments of this view of Augustine (among others, including Thomas Aquinas) on the passions or emotions and their possible transformation appears in McClure's brief overview of thinkers who saw "Emotions as Sinful, Signs of the Fall, and Impediments to Salvation," the title of her second chapter, and in particular the section headed "Emotions Are God Given but Often Misdirected: Augustine."

restlessness of the human heart by offering connection to the transcendent realm and meaningful and joyous life in response to it."[55] The abovementioned *cupiditas* intimacy is a form of such restlessness, which Augustine decries when linked with *concupiscentia* and *libido* in *The City of God*.[56] There the physical "members" (*membra*) that such desire "stirs or fails to stir at its own whim, so to speak, and not at our own choice, should be called our shameful parts."[57] In *Tract. Ev. Jo. XXIX*, however, using "members" to capture his congregation's attention, he redirects it to the intimacy of members who through *credere in eum* are stirred by the rightly ordered love of Christ. The notion that *credere in eum* therefore is deeply relational and constitutive of Christian faith continues to be clear, as Augustine proceeds to assure his hearers:

> *Ipsa est ergo fides quam de nobis exigit Deus; et non invenit quod exigit Deus, nisi donaverit quod inveniat. Quae fides, nisi quam definivit alio loco apostolus plenissime dicens*: Neque circumcisio aliquid valet, neque praeputium, sed fides quae per dilectionem operatur?

> Therefore it is the very faith which God requires of us: and God does not find (in us) what God requires unless God has given what God finds in us. What faith is this, if not that which the apostle in another place has most fully defined, saying "Neither circumcision nor uncircumcision is worth anything, but faith that works through love?"[58]

God is here depicted as wanting so much to put "us" (Augustine and his hearers) in right relationship with God that what God requires of us, God also generously supplies. Augustine earlier connected *credere in eum* with right relationship of the sinner to God by quoting Romans 4:5 and now turns to Paul's other famous "justification by faith" epistle, Galatians. Using Paul's imagery related to the male "member" from the original covenant, he now identifies *credere in*

---

[55] Volf, *Flourishing: Why We Need Religion in a Globalized World* (New Haven, Conn.: Yale University Press, 2015), 83.

[56] Augustine, *The City of God XI–XXII* XIV.7, ed. Boniface Ramsey, trans. William S. Babcock, The Works of Saint Augustine: A Translation for the 21st Century 1/7 (Hyde Park, N.Y.: New City Press, 2013), 107.

[57] Augustine, *City of God* XIV.17, trans. Babcock, 124.

[58] *Tract. Ev. Jo.* XXIX.6 (CCSL 36:287).

eum, an act made possible by God's own gift to us, as faith working through love. He emphasizes the relationship of the Sender and the Sent and the surrender of Jesus' ownership of his own teachings, because he is so rooted in relationship with the One who sent him.

Augustine distinguishes *credere in eum* again, but this time from *credere eum*, instead of *credere ei*, in a sermon on a portion of the Farewell Discourse in which Jesus is about to surrender himself to be crucified.[59] In *Serm.* CXLIV (Sermon on the New Testament 144), Augustine addresses John 16:8-11, about the Holy Spirit's role in challenging the world with regard to sin, justice, and judgment. Even as Augustine wonders with his listeners why, as he interprets it, the sin of not believing into Christ is the sole source of the Holy Spirit's challenge, he draws a distinction between proud unbelievers and believers into humble Christ:

> *Credere Christum, et credere in Christum, differunt. De peccato igitur arguuntur infideles, id est, dilectores mundi: nam ipsi significantur mundi nomine.*[60]

> To believe in Christ, and to believe into Christ, differ. Therefore the unbelievers are challenged about sin, that is, the lovers of the world: for that is what is meant by the name "the world."

Here Augustine seems to suggest that those who love the world don't even know what it is to believe into God. It is important to understand that Augustine is not representing the kind of asceticism that rejects and despises the world. On the contrary, the fundamental difference between Donatism and Augustine's Catholicism is the issue of whether to abstain from the world completely and set Christian communities as far apart from it as possible in order to keep them unstained by evil (the Donatist view), or to see the mission as that of risking relationship with outsiders who can be positively influenced by being absorbed into and transformed by

---

[59]   While this text is from John's Gospel, this sermon is not part of the *Tractatus* project on the entirety of John's Gospel, which, at the time that *Serm.* CXLIV was preached most likely was still in progress.

[60]   Augustine, *Serm.* CXLIV.2 (PL 38:788). My translation differs from but is corroborated by that in Augustine, Sermon 144, in *Sermons on the New Testament* (94A–147A), ed. John E. Rotelle, trans. Edmund P. Hill, The Works of Saint Augustine: A Translation for the 21st Century 3/4 (Brooklyn, N.Y.: New City Press, 1992).

Christian community.[61] An increasingly strong tone of resistance to imperial domination does arise in his mature work, as Augustine sees the Roman Empire's neglect of North African provinces, plundering Punic material and human resources through the slave trade and its treatment of the region as Europe's breadbasket, even while leaving it vulnerable to occupation and attack from other forces.[62] Epistolary exchanges between himself and fellow North African bishops reveal the tension between Augustine's identities as Roman and African of Punic descent.[63] So he preaches this message

[61] As identified by Brown, *Augustine of Hippo*, 220. As Brown frames it, the purity-focus of Donatists was intended, in keeping with the warnings of Israel's prophets, to keep pure the community's relationship with God (216). So relationship itself is not new or unique to Augustine or the Catholics (or Caecilianists), but what is unique is his push against what he perceives to be the loveless, slavish-obedience model of relationship that the Donatists espouse, which made the mistake of suggesting that human will could "stand in the way of the omnipotence and foresight of God" who predestines the elect, potentially solving one problem with a doctrinal foundation of predestination that may be seen as raising other theological problems after Augustine, in order to involve a greater swath of the earth than just a corner of Africa (217). Here, Brown directs readers to the *Ennarat. Ps.* 32.14, and *Parm.* I.4.6 for Augustine's frustration with Donatists' failure to understand predestination, and to *Ennarat. Ps.* 95, 11 for his comparison of the Donatists to frogs who "sit in their marsh and croak, 'We are the only Christians!'" Against this background, J. Patout Burns has argued that Augustine's doctrine of election was a "common sense" approach to the confusion sparked by Donatism among African Catholics in the face of a certainty of proper rule-following for salvation on the part of European (read: Roman) Catholics—see Burns, "The Atmosphere of Election: Augustinianism as Common Sense," *Journal of Early Christian Studies* 2, no. 3 (1994): 337.

[62] Robert B. Eno, introduction to Letter 10*, in *Letters*, vol. 6 (1*–29*), The Fathers of the Church 81 (Washington, D.C.: Catholic University of America Press, 1989), 74.

[63] Wilhite, *Ancient African Christianity*, 253–55. Wilhite identifies with an effort to fill the gap in scholarship on Augustine's African identity. In his chapter "Augustine the African," he considers several letters that Augustine writes over the course of his career, including Letter 17.2, chastising Maximus of Madauros for having denigrated indigenous heritage of North Africa (a move he describes negatively as "Roman"); Letter 22.2,4, encouraging Bishop Aurelius of Carthage that he couldn't lead any more wisely even if he were African himself and inviting him to join Augustine in prayer for the healing of the African Church (from Donatist schism, it is implied); Letter 199.46–47, assuring Bishop Hesychius of Dalmatia that the end of the world could not be near, as the gospel had yet to be preached among "barbarians" living "among us (Africans)" and declaring, "For the Lord swore an oath to Abraham that all nations, not just the Romans, would be of his seed"; and Letter 10*.2.5, a more recently discovered text centering on

to a likely mixed congregation, whom he hopes will hunger for the "more than *credere deum*" that he describes.

> *Cum enim dicitur, Arguet mundum de peccato; non alio quam quod non crediderunt in Christum. Hoc denique peccatum si non sit, nulla peccata remanebunt, quia justo ex fide vivente cuncta solvuntur.*

> For when it says, "(The Spirit) will challenge the world about sin," it will not be about any other than that they did not believe into Christ. In fact, if this sin did not exist, no sin would remain, because for the just one living by faith, all (sins) are released.

Now Augustine is identifying a lack of *credere in eum* as the root of all sin. He is not abandoning a doctrine of original sin here. Rather, if pressed on the matter, he would likely identify in Eve and Adam the error of having believed in God's existence as their Creator but not believing into God by, in the terms established in *Tract. Ev. Jo.* XXIX, loving, holding God dear, going into God (instead of being taken in by the serpent), and being made one with God's hands and feet, such that theirs then would not have reached for forbidden fruit nor fled from God's sight. For that matter, in *Tract. Ev. Jo.* XXIX terms, he could argue that humanity's first parents did not even believe God, taking the serpent at his word instead. However, Augustine has yet to establish the terms, within the parameters of this sermon, for the distinction that he is making. He has only pointed out that the one who believes into Christ has faith that frees from all sin. So we cease speculating and continue:

> *Sed multum interest, utrum quisque credat ipsum Christum, et utrum credat in Christum. Nam ipsum esse Christum et daemones crediderunt, nec tamen in Christum daemones crediderunt.*

> But it makes plenty of difference, whether someone believes in Christ (i.e., affirms Christ's existence and identity/believes him

---

complaint to his friend residing in Italy about the ways that slavery threatened to deprive Africa of its native population. There are obvious complexifying factors in his choice of language about barbarians and about Abraham, but the tensions between African and Roman identity are nevertheless clear. Wilhite also notes an increasing awareness on Augustine's part of the temporary nature of the Roman Empire's role in the spread of Christianity.

to be actually Christ), or whether they believe <u>into Christ</u>. For even the demons believed him to be actually Christ, nevertheless the demons did not believe <u>into Christ</u>.

Once again, the demons set the example of insufficient belief for constituting Christianity. He does not elaborate here on the distinctions from demons, as he does elsewhere, for example, in *Enarrationes in Psalmos* CXXX (Exposition of Psalm 130). There he lays out that to believe into Christ is to hold Christ dear; not how demons believe in Christ but don't hold Christ dear and instead question, "What do you have to do with us?" With that reference to Matthew 8:29, he advises believers into Christ not to ask that question but instead to declare that we belong to Christ, for he has redeemed us.[64] For now in *Serm.* CXLIV, however, he finally begins to lay out the terms of *credere in Christum*:

> *Ille enim credit <u>in Christum</u>, qui et sperat in Christum et diligit Christum. Nam si fidem habet sine spe ac sine dilectione, Christum esse credit, non <u>in Christum</u> credit.*

That is to say, you[65] believe <u>into Christ</u> when you both hope in Christ[66] and hold Christ dear. For if you have faith without hope or without love (lit. without holding him dear), you believe in Christ, but you do not believe <u>into Christ</u>.

---

[64] Augustine, *Ennarat. Ps.* CXXX (CCSL 40:1898). I have here translated: "*Hoc est enim credere in Christum, diligere Christum: non quomodo daemones credebant, sed non diligebant; et ideo quamvis crederent, dicebant,* Quid nobis et tibi est, Fili Dei? *Nos autem sic credamus, ut in ipsum credamus, diligentes eum, et non dicamus,* Quid nobis et tibi est? *sed dicamus potius,* Ad te pertinemus; tu nos redemisti." Note that English translations tend to omit this portion of Augustine's exposition of this psalm, which they designate as Psalm 131. Perhaps they do so to avoid the awkwardness of believing into Christ, whom Augustine sees as the lens through which to view even the psalms of the Hebrew Bible, as do his contemporaries. An exception is Hill's full translation in Augustine, *Sermons on the New Testament* (94A–147A).

[65] Literally "one" or "one who," but for flow and ease of pronoun selection, I am siding with Hill and selecting the second person singular.

[66] In this instance, one might translate *sperat in Christum* as "hope <u>into</u> Christ," though Augustine does not expound upon the *in* + accusative object for "hope." Perhaps he has chosen this construction and used it without explanation because he considers the theological virtues to be so intertwined that explanation is unnecessary.

Here, Augustine links the three theological virtues of faith, hope, and love with regard to *credere in eum/Christum*. Without making direct reference to the famous thirteenth chapter of Paul's letter to the contentious church at Corinth,[67] Augustine is in agreement with the apostle that the three virtues are bound together. He further concurs with Paul that love, when paired with hope, is supreme in its ability to transform faith into the "believing into Christ" that frees the believer from sin.

> *Qui ergo in Christum credit, credendo in Christum, venit in eum Christus, et quodam modo unitur in eum, et membrum in corpore ejus efficitur. Quod fieri non potest, nisi et spes accedat et caritas.*

> When you believe into Christ, therefore, by your believing into Christ, Christ comes into you, and you are in some way made one with him (literally "united into him"), and made a member in his body. And this cannot be, unless both hope and charity are added.

Again, he has emphasized that righteousness in the Christian faith relies on the act of *credere in Christum* and now describes what it entails. The language of body and members appears here, as in *Tract. Ev. Jo.* XXIX, and there is a counterpoint to the movement described in that sermon. For here it is Christ who comes into the believer. Once again, Augustine seems to risk *double entendre*, perhaps to startle sleepy listeners, with language of union that recalls fleshly union for emphasis on the intensity of holy intimacy. Christ, in this mutual indwelling, equips the believer with love of neighbor, which Augustine then describes in terms of Christlike humbling of self for others.[68] This whole section of the sermon is a rehearsal of the Christ Hymn of humility in Philippians 2:3-11, encouraging Christians to seek the advantage of others.

Between the two types of *credere* he describes here (*credere Christum* and *credere in Christum*) and the two in *Tract. Ev. Jo.* XXIX (*credere ei* and *credere in eum*), there are three identifiable types of Christian belief: *credere eum/Christum, credere ei/Christo,* and *credere*

---

[67]   Corinth is perhaps the best biblical example of the kind of risks Augustine is willing to let the church take in welcoming worldly sinners and in absorbing the world in order to transform Christians' love of it into love of God.

[68]   *Serm.* CXLIV.4.

in eum/*in Christum*. The order of the first two is not as important for Christianity as is the constitutive nature of the third. This three-part formula (using *Deum*/*Deo*, "God" as placeholder for the object) might be taken as the framework by which one can view Augustine's understanding of the Christian faith.[69]

A Discovery Reveals the Three Types of *Credere* Together

Until recently, any scholars examining the three types of *credere* considered the resulting formula as if it had been compiled from across the Augustinian corpus, with its systematization of the three types as a formula apparent only beginning to emerge in the works of Augustine's inheritors (to be considered in the next chapter). In 1990, François Dolbeau discovered twenty-six sermons, previously lost for hundreds of years—including a sermon now known as the Dolbeau 19/Mainz 51/Sermon 130A, in which Augustine addresses the *credere* formula in all three of its parts.[70] In this sermon, ostensibly on John 6:27 ("Work for the food which does not perish but abides unto eternal life") but rapidly moving to focus the majority of its length on 6:28-29 ("This is the work of God, that you should believe into the One whom God has sent"), Augustine describes at length the three types and explains carefully the whole *credere* formula. The uncertainty of the dating of this sermon (scholars' opinions ranging from 405 to 419) makes it unclear whether Augustine preached it as a foundation from which he drew reflections in the above sermons, or as a culmination of years of exegesis and working out details of the three types as he had continued preaching through the Gospel of John.[71]

It already is clear from the sermons considered thus far that purely propositional *credere eum*/*Christum* merely affirms that God exists or

[69] As suggested by TeSelle, "Faith," 348. He is drawing from writings such as the *Enchiridium* and *The Spirit and the Letter*.

[70] John E. Rotelle, introduction to *Newly Discovered Sermons*, ed. John E. Rotelle, trans. Edmund Hill, The Works of Saint Augustine: A Translation for the 21st Century 3/11 (Brooklyn, N.Y.: New City Press, 1997), 13–14.

[71] Augustine, "Sermons Inédits de Saint Augustin Préchs en 397 (5ème série)," ed. François Dolbeau, *Revue Benedictine* 104, no. 1–2 (1994): 34–72. In publishing the Latin text for the first time, Dolbeau suggests that this sermon's characteristics lie outside those common to the rest of the set published with it, dating it to 404 or later (67–68). Edmund Hill, in the New City Press translation (see previous note), places "405" on the first page but in endnote 27 opines that it bears features suggesting instead that Augustine preached it in his old age, during his final visit to Carthage in 419 (125, n. 27).

that Jesus is actually the Christ and by extension affirms the propositions of the creeds as facts. Whenever the believer observes Christ's promises coming to fruition, then *credere ei/Christo*, believing him, becomes possible—a matter of respecting his divine authority and veracity. Either may accompany or precede the other, but it is *credere in eum/Christum* that results in right relationship with God and ultimately neighbor. Augustine considers saving faith to be viewing the person(s) of God described in the creeds and who keeps promises as the One into whose hands we wish to place our lives, with whom we wish to become one. These implications become even stronger in light of what Augustine reiterates from them and adds to them (assuming a dating later than those sermons previously discussed here) in Sermon 130A.

In this newly discovered sermon, the bishop appears to ramble in his preaching, and the Dolbeau manuscript has a few sections in which the Latin is nearly unintelligible due to possible copyist errors.[72] Yet it makes clear that Augustine fully intended the three parts of the formula to expose the inadequacy of the first two alone and to emphasize the necessity of believing-into. Similar to his treatment of the same ideas in *Tract. Ev. Jo.* XXIX, Augustine urges his audience to recognize "believing into the One whom that One has sent" as the only and utmost way to "do the work of God," and therefore Augustine promises to spend the whole sermon, the Lord being his helper, "explaining what it is to believe into Christ."[73] In the process of presenting this explanation,

---

[72]   Augustine, Dolbeau 19/Mainz 51/Sermon 130A, "Sermon of St. Augustine the Bishop on the Words of the Gospel, 'Work for the Food which Does Not Perish, but Which Abides Unto Eternal Life," in *Newly Discovered Sermons*, 127, n. 13, 128, n. 27. In n. 13, translator Hill admits, "This sentence baffles me completely. My translation plays ducks and drakes with Latin grammar—or assumes that that is what Augustine was doing." He then offers the Latin, as he does in other footnotes, actively inviting the reader to try their hand at translating. In n. 27, Hill observes, "He is really rambling! Admittedly he has just said he is very tired. But his constant loss of the thread of his remarks inclines me to think that the sermon was much later than the date suggested by Dolbeau, after 404. It's the sermon of an old as well as of a tired man. I think it probable it was preached, together with its sequel, 14A (Mainz 52), during Augustine's last visit to Carthage in 419."

[73]   Augustine, *Sermo S. Augustini Episcopi de Verbis Evangelii Ego Sum Panis qui de Caelo Descendi et Operamini Escam non quae Perit sed quae Permanet in Aeternum*, in "Sermons Inédits," 57–58. Here and after, this Latin text will be noted in the following format: Dolbeau 19, 2, 25–26, and 51–53. This sentence includes my translations of the following Latin: *Hoc est . . . opus dei, ut credatis in illum quem ille misit* (25–26) and *Iam tota intentio nostri sermonis innititur,*

features emerge from his previous, partial treatments of the formula that he revisits and upon which he expands. He also introduces several newer features upon which the constructive work of the present volume relies, such that it is important to identify these expanded and newly introduced elements briefly now. Rather than attempt to make sense of the rambling nature of the sermon, the following approach is thematic, acknowledging similarities and presenting at greater length the additions or innovations of 130A in particular.

The Three Types Together

The first appearance of all three types of *credere* uses the first two types to establish what *credere in eum* is not:

> Hoc est *enim* opus dei, ut credatis in eum quem ille misit. *Non dixit "credatis ei" aut "credatis eum," sed* credatis *in eum. Audivimus eloquia prophetarum: credimus eis, sed non credimus in_ eos. Audivimus praedicantes apostolos: credimus praedicationi eorum, sed in eos non credimus. Non credimus in Paulum, sed credimus Paulo.*[74]

> *Indeed,* "this is the work of God, that you believe into him whom that One has sent." He does not say "that you believe him," but that you believe into him. We have heard the prophets' utterances—we believe them, but we do not believe into them. We have heard the Apostles' preaching—we believe their preaching, but we do not believe into them. We do not believe into Paul, but we believe Paul.

Augustine is covering the same general rhetorical territory as in *Tract. Ev. Jo.* XXIX.6, contrasting propositional belief that the words of the prophets (uniquely mentioned here) and apostles, including Paul (also mentioned in *Tract. Ev. Jo.* XXIX.6), are true with belief into Christ, the relationship of trust that Christ invites in the sermon's selected Bible passage. While he has named all three types here, he does not unpack all three until later, when he commands his hearers to "examine now these things for yourselves," or, as Edmund Hill

---

in quantum possumus, si domino adiuuante possumus, explicare quid sit credere in Christum (51–53). Hereafter all translations of the Dolbeau 19 text are mine unless otherwise indicated.

[74] Augustine, Dolbeau 19, 3, 54–58.

interprets it in the New City Press translation, "now see the difference between these three in yourself."[75] Augustine names and explains
the three both before and after this command, the second time with
added explanation:

> . . . *distinximus aliud esse credere illi, credere illum et credere in*
> *illum—credere illi est credere vera esse illa quae loquitur, credere*
> *illum est credere quod ipse sit Christus, credere in illum diligere*
> *illum . . . credere quae loquitur vera esse, credere ipsum esse Chris-*
> *tum, diligere Christum. Credere vera esse quae loquitur, multi*
> *et mali possunt. Credunt enim esse vera et nolunt facere ei: ad*
> *operandum pigri sunt. Credere autem ipsum esse Christum, hoc*
> *et daemones potuerunt.*[76]

> . . . we have distinguished between believing him (literally "that
> One"), believing in him and believing into him—to believe him
> is to believe what he says is true, to believe in him is to believe
> that he is the Christ, to believe into him is to cherish him. . . .
> to believe what he says is true, to believe him himself to be the
> Christ, to cherish Christ. To believe what he says to be true, even
> many evil ones can do. For they believe (it) to be true and do not
> will to do it: they are lazy about working. To believe him to be
> Christ himself, this even the demons can do.

Much of this language is familiar from *Tract. Ev. Jo. XXIX*. Note that
here, however, having first named *credere in illum* with its contrasting
alternatives, and then having described it as cherishing Christ, he sub-
stitutes *diligere Christum* for *credere in Christum* in the summary set
listed as he sets up for the discussion of evil ones.

Evil Ones Do vs. Love Is Done

Just as he has brought up demons in *Tract. Ev. Jo. XXIX* and the
Exposition on Psalm 130, so now he turns his hearers' attention to
the question of whether they want to believe better than demons do.
In fact, he has introduced them quite early in this sermon and is only

---

[75]   Augustine, Sermon 130A.5, in *Newly Discovered Sermons*, trans. Hill, 121.
Both Hill and I take a little poetic license with the short phrase from Dolbeau's
text (19A, 5, 107), *iam discutate tua ista*, which verbatim we could translate "now
examine your things of yours." Hill has inserted the implied extension of the
object of examination in Augustine's exhortation, "these three."

[76]   Augustine, Dolbeau 19, 5, 104–7, 108–11.

now returning to the subject in order to elaborate on his earlier statement, which paired them with Peter for comparison and contrast in the types of *credere*:

> *Et quid est quod ei dicunt*: Scimus qui sis? *An forte mentientes dicunt? quod nesciunt, dicunt? Ecce alio loco planius*: Tu es sanctus dei *dicunt, etiam* Tu es filius dei *dicunt. Quod cum Petrus dixisset, audivit a domino*: Beatus es, Simon Bariona, quia non tibi revelavit caro et sanguis, sed pater meus qui est in caelis. Et ego dico tibi, Simon Bariona, quia tu es Petrus, et super hanc petram aedificabo ecclesiam meam. *Propter quod totum hoc? Quoniam dixit*: Tu es Christus, filius dei vivi. *Hoc dixerunt et daemones, quibus dictum est*: Obmutescite. *Quis ista facile discernat, unde non laudatur vox par, nisi quia cor dispar? Intellegite ergo, carissimi, admonentibus nobis, quod cottidie, legitis et dicitis.*[77]

Then what about what they (the demons) say to him, "We know who you are"? Or perhaps they are telling lies? They are saying that, when really they do not know? See, in another place more plainly, "You are the holy one of God," they say, and also, "You are the Son of God," they say. When Peter said that, he heard from the Lord, "Blessed are you, Simon son of Jonah, because flesh and blood have not revealed this to you, but my Father who is in the heavens. And I say to you, Simon son of Jonah, that you are Peter (the Rock), and upon this rock I shall build my church." Why all this? Because he said, "You are the Christ, the Son of the living God." This the demons also said, to whom he said, "Be silent!" How does he distinguish that readily, whence is an equal voice not praised, unless because of unequal hearts? Therefore understand, dearest ones, with our prompting, what you read and say every day.

Apparently Augustine is concerned that his hearers may be missing the drastic difference that the grammatical distinction describes, thinking their daily reading and profession of belief in Christ, that he is the Son of God, is all there is. There is a difference of heart, the difference-maker in *credere* in *eum*.

This difference of heart he goes on to explain later in the same section, in which he enumerates the three parts of the formula together.

[77] Augustine, Dolbeau 19, 2, 40–50.

Fear was at work in the hearts of both the demons and Peter, but two different kinds of fear:

> *Petrus ergo*: Tu es Christus, filius dei vivi *amando dixit; dae-mones hoc timendo dixerunt. Non autem omnis qui timet amat, omnis qui amat timet. Sed . . . timore casto*—timor *enim* domini castus permanens in saeculum saeculi, *non timore servili. Nam* consummate caritas foras mittit timorem.[78]

> Therefore Peter said, "You are the Christ, the Son of the living God" by loving; the demons said this by fearing. Moreover, not all who fear love, but all who love fear. But . . . with a chaste fear—for "the fear of the Lord is chaste, remaining for ever and ever," not servile fear. For "perfect love casts out fear."

Even evil ones do the work of identifying Jesus as the Christ, which is for them a terror that causes them to wish Christ away, but whoever does the work of God, believing into the One whom God has sent, does it with love and the desire for him to remain with them always. This love is done—in the sense of finished—with fear, casting it out and replacing it with the notion that the only thing that would be frightening would be the absence of Christ.

Augustine continues quoting Scripture throughout the remainder of the section on the types of fear and the presence of love that believing-into entails, which is the difference-maker between *credere in eum*, versus *credere eum* alone.[79] His selection of prooftexts spans from the Hebrew Bible through the New Testament (here Ps 19:9 and 1 John 4:18) to underscore the difference between being praised and being cast out by Christ, depending on whether one merely believes in Christ or also believes into Christ. Augustine later will turn the concept of praise in a different direction and apply it to believers' own actions in sacramental life.

"The Food Which Does Not Perish": Sacraments and Flourishing

The selected sermonic theme-text of "the food which does not perish but which abides unto eternal life" clearly sets up Augustine's hearers

---

[78]   Augustine, Dolbeau 19, 5, 111–16.

[79]   Later, in section 11—a section impossible to separate from its antisemitic language and therefore not worthy of discussion here—Augustine will contrast "a fear of damnation" with "the fire of love" (Augustine, Sermon 130A, in *Newly Discovered Sermons*, trans. Hill, 125).

for an exegesis related to the Eucharist. In the initial section, Augustine suggests that when the inner person is sin-sick, one "can praise good bread, but can't eat it," for such a person "is not inclined to eat such heavenly bread . . . and . . . takes no pleasure in eating it."[80] A healing change, however, seems to begin with or be marked by baptism, such that it is important to get believing-into right. The few direct references to baptism emerge in drawing the contrast between believing and believing-into.

The first explicit mention of baptism comes in drawing the contrast between believing Paul and believing into Paul. He turns to Paul's own words, before drawing contrasts in types of *credere* once again, and finally noting that only the God in whose name baptism occurs is worthy of belief-into:

> Numquid Paulus pro vobis crucifixus est, aut in nomine eius baptizati estis? *Denique non solum apostoli doctoresque sancti, sed etiam nos ipsi, minimis vestigiis non comparandi, cottidie dicimus:* Crede mihi; *numquam audemus dicere:* Crede in me. Crede mihi: *quis non dicit?* Crede in me: *quis dicit ait quis non insanit qui dicit? In quem ergo credendum est? De quo idem Paulus ait:* Credenti in eum qui iustificat impium, deputatur fides eius ad justitiam.[81]

> "Is it possible that Paul was crucified for all of you, or were you all baptized in his name?" Finally, not only the apostles and holy teachers, but also we ourselves, not to be compared with them in the slightest trace, daily say "Believe me"; never do we dare to say, "Believe into me." "Believe me"—who does not say it? "Believe into me"—who does say it, or who does say it who is not insane? Well, then, into whom is one believing? Into the same One about whom Paul said, "Believing into him who justifies the ungodly, their faith is reckoned as justice."

Augustine goes on to discuss why Paul is not that One. To the observations we have seen him make in *Tract. Ev. Jo.* XXIX.6, regarding the difference between believing Peter and Paul and believing *into* them, there is added here in 130A the observation that Paul's focus on crucifixion and baptism reorients Paul's audience away from Paul and toward Jesus as the One in whose name baptism occurs. Paul is not the

---

80 Augustine, Sermon 130A, in *Newly Discovered Sermons*, trans. Hill, 118.
81 Augustine, Dolbeau 19, 3, 60–67.

One who justifies the ungodly described in the words of Romans 4:5 (a passage also briefly quoted in *Tract. Ev. Jo.* XXIX.6). That One alone is the one into whom faith should be placed in order for faith to be reckoned justice, in the sense of justification.[82]

Baptism emerges explicitly one more time in Sermon 130A, when he names it in response to the question posed by the psalmist (in Ps 116:12), "How shall I recompense the Lord?" With reference to Psalm 103 to describe the gifts for which recompense may be required, Augustine answers, *Hoc factum est, quando abluti sumus*, that is, "This was done, when we were washed."[83] Augustine appears to treat baptism here as a response, in a sense of repayment, to the grace extended in pardon for sin that the psalmist describes (103:2-3). Without straying too far from his emphasis on grace (lest one slip into Pelagianism), such a construal makes sense in light of the previous baptismal reference in this sermon and its images related to justice. A hearkening to a process of sanctification follows, as he then notes, *Sed quod sequitur fit: Qui sanat omnes languores tuos*.[84] While the phrase from Psalm 103 in this sentence suggests the translation "But what follows is still happening: 'who heals all your feebleness (or ills, infirmities, faintnesses),'" the last word can also be translated "apathies," which, as will become clear, is a fitting translation for this context.[85]

He next proceeds to the place where he began both the section and the sermon, a focus on the bread of life that is Christ and the need of healing from sin-sickness in order to have an appetite for it:

> *Quantum sanantur languores, tantum delectat esca caelestis; tantum delectat panis vitae qui de caelo descendit, quantum sanantur*

---

[82]   Regarding faith, philosopher Isabelle Bochet's recent work is among the first (if not the first) sustained reflection(s) on this sermon (Dolbeau 19/Mainz 51/Sermon 130A). Her research and teaching explore *fides*, "faith," as a concept in Augustine's sermons, culminating in this one (that she dates to late 414 or shortly thereafter), upon which she presented at the International Conference on Patristics Studies on August 20, 2019. A publication based on this presentation is expected, "*Credere in Christum*: The Development of the Augustinian Notion of Fides," *Studia Patristica*, Papers Presented at the Eighteenth International Conference on Patristics Studies Held in Oxford 2019 (Leuven: Peeters, forthcoming).

[83]   Augustine, Dolbeau 19, 7, 155–58.

[84]   Augustine, Dolbeau 19, 7, 158.

[85]   "Languor, oris," *Oxford Latin Desk Dictionary*, 104. Hill uses "ills" and related forms of "ill" throughout for all forms of *languor* (Augustine, Sermon 130A, in *Newly Discovered Sermons*, trans. Hill, 122–28).

languores nostri. Sed a quo sanantur, nisi cui diximus: Converte
nos, deus sanitatum nostrarum? Converte nos: *tu nos converte,
quia, antequam sanes, adversamur et panem laudatum fastidio
adtingere nolumus. Adversamur languidi, convertimur sanati.*
Converte *ergo* nos, deus sanitatum nostrarum, et averte iram
tuam a nobis. *Languor enim ipse ira dei est.*[86]

As much as the apathies are healed, so much does the heavenly
food delight; so much does the bread of life, who came down
from heaven, delight, as much as our apathies are healed. But
by whom are they healed, if not by the One to whom we said,
"Convert us, God of our healings?" Convert us, oh, convert us,
because, until you heal, we are turned and do not want to touch
the praised bread, out of pride.[87] We are turned, weak; we are
converted, healed. Therefore "convert us, God of our healings,
and turn away your wrath from us." For the wrath of God actually is the apathy.

Here, as Augustine draws from Psalm 85 (apparently the responso-
rial psalm for the day's worship), is a place in which the translation
of *languor* as "apathy" becomes useful.[88] What Augustine goes on to
describe as the appetite suppressant and source of God's wrath is a
lack of care for others in favor of greed for oneself.

He later sketches this apathy, driven by greed, *Fallere hominem vis,
falli te a nemine vis. De malo alieno ditari vis, non vis quemquam de
malo tua ditari,*[89] which is to say, "You want to deceive a person, you
want to be deceived by no one. You want to enrich yourself by another's misfortune, you do not want anyone to enrich themselves by your
misfortune." In contrast to his description of delighting in the bread
of life who came down from heaven, the mirror that he now holds
up to the congregation exposes a false concept of flourishing held
by any who do not believe into the converting One but instead seek
only their own gain. If you enjoy, even delight, in not caring about
anyone but yourself, in building up your own power and strength
at the expense of others for whom you do not care, he warns, you

---

[86] Augustine, Dolbeau 19, 7, 159–68.
[87] Note that *fastidio*, translated "out of pride" here from the ablative singular
of *fastidium*, could also be "out of loathing" or "out of digust."
[88] The verse to which Augustine refers is Ps 85:4.
[89] Augustine, Dolbeau 19, 177–79.

may insist you enjoy it, but you are not experiencing wholeness and flourishing.[90] True flourishing results not from filling one's stomach with rich feasting but from feasting on the bread of life, an implicitly eucharistic image. But your appetite for it is diminished when you merely declare the truth of (but decline to enact) the golden rule, which Augustine poses in the negative words of Tobit 4:15, "What you do not want done to you, do not do to others."[91] What hope is there, then—so long as you delight in this apathy and are so stuck in your ways, turned inward and away from God and others—of being turned around, turned toward the God of healing and toward those for whom God calls you to care? Augustine reiterates the necessity of the cry for conversion from Psalm 85:4.

Bold Surrender and Deification

Such a cry requires a recognition of one's own weakness and what I call a "bold surrender" of all the trappings of our own bid for power and strength, to which Augustine then turns his attention. While Augustine mentions the bread, implicitly associated with Eucharist, without ever mentioning the wine in this sermon, he does mention fruit and pouring, as he draws on a later verse of Psalm 85, in order to emphasize the necessity of owning one's weakness. He likens our hearts and souls to the earth that must be softened or "sweetened" by God's gift of rain in order to yield fruit:

> Dominus dabit suavitatem, et terra nostra dabit fructum suum. Fructus autem spiritus, caritas. *Unde iste fructus, nisi dominus det suavitatem*, qua caritas dei diffusa est in cordibus nostris? *Non a nobis ipsis, sed* (per) spiritum sanctum qui datus est nobis.

> "The Lord gave the sweetness, and our earth gave its fruit." "But the fruit of the Spirit is love." Whence this fruit, unless the Lord gave the sweetness, "because the love of God has been poured out in our hearts?" Not by us ourselves, but "(through) the Holy Spirit who has been given to us."[92]

---

[90]   This is an English gloss of lines 180–82: "*Quare tibi non vis fieri? Si bonum est, quare fugis? Si malum est, quid respondebis, quid dices?* Delectat me facere et delectat me facere, hoc delectat et hoc delectate: *languentis uerba sunt.*"

[91]   The Latin is *Quod tibi fieri non vis, alio ne feceris.* Dolbeau 19, 7, 176.

[92]   Augustine, Dolbeau 19, 8, 184–88. With reference to Ps 85:12, Gal 5:22, and Rom 5:5.

Proceeding along this rambling path of prooftexts, Augustine reminds readers that Paul identified himself and Apollos as merely instruments through whom believers came to experience the softening rain that moved the earth to be "moved" and "grow weak" in order to bear fruit and, in the words of yet another psalm, be "perfected."[93]

He proceeds from "sweetness" to "infirmity" to unpack what "grew weak" means, in terms descriptive of bold surrender:

> *Quid est* infirmata est? *Non de se praesumpsit. Quid est* infirmata est? *De te totum speravit. Quid est* infirmata est? *Quando infirmor, tunc potens sum. Ergo* infirmata est, *intellexit gratiae dei esse, non meritorum suorum, virium suarum; intellexit,* infirmata est, *et perdidit praesumptionem, ut acciperet benedictionem.* Infirmata est. *Non ergo de se praesumat, clamet ad dominum infirma*: Converte nos, deus sanitatum nostrarum.[94]

> What is "it grew weak"? It did not presume about itself. What is "it grew weak"? From you it hoped for everything. What is "it grew weak"? When I am weakened, then I am powerful. Therefore "it grew weak," it understood all to be by God's grace, not by its own merits, its own strength; it understood, "it grew weak," it lost presumption, that it might accept blessing. "It grew weak." Therefore let it not presume about itself, let it in weakness shout to God, "Convert us, God of our healings."

Bold surrender involves precisely this casting aside of privilege and power, if one is in a position to take advantage of others, to recognize and embrace one's relative weakness and inability to save oneself, crying out for conversion. If one is not in such a position, perhaps identifying with the one of whose misfortune the powerful take advantage, then bold surrender involves crying out in weakness and avoiding presumption based on the lauded self-reliance that is the hallmark of the positive fruit of self-control but can go awry in opposition to God, seeking to hoard control for one's self.

When either loses presumption, what of the "blessing" that comes in return? Augustine recalls the words of the biblical author "unworthy to be called an apostle," Paul, in 2 Corinthians 12:9, that "My grace

---

[93]   Augustine, Dolbeau 19, 8, 193–205. With reference, among many other prooftexts, to "perfecting" in Ps 68:9.ᐧ

[94]   Augustine, Dolbeau 19, 9, 206–12.

is sufficient for you, strength is made perfect in weakness." This "grow-ing weak" by surrender of pretense and presumption opens up the one who thus embraces vulnerability to receive with hands empty of all other obstacles the gift of God's perfecting grace.[95] Furthermore, the outstretched hand is not filled with grace as if it were a commod-ity; rather, the God of grace in Jesus Christ grasps the hand and pulls the believer-into into God's own self. This aspect of bold surrender is a feature of doing the work of God, believing into the One whom that One has sent.

Movement Into

The pulling movement is initiated by God, but from the beginning of this meandering sermon, Augustine has been making it clear that even God-initiated faith-in-action involves movement on the part of the believer, too. And this movement is not simply of the mouth, not just pronouncement of words. Of the answer to those who asked Jesus what to do in order to work the works of God, namely believing into the One whom that One has sent, Augustine notes:

> *Cito dicitur, non facile perficitur. Ait mihi aliquis de tam magna multitudine circumstantium, ait*: Quis est nostrum qui in Chris-tum non credidit? Si ergo omnes in Christum credidimus, iam quod moneatur non invenimus. *Quare? Quia* hoc est opus dei. *Numquid quaeris aliud quam opus dei facere et exspectare mercedem dei? Quid ergo te turbas, quid per magnas scripturae paginas occuparis et eas discurrendo laboras quaerere et inve-nire quomodo facias opus dei? Ecce habeas, apud tuum domi-num loquentem tibi, veritatem et brevitatem: non te extendas, non sudes, non labores, non aestues.* Hoc est opus dei, ut credas, *inquit*, in eum quem ille misit.[96]

> Quickly said, not so easily accomplished. Someone says to me from such a great crowd standing around here, he says "Which of us is here who has *not* believed into Christ? If therefore we all have believed into Christ, we do not man-age to get why this is advised now." Why? Because "this is the work of God." Can it be that you seek to do something other than the work of God and expect the reward of God?

---

95   Augustine, Dolbeau 19, 221–23.
96   Augustine, Dolbeau 19, 2, 26–36.

> Therefore, for what are you disturbing yourself, for what are you occupied and you go running about and you labor through extensive pages of Scripture to seek and to find how you may do the work of God? Look, you have it, in the presence of your Lord telling you, truth and brevity: no need to overextend yourself, do not sweat, do not labor, do not get agitated. This is the work of God, that you believe, he says, into the One whom that One has sent.

Augustine clearly is growing frustrated with how easily his hearers take for granted the uniqueness of the grammatical construction of *credere in eum* and is seeking a way to remind them that it's more than just *credere eum*. It is not merely the proclamation of propositional belief in Christ. On the other hand, neither is it proving ourselves proper holders of said propositions by means of busy activity. What Augustine charges his hearers with doing is too much! They think they understand believing into Christ as a frenetic pace of striving, impressing, moving in all directions, except into Christ. At the same time that they sweat and strain to do enough and look appropriately busy as God's workers, it is yet not the believing-into that is exactly enough to build relationship with God through Christ. The "truth and brevity"—what Edmund Hill translates "in a nutshell"[97]—bound up in this simple phrase, *credere in eum*, is the summation of doing the work of God. It is the Christian faith.

His hearers must have kept murmuring about what the big deal was, however, because shortly thereafter—the demonic example already having been offered—he returns to identifying the thoughts of his hearers and reaches for another biblical parallel. In their reliance on their own perceived proficiency at professing *credere in eum* and their seeking more suggestions on what else to do in order to obtain their reward, Augustine hears echoes of the question that the rich man asks in the synoptic Gospels about what to do in order to have eternal life.[98]

The way that they are treating *credere in eum* as a stepping-stone to whatever else may be required to complete the transaction of heavenly reward is like the rich man approaching Jesus and treating the relational Decalogue, intended to maintain covenant-keepers' relationships with

---

[97] Augustine, Sermon 130A, in *Newly Discovered Sermons*, trans. Hill, 119.
[98] Augustine, Dolbeau 19, 4, 79–87.

God and neighbors, instead as a transactional ticket to eternal life.[99] So
Augustine wonders aloud why Jesus brought up the commandments
to the rich man (and, we should note, though Augustine does not, the
order to go sell all he had and give to the poor) instead of the same
simple definition of the work of God as believing-into that he gave the
crowd during the "bread of life" sermon and that by extension he gives
Augustine's hearers.[100] Based on what follows, the difference lies in that
the "truth and brevity" of the love involved in believing-into has been
lost on the rich man, as he hopes it will not be on his present hearers.

> *Intellegamus ergo, si possumus . . . quid sit credere in Christum, et
> id agamus, hoc operemur, in hoc cottidie proficiamus, huc de die
> in diem accedamus, donec accedendo perveniamus.*[101]

> Let us understand, therefore, if we can . . . what it is to believe into
> Christ, and let us go to it, work at this, progress in this daily, come
> near to this point day by day, until by coming near, we arrive.

The language of movement and daily rhythm emphasizes the difference in this kind of belief, the ongoing relational aspect of it, versus a
punctiliar convincing of a particular proposition.

After identifying the three types of *credere* together and the excursus on love and fear, Augustine soon elaborates on the way in which
this daily walk is powered by cherishing-love and renders the believer-
into inseparable from Christ and from God's love:

> *Cum sic credideris in Christum, ut eo ardore diligas Christum,
> vide si non verba ista tua erunt: Quis nos separabit a caritate dei?
> Noli ergo diu quaerere ut facias quae jubeat Christus: non potes
> non facere, si diligis Christum. Dilige, et facis. In quantum diligis,
> in tantum facis: in quantum minus feceris, minus diligis. Imple
> dilectionem, et perficis operationem. Ecce quam verum dictum
> est: Hoc est opus dei, ut credatis in eum quem ille misit, hoc est
> ut diligendo eatis in eum, id est incorporemini ei.*[102]

> When thus you have believed into Christ, so that you cherish
> Christ ardently, see if these words aren't yours: "Who shall

---

[99] Augustine, Dolbeau 19, 4, 85–90.
[100] Augustine, Dolbeau 19, 4, 90–92.
[101] Augustine, Dolbeau 19, 4, 97–100.
[102] Augustine, Dolbeau 19, 5, 124–31.

separate us from the love of God?" Therefore do not seek all
day that you may do what Christ commands—you cannot not
do it, if you cherish Christ. Cherish, and you do it. As much as
you cherish, that much you do—as much as you do less, you
love less. Fill up the cherishing, and you complete the work. See
how truly it was said, "This is the work of God, that you believe
into the One whom that One has sent," that is, that by cherishing you may go into him, that is, may be incorporated in him.

Here imagery from every sermon and commentary dealing with *credere in eum* comes together, with the themes of moving, going into,
and incorporation made possible by the *diligere* cherishing-love that
unites the believer-into to Christ. It is abundantly clear that no mere
going through the motions will complete a transaction to the benefit
of the believer in terms of eternal reward. Rather, the love that moved
God to become human moves believers to respond in such a way that
we turn away from our own pursuit of power and privilege at others'
expense and toward the One into whom we move by love and with
whom we then move in love to the whole world.[103] *Credamus in eum,
hoc est tamquam deum diligamus eum, ut diligendo in illum eamus, a
quo neglegendo recesseramus*, Augustine clearly states, "Let us believe
into him, that is, let us cherish him as God, that by cherishing we may
go into him from whom we have withdrawn by neglecting."[104]

Not Neglect, but Correct Belief

Returning then to *Tract. Ev. Jo*. XXIX, it is clear that Augustine
would find this relational, touching, and incorporating understanding of believing into God useful even in having proper propositional belief, combating heresy. The hearers he urged to understand by believing into God would, by believing to love, hold dear,
go into, and be incorporated in Christ's members, see through the
Sabellian heresy, which denies the distinctions of three persons in
the Godhead. They would now understand that the teaching that
is "not mine" according to Jesus, because it was "from the Father,"
affirms the distinction of persons. Augustine seems confident that
his hearers, now clear on what believing into God is, will be able
to understand the Trinity, because they can know God intimately.

---

[103] Augustine, Dolbeau 19, 6, 144–49.
[104] Augustine, Dolbeau 19, 6, 150–51.

Incorporation in Christ's members enables believers to recognize
the Father and the Son in right relationship to each other's distinct
persons, because believers are in right relationship with the Father
and the Son themselves.[105] He charges the Sabellians with saying
that Jesus and the Father are the same person with two names. The
way in which Jesus has indicated that the work of God is to believe
into him whom that One has sent, together with the way in which
Jesus refers to his own teachings, falsifies the Sabellians' contention.

Along similarly clarifying lines of Trinitarian doctrine and relational belief, though he does not extensively parse it out as thoroughly
as in *Tract. Ev. Jo.*, Augustine, in *De Trinitate* (*The Trinity*) deliberately
uses the construction of *credere in* + accusative in at least two of the
fifteen books that make up this work. Seemingly less concerned specifically about the Sabellians here, he quotes Jesus as using the construction to direct belief into himself beyond himself into the Father
as well.[106] Later he uses the construction in a way that is subtle but
rich in its uniquely Trinitarian depiction, referring to the promise of
Jesus that the Holy Spirit will flow forth from the bellies of those who
believe into Christ.[107]

In *Ennarat. Ps.* 77, he will even go so far as to insist that by believing into God, the human's spirit entrusts itself to the Spirit of God,
and rather than merely believing God the way one does any fellow
human, one is able "to cling by faith to God, who effects good works
in such a way that we (believers-into, for the present purpose) collaborate well with God, for we are told, without me you can do nothing."[108] Such clinging and collaboration certainly align with Volf's

---

[105] Augustine, *Tract. Ev. Jo.* XXIX, 7. All quotations in this paragraph come
from this section of Augustine's sermon.

[106] Augustine, *De Trin.* 1.12.27 (CCSL 50:68). This sentence summarizes the
following Latin excerpt: "Non in me credit sed in eum qui me misit, *non utique
se a patre, id est ab illo* qui *eum* misit, *voluit separari, sed ut sic in eum crederetur
quomodo in patrem cui aequalis est. Quod aperte alio loco dicit*: Credite in deum et
in me credite; *id est sicut* creditis in deum, *sic* et in me *quia* ego et pater unus deus."

[107] Augustine, *De Trin.* 15.19.33 (CCSL 50A:508). This sentence summarizes:
*Qui credit in me sicut dicit scriptura flumina de ventre eius fluent aquae vivae.
Porro evangelista secutus adiunxit: Hoc autem dixit de spiritu quem accepturi erant
credentes in eum.*

[108] Augustine, Exposition 77.8, in *Expositions of the Psalms* (73–98), ed.
John E. Rotelle, trans. Maria Boulding, The Works of Saint Augustine: A Trans-
lation for the 21st Century 3/18 (Hyde Park, N.Y.: New City Press, 2009), 98.
Latin available in PL 36:988. This relevant passage dealing with *credere in Deum*

portrait of flourishing and his image of "when we come to love God and surrender to God in faith, . . . the relation to the divine becomes the axis of our lives."[109]

Rhetoric and Formula

Volf's own description of flourishing owes a debt to Augustine's aforementioned defense of preaching with a rhetorical flourish. Augustine's choice to evoke from grammatical uniqueness a distinctly Christian rhetoric of believing-into represents well his effort to rescue rhetoric from the condemnation thereof as tool of paganism.[110] In the same way in which the Donatist controversy emerged from an understandable suspicion among Christian leaders of the Roman Empire's sanction of Christianity after previously having persecuted it, a certain suspicion of the devices of that empire lingered as well. As the empire itself evolved, in the secular realm rhetoric went from being a ubiquitous tool of the Roman Republic to being a more obscure academic subject and specialty of the Sophists. As the Edict of Religious Tolerance (313 CE) afforded Christianity protections, there was plenty of resistance by heads of the church to the use of what they deemed to be tools once held by pagan hands. Augustine, meanwhile, recognized that preachers who wanted to draw first-time hearers of the Gospels into relationship with Christ needed to deliver good news using the same method and means by which would-be believers into Christ had come to receive ordinary news, and that method and means was rhetoric.

---

and introducing the clinging in context is: *Hoc est etiam credere in Deum; quod utique plus est quam credere Deo. Nam et homini cuilibet plerumque credendum est, quamvis in eum non sit credendum.* **Hoc est ergo credere in Deum, credendo adhaerere ad bene cooperandum bona operanti Deo: Quia sine me, inquit, nihil potestis facere** (*Joan. XV*, 5). *Quid autem plus hinc Apostolus dicere potuit, quam quod ait: Qui autem adhaeret Domino, unus spiritus est.*

[109] Volf, *Flourishing*, 81.

[110] Hermanson et al., "Saint Augustine," 3–4. This opening essay notes the changing place of rhetoric from ubiquitous tool of the Roman Republic to academic subject and specialty of the Sophists. It claims that as the Edict of Religious Tolerance (313 A.D.) afforded Christianity protections, "Many church leaders, skeptical and suspicious of 'pagan' rhetoric, used their new authority to confront what they believed were rhetoric's dangerous worldly aims and pragmatic perspectives." Augustine meanwhile recognized that "the need to win souls for the Christian faith necessitated that clergy be able to reach audiences unfamiliar with Scripture and to move them toward Christ, making rhetoric attractive as an evangelical tool."

Augustine supports his advocacy for the church's use of rhetoric by identifying certain rhetorical devices as having been used by
inspired writers of Scripture. We now may observe that his rhetoric
of "believing into" uses the types of devices he claims these inspired
writers have used. Both his *credere* formula, in general, and the *credere in eum* as it appears in *Tract. Ev. Jo.* XXIX, in particular, can be
perceived to use the figures of speech that he will claim in book IV of
DDC to see in Paul's letter to the Romans. The Romans passage is but
one example that Augustine gives of biblical writers using rhetorical
devices (while acknowledging that it is laughable to suggest they had
striven to observe the rules of rhetoric).[111] He identifies two different
devices in this one example, both of which are useful in describing the
rhetoric of Augustine's own *credere* formula. He lifts up Paul's use of
κλῖμαξ (*klimax*) in Greek, *gradatio* in Latin, in Romans 5:3-5, building in stages from tribulations, to patience, to approbation, to hope,
to the love of God that is poured into believers' hearts. Similarly, as
Augustine's formula comes together across Augustine's writings, it is
possible to see him employing a form of this device in building from
believing God and believing that God exists/that Jesus is Christ—like
demons do—to believing into Christ.

Further, within the culminating step of the formula, *credere in eum*,
as it is described in *Tract. Ev. Jo.* XXIX, the abovementioned *credendo*
crescendo provides another climax. Recall the way those phrases build
upon one another with each phrase following the repeated first word,
credendo, "by believing," escalating in intensity. Augustine takes the
phrase he finds in John's Gospel to describe belief and does with it what
Paul does in describing hope, both of them involving love. As he builds
from "by believing to love," to "to cherish," to "to go into him," he both
builds to a climax and arrives at a point, which evokes the second set of
devices he sees at work in Romans 5:3-5 according to *DDC* IV, "another
embellishment to be observed."[112] The κόλα/κόμματα (*kola/kommata*)
and περίοδος (*periodos*), which are related to the modern English language punctuation terms comma and period, involve a series of phrases
followed by the use of a pause and concluding phrase (signaled in Augustine's case by a phrase not beginning with *credendo*). As Paul uses a *periodos* to describe the hope that does not disappoint because of the love
of God poured out through the Holy Spirit, so Augustine punctuates

---

[111] Augustine, *Teaching Christianity* IV.7.11, trans. Hill, 206.
[112] Augustine, *Teaching Christianity* IV.7.11, trans. Hill, 206.

the series of "by believing" phrases with a description of *credere in eum* as being incorporated in (Christ's) members. In the only known place where Augustine enumerates the three parts of the formula in the same location, Sermon 130A, he draws contrast between the three types of *credere*, but we are left to wonder whether he ever considered presenting them in a way that would suggest culmination using these devices.

With all these elements now reviewed, before proceeding in the next chapter to examine the further systematization, reduction, and loss in translation of *credere in eum*, we do well to consider some related implications, drawn from across the Augustinian corpus.

The Spiritual and Fleshly Dimensions of Augustine's Theological System

The *credendo* crescendo offers Augustine's hearers an exciting invitation to *credere in Christum*, but what is to prevent the believer from settling for remaining turned inward instead and merely believing in God and believing God? *Credere in eum*, with the same satisfaction to the soul that a physical stretch brings to the body, unfurls the believer to turn toward and cling to God by incorporation in Christ through the power of the Holy Spirit, whom Augustine describes as the bond, bend, or curvature of love between Father and Son.[113] This notion directly contradicts the Platonist notion, which the mature Augustine had come to reject, that "the way to God is by an inward turn, a kind of solitary contemplation that enables the ascent to a vision of truth."[114] Augustine's early works display evidence of contemporary influences that emphasized an inward turn to escape the world of flesh and attain a solitary vision of truth.[115] Yet Augustine's later works show that he

[113] David Meconi, *The One Christ: St. Augustine's Theology of Deification* (Washington, D.C., Catholic University of America Press, 2013), 148–49. Meconi presents this notion as Augustine's effort to overcome the unfortunate tendencies of his predecessors to neglect the Spirit's equality with the other two persons of the Trinity. Meconi credits the translation as "curvature" to Olivier Du Roy.

[114] Lee, *Augustine and the Mystery*, xxii. Lee repeatedly identifies evidence of Augustine's maturing beyond this view, in favor of the notion that the turn toward truth cannot be accomplished by humans alone by means of philosophy and the liberal arts. The alternative Augustine chooses, "by participation in a communal body celebrating the sacraments" (xviii) occupies much of the remainder of the present chapter.

[115] Lee, *Augustine and the Mystery*, 31. Now known within the study of philosophy as "Neoplatonists" and most notably represented by third-century Roman figure Plotinus, these thinkers considered themselves simply "Platonists" and

found them insufficient to heal the sin-sick soul's turn to self. He perceived this turn as having a precedent even before the Fall of humans in Genesis, in the turning of evil angels away from God toward themselves.[116] By contrast, "the truest cause of the happiness of the good angels is that they cling to (that One) who supremely is."[117] The belief of demons and the language of "clinging" used to elucidate the *credere* formula is recognizable here, prompting consideration of the kind of turns in operation in the formula. Then it is possible to explore the ways in which the alternative understanding that Augustine reached of coming to God in community both bears out the workings of the formula and is enriched by *credere in eum.*

The notion that the turn toward self is a turn away from God captures how dangerously incomplete the absence of *credere in eum* renders belief. *Credere eum* and *credere ei* by themselves allow the believer to turn inward still and to contemplate only the believer's own assent to God's existence and to Christ's identity as Son of God. One may congratulate oneself on having recognized the veracity of the words Christ has spoken and that are spoken about him. The believer having salvation squared away, as it were, there may be nothing more to the Christian faith and life than to keep thinking about these good things and looking forward to attaining the heavenly vision they promise. It is entirely self-serving, as the believer needs only express assent to and appreciation of Christ's death on the cross to obtain the benefits of religion for themselves, primarily eternal life and a heavenly home, reductive, transactional, and

---

focused on Plato while drawing from what they deemed the best contributions from a millennium of Greco-Roman schools of thought (except for those emphasizing corporealism, such as the Epicureans). For more information, see https://plato.stanford.edu/entries/neoplatonism/.

[116] Augustine, *City of God* XII.6, trans. Babcock, 41: "And when we ask about the cause of the misery of the evil angels, what rightly comes to mind is that they turned away from (that One) who supremely is and turned to themselves." The Latin shows the compound forms of the words "turned away from" or "opposed" (*aversi*) and "turned to" or "converted" (*conversi*), though the action is arguably one and the same. *De Civitate Dei* XII.6 (CCSL 48:359): *Cum vero causa miseriae malorum angelorum quaeritur, ea merito occurrit, quod ab illo qui summe est aversi, ad se ipsos conversi sunt, qui non summe sunt.* See also J. Patout Burns, "Augustine on the Origin and Progress of Evil," *Journal of Religious Ethics* 16, no. 1 (1988): 9–27.

[117] Augustine, *City of God* XII.6, trans. Babcock, 41.

not very relational.[118] Whatever attention is turned to Christ quickly turns right back to the believer's self.

Love is what prevents faith from being just one more opportunity to turn inward. Love is what distinguishes the operation of *credere in eum* from *credere eum* and *credere ei*. Recalling the *credendo* crescendo and the clinging that *credere in eum* entails, the believer-into certainly still may feel free to contemplate God's existence and God's truthful promises but does so in service to an awe-inspired, committed relationship. This relationship turns the believer ever outward, toward God and toward neighbors, as cherishing-love *dilectio* dictates. To keep the believer-into from devolving into an inward turn, the Holy Spirit also serves as the glue ensuring that the believer's God-ward bond to the body of Christ holds.[119] "For when you reach (Christ)," Augustine insists, "you also reach the Father, because it is through his equality that the one [*sic*] to whom he is equal can be recognized, with the Holy Spirit binding and so to say gluing us in there, so that we may abide forever in that supreme and unchangeable good."[120]

Outward Participation through Incorporation: Sacraments, Creeds, Community

But how does it all work? What does movement into, incorporation in members, Christ coming into and being united with the believer, clinging and collaboration, becoming weak, and being perfected look like in the life of a believer? Fortunately, all of this figurative language has very tangible referents. When he was preparing for his own baptism, Augustine withdrew on a retreat he hoped to make permanent with his mother and friends at a friend's estate in Cassiciacum, the rural town outside his metropolitan secular workplace, Milan. As Augustine went from being contemplative catechumen on private

---

[118] H. H. Price, *Belief* (New York: Humanities Press, 1969), 444–52. Price is the analytic philosopher appearing in this introduction who wrote at greatest length about belief. At best, transactional belief, such as agreeing that it is a "good thing that" Christ died for sins in order for those who declare it to be true to get the benefit of eternal life, is what Price dubbed "interested belief-in," easily reducible to a merely propositional "belief-that."

[119] Meconi, *One Christ*, 149. I am indebted to Meconi's mention of Augustine's treatment of the Holy Spirit as glue and directing attention to the next passage, among others.

[120] Augustine, *Teaching Christianity* I.34.38, trans. Hill, 123.

retreat, to reluctant public priest, and then to bishop of the large con-gregation at Hippo, he left the environment that had made the inward turn to a solitary vision of God appealing and entered the real world of life in ministry that offered "outward participation in a visible com-munity."[121] There he delved deeply into and even imagined himself in the Scriptures of both Testaments in the midst of and for the sake of people bound together in sacramental life.[122] What he would dis-cover is the power of deification as unity with the "whole Christ." As Meconi notes, "The unifying power of the church and the sacraments celebrated therein cannot be overemphasized for Augustine. This is because the church is nothing other than 'the whole Christ,' a con-tinuation of the incarnation where union with the perfect man Jesus Christ is made possible."[123]

Baptism

For Augustine, therefore, baptism is not merely going through the motions of initiation into a club, but rather it is a movement into relationship with the Trinity and all who participate in the life of the Father, Son, and Holy Spirit. Baptism involves nearly everything Augustine preaches about what "believing into Christ" entails. From the *credendo* crescendo of "by believing to love, by believing to hold dear, by believing to go into him, and to be incorporated in his mem-bers" to being "made a member in his body," and the presence of the theological virtues, as Christ coming into the believer "cannot be, unless both hope and charity are added," as well as the washing as beginning point of healing, some aspect of baptism covers each.

How is the one who wishes "to do the work of God by believing into him whom that One has sent" able to love or to cherish? It requires opening up to the activity of the Holy Spirit. While any encounter with the Trinity is an encounter with the One whose very name is Love, Augustine applied that name not only to the whole Trinity and each

---

[121] Lee, *Augustine and the Mystery*, xxii.

[122] While outside the scope of the present project, the ways that Augustine experimented with transposing himself and his own voice into the texts of Scrip-ture with a view to helping his hearers do so are detailed in Michael Cameron's *Christ Meets Me Everywhere: Augustine's Early Figurative Exegesis* (New York: Oxford University Press, 2012).

[123] Meconi, *One Christ*, 176.

of the Persons, but especially to the Holy Spirit.[124] Augustine claims to have arrived, in his fifteenth and final book of *The Trinity*, at his own best understanding of the Trinity when he sees the "triad" as Lover, What is Loved, and Love.[125] As humans are not God, whose absolute substance is Love, it is not our nature to desire to die and to be buried with Christ, even if we intellectually believe that we do so in order to rise again with Christ to newness of life. So, it is the Holy Spirit who enables the one believing into God in baptism to experience this trinitarian reality of being loved and loving/cherishing in return.

For in baptism this being loved and loving, an aspect of entering into the divine life, is the invisible reality of *credere in eum*. The visible reality is that the Glue in-corpor-ates the believer-into in Christ's members, literally adhering the believers' bodies into Christ's limbs, so that the believers-into—body and soul—are transformed visibly into the members of the body of Christ. Augustine provides language and imagery that starts with focus on *Christ's* members, "by believing . . . to be incorporated in his members." He then declares believers-into, once glued in Christ's limbs, to have become his members themselves, "made a member in his body." What makes the transformation visible is that these limbs now follow the Way of Christ and move in the same healing directions in which his limbs have always gone, performing the works of mercy that his hands and words have always done.

As to who applies this Glue in baptism, Christ himself does, though it may be a priestly or episcopal stand-in who physically administers or ushers believers into the water and lays hands on them. Augustine's insistence to the same congregation[126] that it is Christ who does the baptizing and giving of the Spirit both makes this action clear and thwarts the Donatists.[127] Today, when frequent efforts by bishops and baptizands to procure and mix into the font's or baptistry's contents a bit of water from the Jordan River suggest that the water itself conveys

---

[124] R. Kendall Soulen, *The Divine Name(s) and the Holy Trinity*, vol. 1, *Distinguishing the Voices* (Louisville: Westminster John Knox, 2011), 70–71, with reference to *Trin.* XV.5.29.

[125] Soulen, *Divine Name(s)*, 71.

[126] Albeit much earlier in the *Tract. Ev. Jo.* XXIX series, *Tract. Ev. Jo.* V and VI. See Augustine, Homily 5.6 and 6.7, in *Homilies on the Gospel of John* (1–40), trans. Hill, 106 and 126–27.

[127] Adam Ployd, *Augustine, the Trinity, and the Church: A Reading of the Anti-Donatist Sermons* (New York: Oxford University Press, 2015), 152.

the Glue, we need again the force of Augustine's argument that neither the water itself, nor the bishop or priest handling it, does the baptizing. Augustine preaches two consecutive sermons on a single verse, John 1:33 (from a pericope previously preached), in an effort to dismantle Cyprian's proposal that the church's task—safeguarded by the ministers' own purity preserved in apostolic succession—was stewarding the Spirit breathed on the believers by Christ in John 20:20-33.[128]

In this pair of sermons Augustine appears to be in a holy conspiracy with his congregation against what "bothers (him) a lot" from the Donatists' efforts to "cloud the minds of simple people and spread out their nets to catch flying birds."[129] Inviting them into the text to ask John the Baptist what he knew and did not know about Jesus leads to a lesson in who it is that really does the baptizing.[130] When the dove descends on the Beloved in the baptism of Jesus, it signifies to John—who already knows that Jesus is Lord,[131] hence saying he should rather be baptized by him—that Jesus was the One promised who would baptize in the Holy Spirit.[132] It is not the minister nor the water itself that does the baptizing, but Christ. The believer-into is not believing into the minister, nor into the local congregation, but into Christ himself.

The Spirit-Glue is too strong for its bond to be broken by any brokenness of the hands of whoever handles the water in baptism. Because it is the divine-human Christ who applies the Glue, there is no fear that flesh, nor anything that traditional hamartiology sees as sticking to the flesh like dirt, can keep the bond from holding the human to the divine. This body-based gluing-into undergirds the mutual indwelling imagery in the sermonic passages on *credere in eum* that continued the development in the mature Augustine[133] of

---

[128] Ployd, *Augustine*, 149–51.

[129] Augustine, Homily 4.16, in *Homilies on the Gospel of John* (1–40), trans. Hill, 99–100.

[130] Augustine, Homily 5.1, in *Homilies on the Gospel of John* (1–40), trans. Hill, 102.

[131] It is helpful to note that Augustine's understanding of the title "Lord" as it applied to Jesus lacks the uniqueness that arises from its having been "employed as a surrogate from the unspoken Tetragrammaton," of which Soulen suggests Augustine seems to have been unaware. Thus Augustine uses John's awareness of Jesus' Lordship as describing his relationship with creation, not with the Holy Spirit (Soulen, *Divine Name[s]*, 72–73).

[132] Augustine, Homily 5.9, in *Homilies on the Gospel of John* (1–40), trans. Hill, 109.

[133] Lee, *Augustine and the Mystery*, 28. As described previously, this mature period refers to the time after his entry into parish life and deep engagement with

a revaluing of the body in Christianity for the sake of the body of Christ.[134] As the believer-into boldly surrenders to die and rise with Christ and is washed clean of sin in the sacramental act, the Glue bonds the members so tightly to Christ that it is as if a new vascular connection is made. The relationship of Christ's body to the head is then maintained by a circulatory system that causes hope and charity to be added to faith as all three flow through the members. Across Augustine's works are hints at precisely how "both hope and charity are added" to the faith of them who *believe into* Christ, such that incorporation into Christ's body does not occur apart from all three theological virtues. In response to Augustine's comments in the *Ennarat. Ps.* about "the body's linkage with its Head through the bond of charity, so close a link that Head and body speak as one," and that "Your fear is your own, your hope is God's gift in you . . . for divine mercy does not desert us in our fear," Lee reflects:

> By the bond of charity, the head and members can speak as one, and Christ is mysteriously present in his members on earth. This is why Christ declares to Saul in Acts 9:4, "Why are you persecuting me?"
>
> . . .
>
> The church is the mysterious presence of Christ on earth. The head remains distinct and does not suffer in his human nature in heaven, yet there is a real identity between Christ and the members of his body, such that head and members can speak in "one voice" (*una vox*). In the act of crying out, the members of the body are transfigured in hope.[135]

---

the Scriptures, in Lee's assessment, "following the biblical, incarnational shift in his thought in the 390s." Then the Pauline language of the "body of Christ" became one of his dominant metaphors for the church, eventually woven in occasionally with the imagery of the bride of Christ.

[134] Margaret Miles, *Augustine on the Body* (Missoula, Mont.: Scholars Press, 1979), 129. Miles is careful not to deny that "the period of greatest conscious affirmation of the body—Augustine's old age—coincides exactly with the time of his strongest negative focus on sexuality." She enlists Freudian theory to ascribe this contradiction to emphatic denial as the initial response to conscious attention to repressed or denied longings, even as she distinguishes his struggle from the hatred and mortification of the flesh exhibited by desert fathers.

[135] Lee, *Augustine and the Mystery*, 54, with reference to *Ennarat. Ps.* 37:6, 142:3, and 30:3. He also cites Michael Fiedrowicz, *Psalmus vox totius Christi: Studien zu Augustins "Enarrationes in Psalmos"* (Freiburg: Herder, 1997), 298–375, for the sentence ending "(una vox)."

Faith, hope, and charity together not only ensure that "divine mercy does not desert us in our fear," but also make possible the works of divine mercy carried out by the members. While the congregation itself is not the object of faith (contrary to the confusing suggestion in the third clause of the Nicene Creed), the resulting relationship there is vital. The Glue holds together the body's members and empowers them to practice mercy toward one another and to move together in works of mercy in the world.

The texts of three baptismal creeds can be reconstructed from his writings, all beginning with *cred(ere) in Deum*.[136] Candidates for baptism were given the creed a few weeks beforehand, *traditio symboli*, and expected to "give it back," *redditio symboli*, upon their baptism (phrases used often by Augustine). Under Augustine's instruction, such as what is evidenced in the sermons here considered, what do new believers know believing to entail as they go into the water? They know that believing into the God whom their creed describes is a gift of that God and unites them intimately, almost bodily, with the Son of God in such a way that where his limbs go—to surrender self on behalf of the sinner, the needy, the sick—they will now go, too. This going will be unavoidable, as Augustine notes in Dolbeau 19/Mainz 51/Sermon 130A, for "When thus you have believed into Christ, . . . do not seek all day that you may do what Christ commands—you cannot not do it, if you cherish Christ."[137]

In another sermon, Augustine is so convinced of this reality that he defends infant baptism, because the parents who are believers into Christ are so united with Christ that (since it is through them that the infant inherits original sin) their vows are sufficient to answer the

---

[136] Joseph Leinhard, "Creed," in Fitzgerald and Cavadini, *Augustine through the Ages*, 254.

> Creed of Milan (*De Fide et Symbolo, Serm. 212–14*)
> **Credo in Deum** Patrem Omnipotentum . . . ascendit **in caelum** (**I believe into God** the Father Almighty . . . he ascended **into heaven**)

> Creed of Hippo (*De Fide et Symbolo, Serm. 215*)
> **Credimus in Deum** Patrem Omnipotentum . . . ascendit ad caelos (**We believe into God** the Father Almighty . . . he ascended **into the heavens**)

> Creed from *De Symbolo ad Catechumenos*
> **Credimus in Deum** Patrem Omnipotentum . . . ascendit **in caelum** (**We believe into God** the Father Almighty . . . who ascended **into heaven**)

[137] Augustine, Dolbeau 19, 5, 124–26.

prayers embedded in their babies' cries by declaring the infant's own belief.[138] He further emphasizes the motion of the believer into Christ's presence and connection with him in another sermon, as he points to the woman with the hemorrhage who touched the hem of Christ's robe as demonstrating "the approach of the person believing."[139] A contrast here arises that makes it necessary to identify and consider a potential problem. As infants are not responsible for their own approach to the baptismal waters, does the language and relational aspect of "believing into" break down in the circumstance of infant baptism, with Augustine curiously seeming to endorse causal efficacy of the sacrament? It is a problem that Augustine does not consider in what Edmund Hill calls this "extraordinary, important, interesting, and yes, rather bad sermon."[140] Its logic is as muddled as its superscription, "Preached in the Basilica of the Ancestors on the birthday of the Martyr Guddens on 27 June (On the Baptism of infants, against the Pelagians)," so it is tempting simply to dismiss the issue altogether.

On the contrary, it is wise to consider here how the language of "believing into Christ" works with infant baptism. We may struggle to embrace Augustine's notion of baptized infants' believing "with the faith of their parents," but it makes more sense in the context of antiquity, wherein we find an understanding of the individual believer and

---

[138] Augustine, Sermon 294.12, in *Sermons on the Saints* (273–305A), ed. John E. Rotelle, trans. Edmund Hill, The Works of Saint Augustine: A Translation for the 21st Century 3/18 (Hyde Park, N.Y.: New City Press, 1994), 187–88. Latin available at PL 38:1342.

[139] Augustine, *Serm.* CCXLIV.3 (PL 38:591). "*Tactus fidem significat. Tangendo enim acceditur ad eum qui tangitur. Mulierem illam videte, quae fluxum sanguinis patiebatur. Dixit in corde suo:* Sanabor, si tetigero fimbriam vestimenti ejus. *Accessit et tetigit, sanata est. Quid est,* Accessit et tetigit? *Propinquavit et credidit. Ut sciatis eam credendo tetigisse, Dominus dixit:* Tetigit me aliquis. *Quid est,* Tetigit me; nisi, Credidit in me?" "Touching means faith. For touching she came near to him who is touched. See that woman, who suffered from the issue of blood. She said in her heart, 'I shall be healed, if I touch the hem of his garment.' She approached and touched, and she was healed. What is 'She approached and touched?' She drew near and she believed. That you may know that touching is believing, the Lord said, 'Someone touched me.' What is 'touched me,' but 'believed into me?'"

[140] Augustine, *Sermons* (273–305A), trans. Hill, 195, n. 1. Hill continues, "In it we seem to see Augustine arguing for a theological conclusion, which he treated as almost a dogma, of which his intellect was utterly convinced, and from which his heart recoiled: that babies dying unbaptized go to hell. So he is prey to an inner conflict that produces what is, as I have suggested, really a rather bad sermon." Hill goes on to clarify that the church of the late twentieth century—when Hill was writing—is "much less dogmatic on this point than Augustine was."

the believing community of Christ's body the church as not separable.[141] The parents' expression of faith does not itself prove effective for the infant, who certainly does not cease crying or dedicate itself to a life of holiness in relationship with God upon baptism. Nevertheless, as *credere in Deum* engenders bold surrender, the parents' believing into Christ entails their surrendering of self in order to nurture the growth of faith in this little one with the same love with which Christ incorporates children in the kingdom of God throughout the Gospels. In this way infant baptism signifies the grace that will enable the child to become one who believes into Christ as well.

The statement in this sermon that sounds so odd to contemporary ears, that parents are able to interpret their infant's cries as the infant's own renunciation of sin and profession of faith, fits within an ancient worldview of this interconnectedness of the body of Christ. In such a view, the crying infant's voice and parents' voices join the "one voice" of Christ the head and the body. If in fact "Christ assumed flesh in order to forgive sins and to incorporate new members into his body,"[142] then it stands to reason that the newest living persons born to members of his body are also to be incorporated into the body. With baptism as the source that brings about hope and charity to join with faith, this reasoning might suggest, the child would be denied reception of and growth in these theological virtues, one of which is itself twofold. Augustine also claims in *DDC* that those who came to "the holy bath of baptism . . . conceived by the Holy Spirit and gave birth to the twin fruit of charity, that is to love God and neighbor"— the greatest commandment, which parents will want their child to bear and tend, nurtured by the body of Christ.[143]

Euphoria of Eating: Eucharist

The aspect of Augustine's preaching on believing into Christ that connects most strongly with this sacrament is the mutual indwelling he describes. The Eucharist illuminates the operation of the part of the *credere in eum* summary in which by believing into Christ the

---

[141] Augustine, Sermon 294.17, in *Sermons* (273–305A), trans. Hill, 192. I am indebted to Lee for this observation that "the individual believer is best understood in relation to the communal body, and therefore saving faith is communal as well as individual" (personal correspondence, January 11, 2018).

[142] Lee, *Augustine and the Mystery*, 28.

[143] Augustine, *Teaching Christianity* II.6.7, trans. Hill, 131.

believer-into experiences the reality that "Christ comes into you, and you are in some way made one with him, . . . who effects good works in such a way that we collaborate well with God, for we are told, without me you can do nothing." The Eucharist includes an action of ingesting Christ, whether understood physically or meta-physically, and it also comes with the commission to go into the world as Christ's body. It is now necessary to exercise the greatest care to remain relational and avoid commodification and transac-tional language in describing the operations of *credere in eum* here. "Rarely does anyone seek Jesus for the sake of Jesus," Augustine notes in preaching on the same passage that lies at the heart of *Tract. Ev. Jo.* XXIX and Dolbeau 19/Mainz 51/Sermon 130A.[144]

Augustine's eucharistic language in *The Confessions* illuminates the way in which the sign works to make believing-into a reciprocal going-into. Augustine there refers to the Eucharist as the "cup of our ransom" (*poculum pretii nostri*), which "mediates the mercy of the one mediator who entered history in order to redeem a people and a city."[145] This cup is the overt partner of the more subtly named "living bread which came down from heaven" so emphasized by Augustine in Dolbeau 19/Mainz 51/Sermon 130A as "the justice of faith which we preach, . . . healing us so that it might be eaten, strengthening us because it is eaten, satisfying us because it is desired, since it is about this that our soul is told that *he satisfies your desire with good things.*"[146]

Clarifying Confusions: Creeds

That desire can transform the creeds, including the three mentioned above that can be directly traced back to Augustine's writings, from lists of tenets for rote memorization and propositional assent to odes to the One into whom a baptizand is invited to believe. One won-ders, yet again, under Augustine's instruction, so clear in the sermons

[144] Augustine, Homily 25.10, in *Homilies on the Gospel of John* (1–40), trans. Hill, 437. Augustine briefly considers John 6:29 here but does not treat the text of doing the work of God as believing into him whom that One has sent as thor-oughly as with the *credendo* crescendo of Homily 29 nor the extensive treatment given it in Dolbeau 19/Mainz 51/Sermon 130A.

[145] Lee, *Augustine and the Mystery*, 42. Reference is to Boulding's translation of *Confessions* VII.21.27, 182.

[146] Augustine, Sermon 130A, in *Newly Discovered Sermons*, trans. Hill, 12, 126. This concluding sentence of the sermon is one that Hill translates from Latin almost verbatim.

here considered, what do new believers know believing to entail as they go into the water? They know that believing into the God whom their creed describes is a gift of that God and unites them intimately, almost bodily, with the Son of God in such a way that where his limbs go—to surrender whatever power and privilege they have in order to suffer with those who suffer—they will now go, too. To those content with *credere eum* and *credere ei* alone, such suffering is distasteful. What is missing without *credere in eum* is humility of bold surrender to become truly "one with Christ" in his suffering and ours. Augustine's mature ecclesiology reveals the manner in which incorporation leads to deification by which both glory and suffering are fully shared, as Lee notes:

> The church is united with Christ the head in a mystery of solidarity, a union made possible by the incarnation. Christ "came to receive insults and give honors, he came to drain the cup of suffering and give salvation, he came to undergo death and give life." There is a wonderful "exchange" (*commercium*) between the head and members of the one Christ. The head takes on the sufferings of the body "toiling on earth," while the members are given a share of the glory of the head in heaven by baptism. Christ's solidarity in suffering conforms the members to the head, as signified by the head "crying out on behalf of the members," for "the head was transfiguring the members into himself."[147]

Now Augustine's language has gone a step further than incorporation in Christ's members—now it's a transformation of those members into Christ himself! Believers-into have the creeds handed over to them, and even when they have given them back, they cling to their words, so that even in times of trial, the song of the Other to whom they have boldly surrendered comes to mind immediately, and they cling to God's promises as those who have entered into the waters that wash away sin and who have ingested the body and blood of the Son. As they cling, they are reminded of the surgical Glue of the Holy Spirit who keeps them turned out and toward God, and not curled in on themselves. Now more than simply turned Godward, they go Godward, as God, so to speak. But literally transfigured? Almost, but not quite. According to Meconi, what we have here is another deification metaphor without the

---

[147] Lee, *Augustine and the Mystery*, 53. With copious reference to *Ennarat. Ps.* 30.[2].3.

actual word *deificare*: "Augustine's cleaving to God ultimately means to be transformed into God in a nonliteral yet real way."[148] Nonliteral but real. And ultimately more real than the literal things we mistake for the ultimate.

How Did Such a Life-Giving Formula Die Out?

Next we shall look at the first known systematization of the formula after Augustine, by Bede—who sought to follow Augustine's method of commentary closely.[149] Then we shall examine the similar systematization by Lombard—who would draw from the influence of Bede as well as of the growing medieval genre of *sentences* which had begun with Prosper of Aquitaine's own collection of sentences glossing his contemporary and friend, Augustine.[150] We can then consider the ensuing reduction that downplayed the relational aspects of *credere in eum* and hastened its loss in translation.

---

[148] Meconi, *One Christ*, xvi.

[149] Benedicta Ward, SLG, *The Venerable Bede* (Kalamazoo, Mich.: Cistercian Publications, 1998), 46.

[150] Philipp W. Rosemann, *Peter Lombard* (New York: Oxford University Press, 2004), 17.

3

The Formula after Augustine

Systematized, Reduced, Faded

The Venerable Bede: The Formula Systematized

The first to count Augustine as one of the Four Great Church Fathers,[1] the Venerable Bede was an Anglo-Saxon monk of Northumbria at the turn of the eighth century C.E. While most widely regarded for his magnum opus, *Historia Ecclesiastica Gentis Anglorum*, or *Ecclesiastical History of the English Peoples*, Bede declared his primary purpose as "applying myself entirely to the study of the Scriptures" and judged his exegetical works to be at least as important as his *Ecclesiastical History*, listing them first among his works in the catalog thereof with which he concluded the *Ecclesiastical History*.[2] Bede stood in the stream of early church tradition wherein to do theology was to do biblical commentary.[3] Fully immersed in scripture by the Divine Office of his monastic life, Bede also was thereby immersed in readings from the early church fathers, which were woven into the office of matins. Just as Augustine had established the formula across commentaries and sermons, so Bede seems to have distilled the formula from these sources, especially from Dolbeau 19/Mainz 51/Sermon 130A, and further systematized them in one locus of Christian thought.

It is worthy of note that Bede, who pioneered academic citation, did not consider himself much of a theological innovator, offering nothing

---

[1]   Benedicta Ward, SLG, *The Venerable Bede* (Kalamazoo, Mich.: Cistercian Publications, 1998), 8–9. "He was the first to name Augustine, Ambrose, Jerome and Gregory as the four great Fathers of the Church, and their commentaries provided his main source for biblical exegesis."

[2]   Ward, *Venerable Bede*, 41.

[3]   Michelle P. Brown, "Bede's Life in Context," in *The Cambridge Companion to Bede*, ed. Scott DeGregorio, Cambridge Companions to Literature (New York: Cambridge University Press, 2010), 4. See also Ward, *Venerable Bede*, 44.

new (at least nothing that survives) on the works of Paul. He admits in the list of his works that appears in the *Ecclesiastical History*, "On the apostle I have transcribed in order whatever I found in the works of St. Augustine."[4] While his reluctance to identify himself as an innovator may be perceived as an act of self-deprecation, it was also rooted in dedication to a task of transmission to and education of the monks and priests of an emerging people. Brought to the monastery at Wearmouth very young (likely as an orphan) and being perhaps the sole survivor of plague in 686, save the Abbot Ceolfrith, to whom he thenceforth clung, Bede perceived his work as a means of providing continuity with tradition.[5] It is therefore likely that, when he systematized Augustine's formula, he expected it to be perceived as acceptable, even customary, and to carry a pedagogical, catechetical purpose.

It is fitting that Bede should have appreciated Augustine's play on words, as one primary task Bede faced with his own illiterate pupils was improving their facility with and appreciation of the Latin language, from its most basic grammar to the most powerful biblical allegories, en route to the Anglo-Saxons' crafting of a written form of their own language.[6] Bede scholar Peter Blair notes the "abundant evidence" throughout the writings of early Christian authors, like Augustine and many others before Bede, that they highly prized the study of grammar as the key by which students "gained access to the Word of God."[7] Bede follows this tradition closely. His earliest work (ca. 700 C.E.) is believed to have been a helpful handbook, *De Orthographia*, "On the Art of Writing Words Correctly," a loosely alphabetized collection of Latin words and their nuances for interpretation.[8] In addition to biblical usages, many of the entries contain examples culled from the early church fathers.

While the library lists no longer exist for the monastery at Wearmouth-Jarrow, it is known that the abbots' Mediterranean travels supplied Bede with an abundance of patristic works over which to pore as he developed his commentaries. We can determine which

---

4   Ward, *Venerable Bede*, 51.
5   Ward, *Venerable Bede*, 3–4.
6   Ward, *Venerable Bede*, 23.
7   Peter Hunter Blair, *The World of Bede* (London: Secker and Warburg, 1970), 248.
8   Bede, *De Orthographia*, ed. Charles Williams Jones and David Hurst (Turnhout: Typographi Brepols, 1975) (CCSL123A).

early church fathers were most popular in Bede's time and place from the availability today of manuscripts from eighth-century England: Jerome, Augustine, Isidore of Seville, and Gregory the Great.[9] The latter two were closer to Bede's time period, but the influence of Augustine on Bede's method is undeniable.

Bede's method in general displays features common to that of the early church fathers. For Bede, as for them, any part of the Scriptures can be used to interpret any other part thereof, though the first step is always an intent focus on grammar and face-value meaning, referring to original languages to the greatest possible extent.[10] Beyond that, however, Bede demonstrates exact parallels specifically to the method of crafting commentary—the equivalent of preaching[11]—that Augustine describes in *DDC*.[12] First and foremost for Augustine, love of God and neighbor and the Christian life must be the accompanying action and context of reading Scripture. The first step in preparing commentary is to read it in its entirety. Next, Augustine encourages memorization, then awareness of the difficulties presented by reading the texts in a language other than the originals. If no knowledge of or access to these languages is possible, a comparison of available Latin translations is an acceptable substitute for identifying potential nuances of meaning. Both Augustine and Bede go so far as to recommend an understanding of Scripture's original milieus, including flora and fauna and numerological understandings. When exegeting poetic expressions in Scripture, Bede continues the tradition of Augustine and other early church fathers by prioritizing grammatical scrutiny, extrapolating spiritual meaning from beautiful turns of phrase only after careful consideration of the "art of grammar" and its issues.[13]

One possible assessment of Bede's method, therefore, is to declare him wholly unoriginal, a mere compiler of the early church fathers before him. His own humble insistence that he was merely repeating

9   Blair, *World of Bede*, 292.

10   Ward, *Venerable Bede*, 46.

11   J. E. Cross, "Bede's Influence at Home and Abroad: An Introduction," in *Beda Venerabilis: Historian, Monk and Northumbrian*, ed. L. A. J. R. Houwen and A. A. MacDonald (Groningen: Forsten, 1996), 23. "But we recall that a homily is, in effect, a section of commentary," Cross notes in discussing Bede as a standard source for homily collections in the ninth century.

12   Ward, *Venerable Bede*, 47.

13   Ward, *Venerable Bede*, 47.

the wisdom of those who went before him (consider his description, noted above, of his method of copying everything from Augustine on Paul verbatim) appears to undergird this assessment. However, his own self-deprecating description of his work reads more as a rhetorical expression of humility than an accurate self-assessment. Even his compilations involve the making of choices, such as the placing of various voices in dialogue with one another, all of which for him would be themselves instruments to amplify the voice of God. That he saw himself as one such instrument is clear from the acknowledgment, in the opening of his commentary on Luke, of his having added "some token of my own efforts as the Author of Light revealed them."[14] Far earlier than that commentary, Bede similarly mounts a defense of his method in his commentary on Revelation, indicating that his innovations are in obedience to "the commandments which we have received, to return to the Lord with usury the talents which have been committed to us."[15]

Having obeyed these "commandments" by completing his first exegetical work, Bede next applied himself to the exegetical work in which he presented Augustine's formula. This time it is a commentary on the seven Catholic Epistles, *In Epistolas Septem Catholicas*.[16] Based on the number of *In Septem* manuscripts still in existence, it appears that it was Bede's most popular theological work, and no wonder, as there appears to have been a dearth of commentaries available on these epistles (James; 1 and 2 Peter; 1, 2, and 3 John, and Jude), with Augustine's own *Treatises on 1 John* one of the few, if any, commentaries available.[17] Yet it is not in commenting on the First Letter of John that Bede made use of Augustine's formula. Rather it is in the first commentary in the order in which he chose to present them, a commentary on James, the epistle Augustine quoted in Dolbeau 19/Mainz 51/Sermon 130A.[18] It is worthy of note that the formula emerges here

---

[14]   Ward, *Venerable Bede*, 48, with reference to Bede's *In Lucae Evangelium Expositio*, ed. D. Hurst (CCSL 120).

[15]   Ward, *Venerable Bede*, 48, with reference to what appears to be Ward's own translation of Bede's *Revelation* as it appears in the *Patrologia Latina*, a work hitherto only partially translated elsewhere by E. Marshall.

[16]   Bede, *In Epistolas Septem Catholicas*, ed. David Hurst (Turnhout: Brepols, 1955) (CCSL 121). Hereafter abbreviated *In Septem*.

[17]   M. L. W. Laistner and H. H. King, *A Hand-List of Bede Manuscripts* (Ithaca, N.Y.: Cornell University Press, 1943), 30–31.

[18]   Augustine, Dolbeau 19, 2, 38–39.

solely in epistolary commentary, while in the majority of Augustine's sermons, the primary texts are from John (even if he also drew upon other scriptural genres for support). This fact suggests the ubiquity and broad applicability of the *credere* formula in the Christian canon (see appendix).

The logic of his choice to begin his work with James (who comes first, Bede noted here, in the list of three apostles named in Gal 2:9, James, Peter, and John,[19] and who was the first of those three, he had noted in the preface of *In Septem*, to be martyred[20]) is not germane to his presentation of the formula. What is important is that he began his epistolary commentary by examining the New Testament text that most emphasizes a faith that either works or is dead, a fitting corollary of the "faith working through love" that Augustine borrowed from Galatians to describe *credere in eum* in *Tract. Ev. Jo.* XXIX. Bede lays out Augustine's formula in his comments on the second chapter of James, both as exegesis of a specific verse and in an effort at systematizing Augustine's attention to this grammatical structure and its theological implications. As he elaborates on the formula, Bede's systematization appears to have been an effort to develop an ethics of belief. The introduction of the formula might itself seem out of place, as it comes immediately on the heels of Bede's commentary on James 2:14 and 2:15-17, neither of which contains *credere in* + accusative in any form. These verses do, however, discuss *fides*, faith. As important as confessions of faith in the form of creeds are in considering what restoration of the relational sense of belief makes possible in common understanding and practice of Christian faith, it is a worthwhile endeavor now to pause a moment with Bede and consider these verses and his comments on them:

> *Quid, proderit, fratres mei, si **fidem** quis dicat se habere, opera autem non habeat?* (2:14a)

> What will it benefit, my brothers, if anyone claims to have **faith** (itself) but does not have works?

> *Ita et fides, si non habeat opera, mortua est in semet ipsam.* (v. 17)

> So faith, if it does not have works, is dead in itself.

---

[19] Bede, *In Septem* I.1–2, lines 3–5 (CCSL 121:183).
[20] Bede, *In Septem*, prologus line 23 (CCSL 121:182).

Bede's commentary on verse 14 is a direct quotation of Augustine's commentary on the previous verse, which Bede would have found in Augustine's letter to Jerome.[21] In that letter, Augustine suggests that the discussion of works pertains to works of mercy, which are necessary because of how easily unmerciful behaviors such as the favoritism that James describes emerge in human lives, even in those of humans with the best of intentions.[22] Augustine indicates to Jerome that the reason James added the phrase "but mercy triumphs (or "exults in its superiority," in Augustine's interpretation) over judgment" was to console those who would otherwise be disheartened by the previous sentences about transgressing in even one bit of the law being to transgress in all of it.[23] In Bede's application of Augustine's commentary to the next verses, James 2:15-17, there seems to be a suggestion that the comfort against worry about transgressing the law comes in knowing that works of mercy inseparably constitute Christian faith. He then expands in his own words:

> *Manifestum est quod sicut verba sola pietatis nudum vel esuri-entem non recreant, si non et cibus praebeatur ac vestis, ita fides verbo tenus servata non salvat;* **mortua est enim in semet ipsa si non operibus caritatis quibus reviviscat animetur.** *Neque huic sententiae contrarium est quod dominus ait:* Qui crediderit et baptizatus fuerit salvus erit; *subintellegendum namque ibi est quod* **tantummodo vere credat qui exercet operando quod credit.** (lines 148–54)

> It is clear that just as the bare words of faith do not revive the naked or the hungry, if food and clothing is not also provided, so faith does not save the saved by word; indeed, **it is dead in itself if it is not animated by works of charity that revive it.** Nor is what the Lord says contrary to this thought: "Everyone who believes and is baptized will be saved"; for here it is implied that **only the one who practices what he believes by working truly believes.**

---

[21] Augustine, Letter 167 (which in collections of Jerome's letters is Letter 132), in *Letters (Epistulae)* (156–210), ed. Boniface Ramsey, trans. Roland Teske, SJ, The Works of Saint Augustine: A Translation for the 21st Century 2/3 (Hyde Park, N.Y.: New City Press, 2004).

[22] Augustine, Letter 167.6.20, in *Letters* (156–210), trans. Teske, 104.

[23] Augustine, Letter 167.6.19, in *Letters* (156–210), trans. Teske, 103.

Here it is clear that propositional assent to faith terms is insufficient for salvation, as belief impacts (and faith is expressed in) practice.

Thus working through love is a defining characteristic of this faith, not merely one variety of it or a possible result of it. To explain this point, Bede further connects James 2 with two other passages from epistles (one pastoral/Pauline, one catholic) as he continued:

> *Et quia fides et caritas ab invicem separari nequeunt, Paulo attestante qui ait: Et* **fides quae per dilectionem operatur,** *apte* **Iohannes apostolus talem de caritate sententiam qualem de** *fide* **Iacobus profert dicens: Qui habuerit substantiam mundi et viderit fratrem suum necesse habere et clauserit viscera sua ab eo, quomodo caritas Dei manet in eo?** (lines 154–60)

> Because both faith and love cannot be divided from one another, which Paul confirming says: **"But faith working through love"** **(Gal 5:6), so to fit exactly the apostle John saying such things about love as the sort of thoughts about faith James advances: "Anyone who has the wealth of the world and sees his brother to have needs but closes his heart from him, how does the love of God abide in him?"** (1 John 3:17).

Bede's insistence that faith and love are inseparable undergirds a robustly relational conception of faith—both in terms of relationship with God in Christ and in terms of relationship with fellow humans in need. Here lies the heart of the matter for the difference that "believing into Christ" made for Bede and can make for us today. Language of "truly believing," while it may to our ears sound exclusionary, anticipates the robustly relational formula that he is about to systematize for his hearers'/readers' understanding. Settling for faith as believing in the existence of God or recognizing the identity of Christ and as believing that what God in Christ says is true is not "truly believing." It is not Christian faith, said Bede as he echoed James (and Augustine), because if it were, then demons would be Christians! Believing-into, by contrast, is an action that demonstrates love through relationship simultaneously with God and with neighbor, that dares to see believers-into as united with those in need, not crying out "what do you have to do with us" as demons do.

While this pericope from James will frame the Reformation debate of "faith vs. works," Bede's distance from that debate is evident.[24] He did not address James 2:18 at all,[25] with its rhetorical use of an imagined interlocutor, "But someone will say, 'You have faith and I have works,'" and the retort of James, "Show me your faith apart from your works, and I by my works will show you my faith." It is important to note that Bede, though deadly serious about Christian faith, eschews anything approximating the rigid fundamentalism evident in American soteriology today.[26] What follows in Bede's writings is not simply a matter of a shibboleth to determine whether a pilgrim is "in" or "out" of the heavenly kingdom. Bede had no interest in positing potentially adversarial proofs. Nevertheless, the Adversary's minions who are mentioned in the next verse (Jas 2:19) do provide Bede with a fitting contrast between faith that works through love and the merely propositional assent to tenets or doctrine that James dubs "barren." It is in Bede's commentary on this verse that his innovation on Augustine's theme becomes evident.

First, Bede patiently states verse 19, *Tu credis quoniam unus est Deus, bene facis; et daemones credunt et contremescunt* (lines 161–62), "You believe that God is one; you do well. Even the demons believe—and tremble with fear." Then he elaborates on Augustine's example of demons' belief as contrast to belief into Christ, warning his hearers/readers, *Ne putes quia magnum aliquid facis credendo unum esse Deum*, "Lest you should think by believing God to be one you do something great," that even the demons do that and in fact believe in both God the Father and God the Son (lines 161–64)! After shoring up this point by appealing to Gospel accounts of the demonic in both Luke and Mark (lines 164–70), he finally declares that, while no belief at all or propositional belief without fear is worse than demonic, the contrast between believing in God and believing into God shows that believing in God alone is not great:

> *Qui ergo Deum esse non credunt vel creditum non timent profecto sunt daemonibus tardiores ac proterviores aestimandi.* **Sed nec <u>Deum</u> credere et contremescere magnum est si non et <u>in eum</u> credatur, hoc est si non eius in corde amor teneatur.** (lines 161–73)

---

[24]   Ward, *Venerable Bede*, 78–79.
[25]   Furthermore, he omitted similar language previously by use of an "etc." to cap his quotation of 2:14.
[26]   See Ward, *Venerable Bede*, 79: "Bede had no simplistic categories of those who can be known to be saved or damned."

> Therefore any who do not believe God to exist or who having believed do not fear certainly will be judged slower and more shameless than demons. **Yet neither is it great to believe in_ God and tremble with fear unless he [*sic*] also is believed into, that is, unless love of God is held in the heart**.

Believing and trembling in fear alone is not the real Christian faith of *credere in eum* that unites the believer with those in need who are the central concern of James. While lacking the faith expressed in belief and trembling makes one worse than demons, having it alone, in the final judgment, does no more than put one on par with demons. Bede's final sentence above, his last before launching into an explanation of Augustine's formula, identifies the missing ingredient: holding love of God in the heart. It is this distinguishing factor that sets *credere in Deum* apart.

As Bede proceeds to lay out the formula, he does not follow exactly the text of Augustine in *Tract. Ev. Jo.* XXIX, with its *credendo* crescendo and its going into Christ and being incorporated in Christ's members. Bede does, however, clearly enumerate and clarify each of the three types of *credere* all together in one place, with brief explanations of each. Rather than directly citing Dolbeau 19/Mainz 51/Sermon 130A, or any other sources, he simply glosses:

> *Aliud est enim credere illi, aliud credere illum, aliud credere in illum. Credere illi est credere vera esse quae loquitur, credere illum credere quod ipse sit Deus, credere in illum diligere illum.* (lines 174–76)

> In fact it is one thing to believe him (literally "that one"), another to believe in him, another to believe into him. To believe him is to believe to be true any things he says, to believe in him is to believe that he is God himself, to believe into him is to love him (hold him dear/cherish him).

Thus far he merely collects in one place the formula established throughout several of Augustine's writings.[27] Bede's genius is to take

---

[27] Cross, "Bede's Influence," 23. No specific citation for the formula from Augustine's oeuvre appears in *In Septem* in the way it does for his quotation of Augustine's epistle to Jerome in the commentary on the previous verses. Nevertheless, a dominant source of Latin homilies in Bede's day would have been Augustine's *Tract. Ev. Jo.*, so, in addition to his apparent familiarity with Dolbeau 19/Mainz 51/Sermon 130A, he very likely drew some of his understanding of the formula in part from *Tract. Ev. Jo.* XXIX.

these collected pieces and arrange them in such a manner as to create a clear picture of participation (or lack thereof) in divine relationship that operates in each type of *credere*.

One Kind of *Credere*: Believing That What Christ Says Is True

Bede first approaches the contrasting phrase equivalent to what Augustine addressed in both *Tract. Ev. Jo.* XXIX and Dolbeau 19/ Mainz 51/Sermon 130A as *credere ei* (to believe him), and, in parts of Dolbeau 19/Mainz 51/Sermon 130A, also as *credere illi* (the way Bede has rendered it here, to believe that one, who in this case is Christ), which Bede describes as believing that what Christ says is true. Regarding the first of the three types of *credere* that Bede enumerates, he now reiterates what Augustine has said in Dolbeau 19/ Mainz 51/Sermon 130A, that even many evil ones can do it and still ignore Christ, because they're lazy![28] The aspect that he amplifies from Augustine is that the very least one who believes that God the Father sent God the Son could do would be to act on the words that the Son utters. Anyone who merely takes Christ at his word but no further, Bede suggests, with no impact on action and no love in response, has done nothing more than even the worst can do. There appears to be no love required in order to believe thus far and no positive effect in the one believing. As Bede notes, like Augustine in Dolbeau 19/Mainz 51/Sermon 130A and James before him, even the demons believed Christ, albeit trembling in fear.

Another Kind of *Credere*: Believing That Christ Is God

Bede next acknowledges the contrasting phrase *credere illum*, equivalent to what Augustine addressed both in *Serm.* CXLIV and in Dolbeau 19/Mainz 51/Sermon 130A as *credere eum* (to believe in him/ that person, again meaning Christ), in the way that he sometimes addressed it in Dolbeau 19/Mainz 51/Sermon 130A, *credere illum*, which Bede explains as believing "that he is God himself." Bede remains unimpressed—this was just another thing the demons have managed to do, too. He illustrates how far demons believe, which is more than those who don't want to believe in any God at all, but

---

[28]   Bede, *In Septem*, II.19, lines 177–79 (CCSL 121:198). See Dolbeau 19, 5, 108–10, covered here in our previous chapter, in the discussion of the three types of *credere* together in Sermon 130A.

it is still not far enough for Christian faith.[29] Just as he had earlier appealed to examples of demons' willingly acknowledging and identifying Jesus as the Son of God in the Gospels of Luke (4:41, in lines 164–65) and Mark (5:7, in lines 169–70), so here he makes clear that naming Christ in terror for the purpose of begging him not to torture the believer is not a bold surrender in loving relationship but a craven opposition to the love of God.[30] It amounts to a mere assent to God's existence and the divine identity of Jesus as God's Son. There is no love involved and no relationship between believers and the one in whom they believe.

The Kind of *Credere* Unique to Christianity: Believing into God

Finally, Bede arrives at Augustine's ultimate distinction of *credere in Deum* (note his shift now from *illum* to *Deum*, "God," as named object), stating boldly that "in truth" the only ones who "know how to believe into God" are those "who cherish-love God."[31] He goes on to note that such believers-into "are Christians not only by name, but also by deeds and by life, because without this kind of love, faith is void."[32] Consider how close Bede's phrasing is to the present-day prized notion of consistency in "word and deed," often colloquially

[29] Bede, *In Septem* II.19, lines 179–80, 183–84 (CCSL 121:198). ***Credere autem ipsum esse Deum***, hoc et daemones potuerunt (lines 179–80) translates literally, "Moreover, to believe that he is God himself ([him] to be God himself), this also the demons have been able to do." He continues this thought only after naming the final kind of *credere*, contrasting it once more with this believing-in-without-believing-into by saying, *Qui ergo non vult credere Christum adhuc nec daemones imitatur* (lines 183–84), which translates literally, "Therefore anyone who does not want to believe in Christ this far is not even imitating the demons" (that is, in their faith, implying the unwilling one is worse off/has less faith than demons).

[30] Bede, *In Septem* II.19, lines 184–87 (CCSL 121:198). *Iam credit Christum sed odit Christum, habet confessionem fidei in timore poenae non in amore coronae. Nam et illi puniri timebant* translates literally, "For he believes in Christ but hates Christ, he has the confession of faith in fear of punishment, not in love of the crown" (that is, by metonymy, of Christ, though *coronae* also can mean a halo).

[31] Bede, *In Septem* II.19 lines 180–83 (CCSL 121:198). *Credere <u>vero in Deum</u> soli noverunt qui diligunt Deum qui non solum nomine christiani sunt sed et factis et vita, quia sine dilectione fides inanis est, cum dilectione fides christiani, sine dilectione fides daemonis* is very awkward in literal translation. It requires rendering thus: "In truth, they alone know how to believe <u>into God</u> who cherish God, who are Christians not only by name, but also by deeds and by life, because without (this kind of) love faith is void, with (this kind of) love faith (is that) of Christians, without (this kind of) love faith (is that) of demons."

[32] Bede, *In Septem* II.19 lines 180–83 (CCSL 121:198).

expressed as "You must walk the walk if you're going to talk the talk."
For Bede, cherishing-love is the very content of Christian faith. This
love is not merely a fondness or any feeling, but that active *dilectio*
that Augustine so prizes and prioritizes as the cornerstone of religion
and society. Recall from the discussion of the *credendo* crescendo in
the previous chapter that *dilectio* involves for Augustine (on Peter
Brown's analysis) "the orientation of the entire personality, its deepest wishes and its basic capacity to love."[33] As previously mentioned,
Bede sharply contrasts such an orientation of believing-into with that
by which a confession of faith arises solely out of fear of punishment,
which can be stated while still hating Christ.[34] In fact, while the confession of demons may seem to have the same wording as that of "blessed
Peter" when he recognized Jesus as the Christ, the Son of the living
God, nevertheless because demons offer it with hatred for Christ, it
is the cause of their damnation.[35] On the other hand, those for whom
the confession proceeds from *dilectio* within have been rewarded with
everlasting blessedness.[36] Here Bede appears to intensify the language
and imagery used by Augustine in Dolbeau 19/Mainz 51/Sermon
130A, in which the focus is confession from love (Peter) versus from
fear (demons)—not hatred—and a result of Christ's blessing (of Peter)
versus silencing (of demons)—not damnation.[37]

The Body That Bede Left Out

It is surprising that, for all the emphasis Bede places on faith working
through love, he did not include Augustine's language of going into
Christ and being incorporated in Christ's members. There is no reason to suggest a fear of the corporeal in Bede, as his earlier commentary on the epistles of John includes language of touching and members between John and Jesus, to emphasize that John's works (among
which he included the Gospel and Revelation) reflect the authorial
style of one who had most intimate knowledge of Jesus as human. The
Last Supper scene comes to mind, which Bede calls to his readers'

[33] Peter Brown, *Religion and Society in the Age of St. Augustine* (New York:
Harper & Row, 1972), 42. Recall also that *diligere* is the verb used most frequently
throughout Dolbeau 19/Mainz 51/Sermon130A for love and even is used synon-
ymously with *credere in illum* in Dolbeau 19, 5, 108.

[34] Bede, *In Septem* II.19 lines 184–86 (CCSL 121:198).

[35] Bede, *In Septem* II.19 lines 186–89 (CCSL 121:198).

[36] Bede, *In Septem* II.19 lines 190–91 (CCSL 121:198).

[37] Augustine, Dolbeau 19, 2, 40–51; 5, 111–20.

remembrance in commenting on 1 John 1:1 by observing the freedom with which John could touch Jesus' members due to their proximity at the table.[38]

Perhaps, while Bede rejects dualism, his dedication to the preservation of monastic chastity leads him to avoid directing pupils in the monastery to a bawdy double entendre, originally designed to grab sleepy sermon-listeners' attention in the everyday worshiping world centuries earlier. Regardless of whether his omission was a deliberate choice, the notion of physicality, of intimate incorporation into Christ, is still present, if not stated in so many words, in Bede's conception of the *credere* that is love in action. Remarkably, Bede retains Augustine's emphasis on the relational sense even without the sermonic imagery of the believer going into Christ and Christ coming into and being in some way united with the believer.

The Life of the Formula beyond Bede

It might be possible to gain a more comprehensive view of Bede's understanding of the uniqueness of believing-into if he had completed and been able to disseminate his translation of John's Gospel into English, rather than having died translating verse 9 of John 6.[39] Bede was the first to translate the Apostles' Creed into English—albeit into English's earliest form. Knowing how he chooses, in doing so, to express the awkward nature of *Credo/Credimus in Deum* (I believe/ We believe into God) and to convey its distinction from *Credo/Credimus Deum* (I believe/We believe in God) and *Credo/Credimus Deo* (I believe/We believe God) would be immensely helpful here. However, as the only way we have of knowing that he even carried out this translation is that he declared as much in his final work, *Letter to Egbert*, it is impossible to access and analyze his translation choices. In that he was merely making available a tool for memorization by the clergy, whom he deemed too lazy to learn Latin, it is no surprise that

---

[38]   Augustine, Dolbeau 19, 2, 40–51; 5, 111–20. Ward translates the relevant portion of Bede's commentary on 1 John 1:1 thus: "The apostles could not doubt that this was a true body, inasmuch as they proved its genuineness not only by seeing but by touching it, particularly John himself who being accustomed to recline on his lap at supper touched his members more freely as he was nearer" (*Venerable Bede*, 52, n. 23). Ward observes that Bede did praise chastity elsewhere in *In Septem* but not in such a way as to introduce dualism or rejection of the flesh (57).

[39]   Ward, *Venerable Bede*, 15.

no manuscripts in the newly written English language were preserved in the way that his Latin works were.[40]

One strike against the retention of the formula over time is that Bede's biblical works are not as readily available as his most famous work today in anything other than Latin.[41] The most widely available work is not *In Septem*, which contains the formula, nor any other theological commentary, but the *Ecclesiastical History of the English Peoples*. Part of the reason his systematization of *credere* is not better known today is that his commentaries have generally been considered less accessible than the *History*, in terms both of hermeneutical skills required and of language.[42]

Nevertheless, his influence as an exegete-theologian in the immediate wake of his death and for several centuries thereafter is indisputable. During Bede's lifetime, respect for his work grew, and requests for copies of his manuscripts were constant. Abbots at Wearmouth and Jarrow had trouble keeping up with the demand that came from far enough away to have influenced more than just English traditions.[43] Within the English tradition, at the end of the eighth century, in his school at Charlemagne's court, Alcuin of York was heavily influenced by and admiring of Bede, whose scriptural commentaries he placed first in a list of famous scholars'

---

[40]   Joshua Westgard, email message to author, March 18, 2017. Westgard is co-compiler with George Hardin Brown of the "Census of Bede Manuscripts," viewable online at http://www.bedemanuscripts.net/. Dr. Westgard declared of Bede scholarship, "As far as we know, no trace of these translations of the creed or prayers has survived."

[41]   *In Septem* became available in 1985 as *The Commentary on the Seven Catholic Epistles of Bede the Venerable*, trans. David Hurst, Cistercian Studies 82 (Kalamazoo, Mich.: Cistercian Publications, 1985).

[42]   Scott DeGregorio, "Bede and the Old Testament," in DeGregorio, *Cambridge Companion to Bede*, 127–41. Degregorio's lament reflects a common contrast that scholars draw today, as classics scholarship and thus Latin language facility are an increasingly narrow domain. The contrast is between Bede as allegedly accessible historian, for which role he did not become famous until centuries after his death, and Bede as allegedly inaccessible exegete, despite his having been celebrated thus in his lifetime and having continued to be for centuries. The exciting characters and swiftly moving narrative of the *Ecclesiastical History of the English Peoples* are wearily compared to the exegetical works that are locked away in Latin tomes, require theological interpretations for which readers are no more likely to be equipped than they are to read Latin, and do not provide sufficient glimpses of Bede's own era and location to be as exciting as the *History*. DeGregorio's assessment of the commentaries seems harsh, though not unhelpful.

[43]   Ward, *Venerable Bede*, 136–37. For example, requests for Bede's manuscripts came from Boniface for his mission at Frisia, accounting for Bede's influence on Germanic/Dutch Christian traditions.

work in his *The Bishops, Kings, and Saints of York*.[44] Alcuin used Bede's works as manuals, arguably giving Bede "strong claim to be regarded as the formative influence on the West in the early Middle Ages."[45] In fact, it is considered a crucial key to the dissemination of Bede throughout Europe that clergy in Charlemagne's Holy Roman Empire relied for their preaching on an official canon of homilies that was compiled by an associate of Alcuin known as Paul the Deacon.[46]

Bede's influence continued through the turn of the first Christian millennium, as his commentaries became part of the *Glossa Ordinaria* (frequently referred to as "the Gloss") of the twelfth century. This massive compilation of biblical texts with thorough interlinear and marginal commentary and explanations gleaned from patristic texts circulated more widely throughout the twelfth and thirteenth centuries than did the actual Bible.[47] Bede is a source of the Gloss' commentary on several biblical books of both Testaments, but most significant among them for understanding his role in disseminating the formula are the canonical epistles, which rely entirely on Bede's work and its acknowledged reliance upon both Jerome and Augustine.[48] Thus his systematization of Augustine's formula as it appears in the commentary on James 2:19 was disseminated throughout Europe.

With exposure to the Gloss, if to none of Bede's other works directly, Amalarius of Metz in the twelfth century quotes Bede as an "indisputable authority," as does Thomas Aquinas in the thirteenth century, in the Prima Pars of his *Summa Theologiae*.[49] One figure whose work is instrumental in Thomas' exposure to the formula adds his own innovations to those of Bede and arose in the century before Thomas: the bishop of Paris from 1159, Peter Lombard. Referred to alternately as "Peter" and "the Lombard" (with or without the definite article), he is believed to be one of the great teachers responsible for developing the *Glossa Ordinaria* into its final popular form around 1140,[50] which would have put him in very close contact, indeed, with the work of Bede as it pertained to Augustine's formula.

---

[44]   Ward, *Venerable Bede*, 138.
[45]   Ward, *Venerable Bede*, 139.
[46]   Cross, "Bede's Influence," 21.
[47]   Lesley Janette Smith, *The "Glossa Ordinaria": The Making of a Medieval Bible Commentary* (Leiden: Brill, 2009), 1.
[48]   Smith, *"Glossa Ordinaria,"* 53. Smith's footnote specifically refers to the pages from *In Septem* quoted above.
[49]   Ward, *Venerable Bede*, 143.
[50]   Smith, *"Glossa Ordinaria,"* 194.

Peter Lombard: The Formula Systematized Further

Peter Lombard was as careful as Bede, if not more so, to cite his sources.[51] Thus it is that references to the Gloss and also to Bede and Augustine surrounds his presentation of the *credere* formula that he includes in the discussion of *fides* (faith) in his landmark work *Sententiae in IV Libris Distinctae* (Sentences in Four Distinct Books).[52] This work would become foundational for much of medieval Christianity. In his discussion of faith in book III, distinction 23, chapter 4, he addresses the issue of *Quid sit credere Deum vel Deo vel in Deum*, "What it might be to believe in God, or God, or into God."[53] He begins by summarizing Bede's presentation for the first two, in slightly different order and with minor adjustments of vocabulary (for example, earlier use of *Deum/Deo/in Deum*, in God/God/into God, as the object of *credere*—in his introduction of the formula, at which point Bede's presentation had used only pronouns).

> *Aliud est enim credere in Deum, aliud credere Deo, aliud credere Deum. Credere Deo, est credere vera esse quae loquitur: quod et mali faciunt; et nos credimus homini, sed non in hominem. Credere Deum, est credere quod ipse sit Deus: quod etiam mali faciunt.*[54]

> In fact it is one thing to believe into God, another to believe God, another to believe in God. To believe him, is to believe to be true that which he says: which also the evil ones do; and we believe humans, but not into humans. To believe in God is to believe that he is God himself: this also the evil ones do.

It is worth noting here that the choice to use God as proper name opens up potential to emphasize a nuance of translation for this definition: "to believe that God himself exists." Whereas the previous use of pronouns holds the possibility of referring to Jesus as being God himself (such as in Augustine's *Serm.* CXLIV), here the existence of God is clearly more plausible as the proposition in play for the believer.

---

51   Smith, *"Glossa Ordinaria,"* 44.
52   Peter Lombard, *Magistri Petri Lombardi Parisiensis episcopi Sententiae in IV libris distinctae, Tomus II* (Grottaferrata: Editiones Collegii S. Bonaventurae ad Claras Aquas, 1981).
53   Peter Lombard, *Sententiae*, 143.
54   Peter Lombard, *Sententiae*, 143.

His summary then quotes Augustine in *Tract. Ev. Jo.* XXIX with surgical precision, using the *credendo* crescendo and language of incorporation in Christ's members. He also grafts a descriptive phrase from elsewhere in the Augustinian corpus. *Credere in Deum, est credendo amare, credendo in eum ire, credendo ei adhaerere et eius membris incorporari*: To believe into God, is by believing to love, by believing to go into God, by believing <u>to cling to God</u> and to be incorporated in God's members.[55]

Note that he inserts into Augustine's original explanation of *credere in eum* from *Tract. Ev. Jo.* XXIX one more level to the *credendo* crescendo, *credendo adhaerere*—by believing to cling (to God). Between Augustine's "by believing to go into him" and the concluding phrase from *Tract. Ev. Jo.* XXIX, "and to be incorporated in his members," the Lombard inserts this new phrase drawn from a familiar line in one of Augustine's previously mentioned *Expositions on the Psalms*, on Psalm 77:8.[56] "Cling" is appropriate Augustinian language to join to the *Tract. Ev. Jo.* XXIX version of the formula here. It is unsurprising that Lombard chooses to make references to Augustine's work on Psalms into his own systematization of the formula, since he is known to have worked closely with Augustine's material on Psalms as it appears in the *Glossa Ordinaria*. He was, in a sense, revising the Gloss into an accessible, ongoing exegetical text that, thanks to the Gloss' own authors' heavy reliance on Augustine (such as Bede's), is really a multilayered effort, crafted from multiple theologians' revisions.[57]

He appears to have been refining the formula into a neat system that could easily be marked, read, and inwardly digested. He presents a straightforward understanding of the distinctive relational sense of this Christian believing, by which one boldly loves God, goes into God, clings to God, and is incorporated in God's members. Even in a briefer space than that which Bede occupies with his systematization of the formula, Lombard is still careful to include what is missing in Bede, the language of incorporation and members.

---

[55]   Peter Lombard, *Sententiae*, 143.
[56]   Augustine, Exposition 77.8, in *Expositions of the Psalms* (73–98), ed. John E. Rotelle, trans. Maria Boulding, The Works of St. Augustine: A Translation for the 21st Century 3/18 (Hyde Park, N.Y.: New City Press, 2009), 98. Note that he would cite for his next sentence the *Exposition* on Ps 67:32-33.
[57]   Smith, *"Glossa Ordinaria,"* 201.

Why delete, however, the *credendo diligere* of *Tract. Ev. Jo.* XXIX? Did he find it redundant with *amare*? Did he merely need to make room for *adhaerere*, without making the memorable *credendo* crescendo unwieldy in length? Perhaps both; however, it soon becomes clear that he had not eliminated, but rather transplanted, the concept of *diligere*:

> *Per hanc fidem iustificatur impius, ut deinde ipsa fides incipiat per dilectionem operari. Ea enim sola bona opera dicenda sunt, quae fiunt per dilectionem Dei. Ipsa etiam dilectio opus fidei dicitur.*[58]

> By this faith is the wicked one justified, as then faith itself may begin to work through (cherishing) love. For by it alone are works called good, which are done through the (cherishing) love of God. Indeed, (cherishing) love itself is called a work of faith.

Now only present in its noun form, *dilectio*, the concept of *diligere* is no less active than in Augustine and Bede's usages of both the noun and verb form. Rather, Lombard uses it to give a synopsis of all that appears in Augustine, whose tenth *Tractatus* on 1 John Lombard cites for the final sentence, in order to conclude that *credere in* + accusative is the "faith working through love" as stated in 1 John.[59]

To get a sense of how the systematization of the formula was being disseminated at the time, it is helpful to consider how Lombard was using these materials in theological discourse, primarily through teaching at the Notre Dame cathedral school.[60] It appears that he preferred to use the Gloss rather than the Bible itself for regular lectures, drawing from glossed texts of Anselm for lectures on Psalms and the Pauline Epistles, for example.[61] Lest the interpreter of Scripture accuse Lombard of thus crafting doctrine that is too far removed from Scripture, it is important to note that Peter was, in his presentation of *credere in* + accusative, very faithful to the words of Augustine, who lifted the phrase directly from multiple passages of Scripture. Lombard differs from the bishop of Hippo only in the divine object, using not simply "him" (which Augustine usually meant to refer to Christ) but "God."

---

[58] Peter Lombard, *Sententiae*, 143–44.
[59] Peter Lombard, *Sententiae*, 144.
[60] Smith, *"Glossa Ordinaria,"* 200.
[61] Smith, *"Glossa Ordinaria,"* 200.

The only inconsistency with which Lombard might be charged is the order of his phrasing within his own presentation of *credere* + accusative, *credere* + dative, and *credere in* + accusative. However, it should already be clear that his presentation of this formula drawn from Augustine, like Bede's before him, underscores how unimportant the order itself is to the establishing of the fact that *credere in* + accusative is, of the three possible understandings of *credere*, the kind of believing that is the Christian faith that works through love. As the *Sententiae* were broadly disseminated throughout Europe, Augustine's, Bede's, and Lombard's insistence on this loving, relational faith as constitutive of Christianity went with them.

Aquinas: The Formula Reduced

When Thomas Aquinas contributed to the myriad of medieval commentaries on Lombard's *Sententiae* with his own *Scriptum Super Sententiis (Writing about the Sentences)*, he attended to the phrase *credere in Deum* no fewer than five times.[62] His approach to the formula, however, was rather distinct from that of his predecessors, even from the one on whose *Sentences* he was commenting in this work. Thomas does not simply quote verbatim each of Lombard's sentences and then comment. He does not simply present Lombard's systematization of the Augustinian formula and affirm it. Nor does he in this work offer the type of straightforward, three-part presentation of and commentary on the formula that he will in his *Summa Theologiae*.

Instead, with Aristotelian precision of logic, in a structure that presages that *Summa*, he poses and then responds to a series of questions that he imagines (or knows) opponents might raise about each of the subsets of Lombard's distinctions. In each section, he first names several *quaestiunculae*, little questions, which represents

---

[62] Thomas Aquinas, *Scriptum super libros sententiarum magistri Petri Lombardi Episcopi Parisiensis*, ed. M. F. Moos (Paris: P. Lethielleux, 1929–1947) 3: d. 23, q. 1, pr.; d. 23, q. 2, a. 2, qc. 2; d. 23, q. 3, a. 1, qc. 3, arg. 3; d. 25, q. 1, a. 2, args. 4–5. Abbreviated hereafter *Scriptum*. Note: One of very few published translations of any portion of the *Scriptum*, Peter A. Kwasniewski's in Augustine, *On Love and Charity: Readings from the Commentary on the Sentences of Peter Lombard*, trans. Peter A. Kwasniewski (Washington, D.C.: Catholic University of America Press, 2008), includes only one of the excerpts here addressed, d. 23, q. 3, a. 1, qc. 3, in which Kwasniewski translates *credere in Deum* as "to believe unto God" and explains in a footnote, "*credere in Deum*, to believe in such a way that one draws near to God through love" (109, n. e).

the position against which Aquinas plans to argue in the ensuing responses, which in turn he marks in correspondence to the number of the initial *quaestiunculae*. His method is similar to that of his contemporary, Bonaventure, allowing Thomas, who comes to be known as the Angelic Doctor (in the sense of *doctor*, teacher), a great deal more room than other methods might have for his original thoughts and additions to Lombard's work.[63]

His treatment of the formula is found in the questions and responses gathered under a heading of *Utrum credere sit cum assensu cogitare*, "Whether to believe may be to think with assent."[64] Thomas lays the groundwork for commentary on *credere Deum, Deo*, and *in Deum* in his response to the second *quaestiuncula* in which he employs an imaginary objector to pose.[65] Beginning by saying, *Ulterius*, "On the

---

[63]   Russell L. Friedman, "The *Sentences* Commentary, 1250–1320 General Trends, the Impact of the Religious Orders, and the Test Case of Predestination," in *Mediaeval Commentaries on the* Sentences *of Peter Lombard*, vol. 1, *Current Research*, ed. G. R. Evans (Leiden: Brill, 2002), 86–88. Though less "bound to the text," Bonaventure and Thomas generally expressed fewer doubts about Peter's propositions than the *dubia* often enumerated in the *Glossa* style used by an earlier generation of commentators on the *Sententiae*, including Alexander of Hale, Bonaventure's mentor.

[64]   Thomas, *Scriptum* 3: d. 23, q. 2, a. 2.

[65]   Thomas, *Scriptum* 3: d. 23, q. 2, a. 2, qc. 2, args. 1–5 (translation mine).

> 1. *Ulterius. Videtur quod inconvenienter multiplicetur credere, secundum quod est actus fidei. Unius enim habitus unus est actus, ex quo habitus per actus discernuntur. Sed fides est unus habitus. Ergo tantum unus actus debet assignari.*

> 1. On the other side: It seems that to believe is multiplied unsuitably, according as it is the act of faith. For one habit is one act, from which the habit is discerned through the act. But faith is one habit. Therefore it should be assigned only one act.

> 2. *Praeterea, de eo quod demonstratur, non est fides, sed scientia: quia quod demonstratur, non est non apparens. Sed Deum esse, demonstrative probatur etiam a philosophis. Ergo actus fidei non est credere Deum esse.*

> 2. In addition, from this it is proven that it is not faith, but knowledge: because that which is proven is not imperceptible. But that God exists already has been demonstratively proven by the philosophers. Therefore it is not an act of faith to believe that God exists.

> 3. *Praeterea, in actu fidei discernitur fidelis ab infideli. Sed nullus est ita infidelis quin credat quod Deus non loquitur nisi verum. Ergo credere vera esse quae Deus loquitur, non est actus fidei; sed magis cre-*

other side," the opponent offers a view contrary to what the opponent regards as an unnecessary compounding of a simple, single act of faith, and supports this view with four additional statements against the notion of faith as thinking with assent. First, the opponent objects that it is unsuitable to multiply the act of believing, insisting that faith, as one habit, should be assigned only one act. The next point strongly reflects the medieval Christian worldview that, since God's existence is proven, it is a matter of knowledge, not faith, so believing that God exists, the opponent corrects, is not a matter of faith but of knowledge. The third point further reflects that worldview by suggesting that there is no one who would believe that God speaks anything but the truth, so believing God does not separate the faithful from the unfaithful and thus is not an act of faith—believing a human messenger is more an act of faith than is believing God! The penultimate point objects to the notion that faith and love are inseparably united, as they are clearly distinct theological virtues, such that it is charity, and not faith, that leads one to love God. Finally, the opponent objects that it is by love, not faith, that the believer stretches toward, clings to, and is incorporated in the members of God.

Thus, the opposing viewpoints that Thomas raised for his readers primarily object to dividing the single act of faith into three possible

---

dere vera esse quae nuntius Dei loquitur: et sic credere homini magis est actus fidei quam credere Deo.

3. In addition, in the act of faith, the faithful is discerned from the unfaithful. But no one is so unfaithful that they do not believe that God does not speak unless it's the truth. Therefore to believe to be true that which God says is not an act of faith; but greater to believe to be true that which a messenger of God says: and thus to believe humans is a greater act of faith than to believe God.

4. *Praeterea, fides et caritas sunt virtutes distinctae. Sed amare Deum est actus caritatis. Ergo credendo amare non est actus fidei.*

4. In addition, faith and love are distinct virtues. But to love God is an act of charity. Therefore by believing to love is not an act of faith.

5. *Praeterea, per hoc quod homo Deum amat, in eum tendit et adhaeret ei, et membris ejus incorporatur. Ergo videtur quod superflue ponatur ista verborum inculcatio.*

5. In addition, through this according to which the human loves God, he stretches into him and clings to him, and is incorporated in his members. Therefore it seems that this forcing of words is placed superfluously.

aspects in ways that would allow Thomas, in responding, to gesture toward the whole formula, *credere Deum, credere Deo,* and *credere in Deum.* Clearly, Thomas presents the opponent as attacking the formula and especially the relational aspects of belief by insisting that the distinctions between theological virtues do not allow for love to be bound up in faith, and by neglecting the phrase *credere in Deum.* Thus, in the objections, there is no attention to the uniqueness of the grammatical distinction of *credere in* + accusative. Whether these objections represent extant resistance to the formula among Thomas' contemporaries is not clear.

Thomas proceeds to identify the three parts of the formula together in his responses to the objections, beginning with a general statement about the act of faith. In this statement, Thomas hearkens back to another statement he has made in his commentary on a previous question, in which he describes the act of believing as a single act proceeding *ex tribus,* "from three things," which are *intellectu,* the intellect, *voluntate,* the will, and *ratione,* reason.[66]

[66]   The complete Latin text and my translation:

> *Ad secundam quaestionem dicendum, quod sicut ex praedictis patet, actus credentis ex tribus dependet, scilicet ex intellectu, qui terminatur ad unum; ex voluntate, quae determinat intellectum per suum imperium; et ex ratione, quae inclinat voluntatem: et secundum hoc tres actus assignantur fidei. Ex hoc enim quod intellectus terminatur ad unum, actus fidei est credere Deum, quia objectum fidei est Deus secundum quod in se consideratur, vel aliquid circa ipsum, vel ab ipso. Ex hoc vero quod intellectus determinatur a voluntate, secundum hoc actus fidei est credere in Deum, idest amando in eum tendere: est enim voluntatis amare. Secundum autem quod ratio voluntatem inclinat ad actus fidei, est credere Deo: ratio enim qua voluntas inclinatur ad assentiendum his quae non videt, est quia Deus ea dicit: sicut homo in his quae non videt, credit testimonio alicujus boni viri qui videt ea quae ipse non videt.*

> Speaking to the second question, what is clear from what was said before is that the act of believing proceeds from three things, namely, from the intellect, which is restricted to one; from the will, which determines the intellect by its power; and from reason, which bends the will: and according to this the three are assigned to the act of faith. For from this, by which the intellect is restricted to one, the act of faith is to believe in a God, because the object of faith is God, according to which he is considered in himself, or anything around himself, or from himself. From this truly the intellect is determined by the will, according to this the act of faith is to believe into God that is by loving to stretch into

According to Thomas, these three things are responsible simultaneously for different aspects of this one act of believing. The intellect is responsible for belief in a God—that is, that God exists. The will is responsible for believing into God because the will is responsible for loving. Reason is responsible for believing God, that is, believing what God says is true, even as it regards the unseen. Thomas then addresses each of the opponent's five objections.

He dismisses the first objection against describing multiple aspects of the single act of faith, with allusion to the fact that faith is discovered in many ways.[67] Thus it is by any of these ways that a person comes to the one act of believing. Note, however, the lack of attention, such as that which Bede so carefully paid, to the possibility of believing in a God without believing into God, like demons do, for example.

The second objection is the first to criticize a specific part of the formula, stating that it is no act of faith to believe God exists.[68] In response, Thomas allows that anyone may be able to prove God's existence but not the specific details about God, such as God's Trinitarian nature, which cannot be demonstrated. Thus, to believe in a God (*credere Deum*) is an act of faith.

To the third objection, targeting the notion of believing God as an act of faith, Thomas retorts that there are many unfaithful ones

---

him: for to love is of the will. However, when reason inclines the will towards an act of faith, it is to believe God: for reason is that by which the will is inclined toward assenting to the things which it does not see, it is because God says so: just as a man does not see something here, yet believes by the testimony of any good man who sees that which he himself does not see.

[67]   *Ad primum ergo dicendum, quod per omnia praedicta non nominatur nisi unus completus actus fidei; sed ex diversis quae in fide inveniuntur diversimode nominatur: illo enim actu quo credit in Deum, credit Deo, et credit Deum.* "Speaking to the first (objection) therefore, that the one complete act of faith is not called by all the preceding; but from the diverse ways in which faith is discovered, by diverse ways is it named: for by that act anyone believes into God, believes God, and believes in a God."

[68]   *Ad secundum dicendum, quod quamvis Deum esse, simpliciter possit demonstrari; tamen Deum esse trinum et unum, et alia hujusmodi, quae fides in Deo credit, non possunt demonstrari; secundum quae est actus fidei credere Deum.* "Speaking to the second, that whomever you please may be able to prove God to exist; nevertheless, that God is three and one, and other things of this sort, which faith believes about (literally "in") God, they cannot demonstrate; according to which it is an act of faith to believe in a God."

who do not believe God's message spoken through a human.[69] The implication is that their disbelief of God's human messengers is the same as disbelieving God. So, the assumption that everyone believes that God speaks the truth is false, and thus it does take faith to believe God (*credere Deo*).

Thomas most quickly dispatches with the fourth objection, the first half of the two-part rejection of *credere in Deum* as an act of faith, both of which parts address language from the *credendo* crescendo of *Tract. Ev. Jo.* XXIX. After clarifying that to love may be an act of charity, but to believe by loving (note the subtle switch from Augustine's "by believing to love") is an act of faith, however moved by charity,[70] he proceeds to dwell a while longer on the rest of Augustine's language describing *credere in Deum* as Peter Lombard presented it in the *Sententiae*.[71] Here Thomas becomes highly technical, summarizing all parts of the objection to the multiple aspects of faith as arising from the interlocutor's misunderstanding the will, related as it is to both love and faith,

---

[69]   *Ad tertium dicendum, quod fidelis credit homini non inquantum homo, sed inquantum Deus in eo loquitur, quod ex certis experimentis colligere potest: infidelis autem non credit Deo in homine loquenti.* "Speaking to the third, that the faithful believes a man not in as much as man, but in as much as God speaks in him, that from reliable experience he can deduce: but the unfaithful does not believe God speaking in a man."

[70]   *Ad quartum dicendum, quod amare simpliciter est actus caritatis: sed amando credere est actus fidei per caritatem motae ad actum suum.* "Speaking to the fourth, that to love simply is an act of charity: but to believe by loving is an act of faith moved to its act through charity."

[71]   *Ad quintum dicendum, quod illa quatuor pertinent ad fidem secundum ordinem ad voluntatem, ut dictum est; voluntas autem est finis; et ideo ista quatuor distinguuntur secundum ea quae exiguntur ad consecutionem finis. Praeexigitur enim primo affectio ad finem; et ad hoc pertinet credendo amare. Ex amore autem et desiderio finis aliquis in finem incipit moveri; et ad hoc pertinet credendo in eum ire. Motus autem ad finem perducit ad hoc quod aliquis fini conjungatur; et ad hoc pertinet credendo ei adhaerere. Ex conjunctione autem ad finem aliquis in participationem perfectionis finis perducitur; et ad hoc pertinet credendo membris ejus incorporari.* "Speaking to the fifth, that those four pertain to faith according to an order to the will, as has been said; but the will is an end; and for that reason those four are distinguished according to that which is driven toward the effect of an end; for it is driven out ahead by the highest affection toward an end; and to this pertains 'by believing to love.' Moreover, out of love and desire of an end does anyone begin to move into an end; and to this pertains 'by believing to go into him.' Also movement leads to an end in order that anyone may be united to an end; and to this pertains 'by believing to cling to him.' Also from the union to an end anyone is led into participation of perfection in the end; and to this pertains 'by believing to be incorporated in God's members.'"

which are not so rigidly separable as the interlocutor has suggested. The various aspects of the one act of believing emerge from the will being drawn toward a higher end. That higher end is God, to whom the *credendo* crescendo directs the believer, until the believer clings to God. Thomas is the first to frame this notion in terms of the heavenly, beatific vision at the center of his theology, declaring that this union results in participation in that end's perfection, resulting in the act of faith as "by believing to be incorporated in (God's) members."

What is interesting in these responses is that Thomas did not privilege *credere in* + accusative as particularly constitutive of the Christian faith, nor was this presentation an admonishment against the dead faith without works that his predecessors had decried. *Diligere* also has disappeared, with only forms of the standard *amare* used for references to love. Nevertheless, there remains language of movement into God, even as Thomas restricts such movement to the intellect, will, and reason. He retains mention of members and employs relational terms of affection (seated in the will) and love that causes the believer to stretch (or direct one's steps, and by association oneself) into God. His introduction of participation in God's perfection and emphasis on unity, while seeming to deemphasize the bodily notions, do emphasize transforming relationship as a key aspect of believing into God.

Thomas addresses the full formula with fresh thoughts in *Summa Theologiae* IIa-IIae, q. 2, a. 2, "Whether the Act of Faith Is Suitably Distinguished as Believing God, Believing in a God, and Believing into God."[72] Here he eliminates the bodily imagery of Augustine's language of incorporation and members, which Lombard retained and which earlier, in the *Scriptum*, Thomas also retained. Here he replaces that bodily imagery with the will's movement of the intellect toward having an end.

For the formula, he indicates that he was appealing to the authority of Augustine, citing both *Tract. Ev. Jo.* XXIX and a now-lost collection of sermons, the authenticity of which several scholars have called into question (though one wonders if it might have included at least Dolbeau 19/Mainz 51/Sermon 130A). He starts his explanation in the *respondeo* with consideration of belief in God's existence, *credere Deum*: "If it be considered on the part of the intellect, then two things

[72] Thomas Aquinas, *Summa Theologica*, trans. Fathers of the English Dominican Province (Westminster, Md.: Christian Classics, 1981), IIa-IIae, q. 2, a. 2. (Note my replacement of "in" with the proper preposition, "into.")

can be observed in the object of faith, as stated above" (by which he means q. 1, a. 1). He continues, "One of these is the material object of faith, and in this way an act of faith is 'to believe in a God'; because, as stated above, nothing is proposed to our belief, except in as much as it is referred to God."[73] This much is fairly straightforward.

He moves from belief in God's existence to believing God, *credere Deo*: "The other is the formal aspect of the object, for it is the medium on account of which we assent to such and such a point of faith; and thus an act of faith is 'to believe God.'"[74] Note that the verb "assent" enters in, as it did for *credere Deo* previously in the *Scriptum* (as well as in IIa-IIae, q. 2, a. 1). In the *Scriptum* it was paired with *ratio*, reason. He elaborates on the reasoning here: "since . . . the formal object of faith is the First Truth, to Which man [*sic*] gives his [*sic*] adhesion, so as to assent for its sake to whatever he [*sic*] believes."[75] The presence of clinging/adherence at this point is somewhat confusing, as it had been associated previously not with *credere Deo* but with *credere in Deum*, specifically with the *credendo* crescendo for his predecessors and with the equivalent thereof in his own *Scriptum*.

At long last, and yet in brief, Aquinas comes to believing into God, *credere in Deum*, stating, "Thirdly, if the object of faith be considered in so far as the intellect is moved by the will, an act of faith is 'to believe in(to) God.' For the First Truth refers to the will, through having the aspect of an end."[76] This presentation is dry, to say the least. Gone is the relational language of cherishing, of movement of the believer into Christ, of clinging to Christ in this unique way, of being incorporated in Christ's members. There is no mention of faith working through love.

---

[73]   Thomas, *Summa Theologica* IIa-IIae, q. 2, a. 2., *resp*. The Fathers' translation of *Si quidem ex parte intellectus, sic in obiecto fidei duo possunt considerari, sicut supra dictum est. Quorum unum est materiale obiectum fidei. Et sic ponitur actus fidei credere Deum quia, sicut supra dictum est, nihil proponitur nobis ad credendum nisi secundum quod ad Deum pertinet.*

[74]   Thomas, *Summa Theologica* IIa-IIae, q. 2, a. 2., *resp*. The Fathers' translation of *Aliud autem est formalis ratio obiecti, quod est sicut medium propter quod tali credibili assentitur. Et sic ponitur actus fidei credere Deo*. . . .

[75]   Thomas, *Summa Theologica* IIa-IIae, q. 2, a. 2., *resp*. The Fathers' translation of *quia . . . formale obiectum fidei est veritas prima, cui inhaeret homo ut propter eam creditis assentiat.*

[76]   Thomas, *Summa Theologica* IIa-IIae, q. 2, a. 2., *resp*. The Fathers' translation of *Si vero consideretur tertio modo obiectum fidei, secundum quod intellectus est motus a voluntate, sic ponitur actus fidei credere in Deum, veritas enim prima ad voluntatem refertur secundum quod habet rationem finis.*

Further, in his response to the first objection, the sharp contrast in sufficiency between the first two types of *credere* and *credere in Deum* that Augustine had drawn in Dolbeau 19/Mainz 51/Sermon 130A is absent, in the effort Aquinas makes to affirm the three types as "one act." He addresses the objector's concern about the irrationality of one virtue's having three distinct acts by insisting to the contrary, "These three do not denote different acts of faith, but one and the same act having different relations to the object of faith."[77] In this effort to defend the formula's rationality, he understandably uses the word "relation," but not in terms of the relational sense Augustine described as unique to *credere in Deum*, rooted in cherishing-love and incorporation, versus the fear-based, limited relationship exhibited in the demons' desire that Christ leave them alone.

In responding to the fourth and final objection, he again uses the language he used in the *Scriptum*, emphasizing the intellect to the exclusion of bodily imagery of movement and incorporation. He refers not to the *Scriptum*, however, but to his article on the intellect's movement of the will in the previous part of the *Summa*, stating, "As stated above,[78] the will moves the intellect and the other powers of the soul to the end: and in this respect an act of faith is *to believe in (into) God*."[79] Here again the loving, moving, connecting, relational sense of *credere in Deum* is unfortunately lost conceptually before it can even be lost in translation.

The curious issue here is not that Thomas departed from Augustine. On the contrary, the language of intellect and will and a bond between them is thoroughly Augustinian—it is just that it is the language of Augustine in his great tome *De Trinitate*, without that of Augustine's *credendo* crescendo in *Tract. Ev. Jo.* XXIX.[80] Thomas now is hearkening to Augustine's treatment of the relationship of the

---

[77] Thomas, *Summa Theologica* IIa-IIae, q. 2, a. 2., *ad* 1. The Fathers' translation of *Ad primum ergo dicendum quod per ista tria non designantur diversi actus fidei, sed unus et idem actus habens diversam relationem ad fidei obiectum.*

[78] Thomas, *Summa Theologica* Ia-IIae, q. 9, a. 1. The Question is "Whether the Intellect Moves the Will" and the article is "Whether the Will is Moved by the Intellect."

[79] Thomas, *Summa Theologica* Ia-IIae, q. 9, a. 1, *ad* 4. The Fathers' translation of *Ad quartum dicendum quod, sicut supra dictum est, voluntas movet intellectum et alias vires animae in finem. Et secundum hoc ponitur actus fidei credere in Deum.*

[80] Augustine, *The Trinity*, 2nd ed., trans. Edmund Hill, The Works of Saint Augustine: A Translation for the 21st Century 1/5 (Brooklyn, N.Y.: New City Press, 1996), I.12.27.

Persons of the Trinity *ad intra*, toward themselves or on the inside, not the relationship between humans and God in Christ *ad extra*, toward others or the outside, through the operation of *credere in eum*, believing into God. Clearly, faith and believing involve the latter. Therefore, while Thomas is indeed faithful to Augustine's coherent word, he is mixing metaphors or at best patterning the relationship of the human *ad Deum*, toward God, after the Trinity *ad intra* by abandoning the language of incorporation in Christ's members and the movement of bold surrender that *credere in eum* engenders.

His minor treatment of the formula's components in the *Scriptum* and his outright sanitization—in the sense of scrubbing out, not ironically (i.e., not linked to *sanus*, health or healing at the heart of salvation, unfortunately)—of the formula from any entanglement with the body in the *Summa Theologiae* signify a shift in emphasis. It is too facile to attribute the shift to the rise of Scholasticism with an attendant dualism that reviles the flesh. Rather, one possible explanation for this shift is exposure to influences and sources in interpreting Augustine other than just Bede and Lombard. Thomas' primary source for Augustine was a compilation of sermons that is no longer identifiable and that thus would receive criticism from twentieth-century scholars. These scholars also have questioned whether the influence of Thomas' mentor, Albertus Magnus, served to weaken the Angelic Doctor's understanding of the *credere* formula.[81] Nevertheless, rather than negate the formula's usefulness in the hands of Thomas as a theological lens, these issues may simply explain the ease with which Thomas reduces the language and arguably diminishes its usefulness.

It is worthy of notice that much of what Thomas and his contemporaries considered theology is what would today fall more within the purview of philosophy.[82] This distinction is not to take away from the theological merits of Aquinas in any way, but it does point to the emphasis on the rational soul and on God *ad intra* as being at the heart

---

[81] Thomas Camelot, "*Credere Deo, Credere Deum, Credere in Deum*: Pour l'histoire d'une formule traditionnelle," *Revue des Sciences Philosophiques et Théologiques* 30, no. 1 (1941–1942): 153. See also Christine Mohrmann, "Credere in Deum: Sur l'interpretation theologique d'un fait de langue," in *Mélanges Joseph de Ghellinck, S.J.* (Gembloux: J. Duculot, 1951), 285. Camelot and Mohrmann were among the very few scholars to address the formula and its history as such.

[82] Eleanor Stump, *Aquinas* (London: Routledge, 2003), 1.

of Thomas' work,[83] rather than the emphases specifically on the concreteness of Christ, incorporation, and members uplifted by Augustine and restored by Lombard.

Late Medieval England: The Formula Used by a Poet and a Politician-Prodding Preacher

Nevertheless, these emphases were not completely lost, at least not immediately. A century after Thomas, Middle English poet William Langland reached back to Bede and Peter Lombard for his pilgrimage poem, *The Vision of Piers Plowman*.[84] Contemporary scholarship of English literature points to the formula in a tradition of commentary allegedly on the creeds that is likely responsible for passing *credere* into the mouth of character "Conscience" in this fourteenth-century Middle English pilgrimage poem.[85] In the poem, when Conscience addresses the King, Conscience starts speaking in Latin and amends the grammatical form of a common phrase from major creeds, *Credo in Ecclesiam*, "I believe into the Church." Instead of the accusative object in the phrase, *in Ecclesiam*, "into the Church," Conscience speaks of the church using the ablative, *in Ecclesia*, "(standing or located) in the church." It is possible that Langland has placed these amended words into the speech of Conscience deliberately, in due deference to the fact that *credere in* + accusative had come to be considered the "proper" way to speak only about belief regarding God, not regarding God's institution, the church (as important as that institution remained).[86] Moreover, Conscience's entire speech attends carefully to grammar as a subject of theology and specifically focuses on the need to use the right case (i.e., accusative, dative, ablative, etc.) in order for each word to relate properly to the things they describe. Conscience draws

---

[83]   Norman Kretzmann, "Philosophy of Mind," in *The Cambridge Companion to Aquinas*, ed. Norman Kretzmann and Eleonore Stump, Cambridge Companions to Philosophy (New York: Cambridge University Press, 1993), 128. One concerning aspect of the mentor's influence is his exposure to competing language about belief from the controversial fifth-century bishop Faustus of Riez.

[84]   Sarah Wood, *Conscience and the Composition of Piers Plowman* (New York: Oxford University Press, 2012), 120–21.

[85]   Wood, *Conscience*, 120–21. What Wood (a scholar of English and comparative literature) dubs a tradition of commentaries "on the Creed" turns out in fact to be the commentaries on Scripture by Augustine, Bede, and Lombard that have occupied the reader's attention in chapter 2 and the first portion of this chapter. It is unclear why she refers to these items as commentaries "on the Creed."

[86]   Wood, *Conscience*, 121.

a parallel between this grammatical necessity and the need of humans (problematically and specifically men) to live the faith that the holy church teaches in order to be in right relationship with God.[87]

During this time, in which grammatical nuance remained as popular a tool of preachers as it had been in the days of Augustine, the theme of *credere in Deum* as describing the "faith working through love" constitutive of Christianity also persisted. This theme is clear in at least one famous sermon delivered by Langland's contemporary Thomas Brinton, bishop of Rochester. Brinton delivered a homily in Latin to a convocation of clergy during the Good Parliament of 1376, in which he insists that the formula provides evidence of the need for his hearers to take action on behalf of the people.[88] With the kingdom in disarray, Brinton turns to the admonishment of James 1:25 against being merely hearers and not doers, asserting that *Factor operis hic beatus*, "A doer of the work (is) blessed." To any who would object (based on their assent to the articles of the Creed and reliance on Jesus' words in Mark 16:16) that salvation depends only on baptism and confession of faith, Brinton responds with a reminder of the formula:

> *Respondeo aliud est credere Deo, aliud credere Deum esse, aliud credere in Deum. Credere Deum est credere Deum esse sicut credunt demones et etiam infideles. Credere Deo est credere quod quicquid nobis promisit in nobis adimplebit. Sed in Deum credimus quando in eo speramus et vere diligimus et fidem nostram opere adimplemus.*

> I respond that it is one thing to believe God, another to believe God to exist, another to believe into God. To believe in God is to believe God to exist, just as the demons and infidels also do. To believe God is to believe that whatever God has promised he will fulfill in us. But we believe into God when we hope in God and truly love (cherish) God and fulfill our faith in works.

---

[87] Wood, *Conscience*, 121–22.

[88] Wood, *Conscience*, 123 (translation mine). Wood in the body of her text quotes Brinton in her own English translation and provides the original Latin in a footnote from *Sermons of Thomas Brinton*. Wood and I make different translation choices due to the different emphases of our fields: she chooses "believe God," "believe God to exist," and "believe in God" for her translation of the *credere* formula, for example. I opt for "believing into" and for nongendered reference to God.

The survival of the formula in this preacher's flourishing prose and in so specific and political a context is remarkable. The embellishments remain faithful to the original sermons and commentaries that established and systematized the formula, regardless of the way in which Brinton inherited it. The slight variations of adding the verb "fulfill" and the verb "hope" remain in the relational realm, even as the language of works appears.

The widespread nature of the formula's reach in medieval England is evidenced in its consideration and use by both this bishop of Rochester and his opponents, the Lollards. In the two decades after Brinton's sermon to the Good Parliament, these Lollards, followers of the Morningstar of the Reformation, John Wyclif, compiled a preaching manual containing numerous extracts from Wyclif's writings.[89] This compilation contains an entry for *credere* that quotes Peter Lombard's presentation of the formula, suggesting that Lollard preachers were encouraged to use the formula with emphasis upon the distinctiveness of *credere in Deum* in their preaching.[90] As Wyclif's followers are considered forerunners to the Protestant reformers, it is appropriate to turn attention next to evidence of the formula in the latter's works.

Luther and the Lutheran Scholastics: The Formula Fades Away

With Luther's own mention of the formula a mere parenthetical that he attributes to Lombard, buried in what is now regarded as a famously antisemitic text, his *Lectures on Romans*, it is somewhat surprising that the formula received any attention from his followers:

> That is, as the Master of the *Sentences* has said: "It is one thing to believe in a God, another thing to believe God, another thing to believe into God." So it also is (to believe) into Christ. For to believe into Christ is to stretch into him with the whole heart and to orient everything toward (literally order everything into) that very one.[91]

[89] Christina Von Nolcken, "Notes on Lollard Citation of John Wyclif's Writings," *Journal of Theological Studies* 39, no. 2 (1988): 413.

[90] Wood, *Conscience*, 123.

[91] Martin Luther, *Lectures on Romans*, ed. and trans. Wilhelm Pauck (Philadelphia: Westminster, 1977), 105, with my belief-into adjustments, according to the original text: Martin Luther, *Römervorlesung*, Martin Luthers Werke Kritische Gesamtausgabe 56 (Weimar: Hermann Böhlaus Nachfolger, 1938). Luther wrote this text in Latin: "*Hoc est, Quod Magister Sententiarum dicit:* Aliud est credere

Wilhelm Pauck, the translator and editor of the English version of this work, wrestles with Luther's disdain for the Scholastics' Aristotelian influences that he claims caused them to wrongly embrace human potentiality instead of see it as stained by sin.[92] The Reformation's emphasis on *sola fide* is clear from Luther's omission of the phrase "faith working through love," which Augustine borrowed from Galatians to describe *credere in Deum*.[93]

Nevertheless, the Lutheran Scholastics stand out among the many branches of sixteenth- to eighteenth-century Protestant Scholasticism for their contribution to the ongoing systematizing of the work of Augustine.[94] All these Protestant Scholastics viewed faith as "having three different aspects: *notitia* (knowledge), *assensus* (assent), and *fiducia* (trust)."[95] However, the Lutheran Scholastic theologians, in the wake of Luther's sixteenth-century systematizers, Philip Melanchthon and Martin Chemnitz, pick up specifically on the *credere* formula to support this threefold understanding.

Both Melanchthon in his *Loci Communes* and Chemnitz in his commentary thereon, *Loci Theologici*, underscore the value to justifying faith of not only intellectual understanding of and assent to the truth of the gospel, but also of the heart's trust in the gospel's saving promise.[96] Augustine's, Bede's, and Lombard's acknowledgment that even the demons are able to do the first two types of *credere* is omitted here, just as it was from Thomas' Scholasticism three hundred years earlier. This omission occurs despite Lombard's being the cited source for Luther's own brief mention of the formula. Melanchthon and Chemnitz frame all three aspects in purely positive terms: by knowledge one comes to understand the gospel; by assent one agrees that

---

Deum, aliud credere Deo, aliud credere <u>in Deum</u>. *Sic etiam <u>in Christum</u>. Credere enim in Christum Est in ipsum toto corde intendere et omnia in ipsum ordinare.*"

[92]   Luther, *Lectures on Romans*, xlvi–xlvii.

[93]   Augustine, *Tract. Ev. Jo.* XXIX.6 (CCSL 36:287). See also Bede, *Commentary on the Seven Catholic Epistles.* The Council of Trent would rely upon the same Scripture in its response to Luther's doctrine of justification.

[94]   Francesca Aran Murphy, Balázs M. Mezei, and Kenneth Oakes, *Illuminating Faith: An Invitation to Theology*, Illuminating Modernity (New York: Bloomsbury, 2015), 45. Murphy et al. make a sweeping gesture in Augustine's direction when referring to the "venerable triad" of *credere* as "found in Augustine, Peter Lombard and Thomas Aquinas" and citing it in "inchoate" form in only one Augustine sermon (47).

[95]   Murphy, Mezei, and Oakes, *Illuminating Faith*, 45.

[96]   Murphy, Mezei, and Oakes, *Illuminating Faith*, 46.

the gospel is true; by trust one believes that one is included in the gospel promises.[97]

In the next century, Johannes Quenstedt and David Hollaz uphold this threefold understanding of faith. Quenstedt explains *credere Deum* as believing "that God exists," *credere Deo* as believing "that what God says is true," and *credere in Deum* as to "love and cling to God."[98] Hollaz hearkens to a more Thomistic gloss of faith's being "in the intellect with respect to knowledge; and assent, in the will with respect to confidence."[99] In this summary, Hollaz appears to have conflated the aspects of assent and trust in a way that obscures the *credere* formula (similar to Luther's presentation), but it may be that he takes for granted the clearer elucidation of the elder Quenstedt.

There is no evidence of engagement with even a fading instance of the formula again after these late Reformation writers and as the Enlightenment emerges on the scene with heightened emphasis on rationalism and the same kind of robust faith in human potential over and against divine love with which Luther charged the medieval Scholastics. As so often happens with the kinds of epistemological crises that arise during movements such as the Enlightenment, vibrant evangelical movements also arose that could have benefited from use of believing-into, had it been available to them, such as Methodism in England or German Pietism.[100]

Well, This Is Awkward: Translating *credere in Deum* into English

At this point the trail of the threefold formula has gone cold, and the difficulties of translation of the Latin into English become apparent soon thereafter. In the nineteenth century, Oxford scholars translating *Tract. Ev. Jo.* XXIX into English for the first time strangely chose the phrase "believe on Him" for *credere in eum*, seemingly inventing a choice of preposition out of thin air, perhaps in an effort to indicate the unusual distinction of *credere in* + accusative.[101] In this matter

---

[97] Murphy, Mezei, and Oakes, *Illuminating Faith*, 46.
[98] Murphy, Mezei, and Oakes, *Illuminating Faith*, 47.
[99] Murphy, Mezei, and Oakes, *Illuminating Faith*, 46–47.
[100] William J. Abraham, *Crossing the Threshold of Divine Revelation* (Grand Rapids: Eerdmans, 2006), 105.
[101] Augustine, *Lectures or Tractates on the Gospel According to St. John*, trans. John Gibb and James Innes in *A Select Library of the Nicene and Post-Nicene Fathers* 7, ed. Philip Schaff (New York: Christian Literature, 1888), 185–86. The

they at least seem to make an effort to emphasize the distinctiveness
for which Augustine had striven, as they did not automatically fall in
line with the only precedent they could possibly draw upon, the King
James translation of the passage to which Augustine referred, John
6:29. From the Vulgate's *Hoc est opus Dei ut credatis in eum quem misit
ille* the King James version had translated, "This is the work of God,
that you believe in him whom he hath sent." John Gibb and James
Innes instead translate that portion, "This is the work of God, that ye
believe on Him whom He has sent." Perhaps if they had been hearkening to a Pauline Greek construction using *epi* (upon), this translation would make sense, but that construction does not apply to this
passage of John's Gospel.[102]

In recent scholarship, translators select the English vernacular "to
believe in Him" or "to believe in Christ" in translating *credere in* +
accusative phrases from *Tract. Ev. Jo.* XXIX and *Serm.* CXLIV,[103] as
well as the *Enarrationes* and Dolbeau 19/Mainz 51/Sermon 130A.[104]
In fact, Edmund Hill goes so far as to translate "in" as "into" in the
footnotes of Dolbeau 19/Mainz 51/Sermon 130A, even explaining the
grammar: "We must remember that 'believing in God or in Christ'
in Latin is *credere in Deum*, etc.; the preposition in with the accusative case, meaning literally 'into.' We believe into God, into Christ, in

---

first English translation appeared in the Oxford "Library of Fathers of the Holy
Catholic Church," Oxford, 1848, in two volumes, and was prepared by Rev. H.
Browne, M.A., of Corpus Christi College, Cambridge. T & T Clark's Nicene &
Post-Nicene Fathers of the Christian Church was published unedited in 1888 by
Rev. John Gibb, D.D., professor in the Presbyterian Theological College at Lon-
don (vol. 1., *Tractates 1–37*), and Rev. James Innes, of Panbride, near Dundee,
Scotland (vol. 2, *Tractates 38–124*), for a series of Augustine's Works edited by a
Dr. Dods, published by T & T Clark, Edinburgh, 1873.

[102] For example, in Acts 16:31, the NRSV translation of οἱ δὲ εἶπαν·
Πίστευσον ἐπὶ τὸν κύριον Ἰησοῦν, καὶ σωθήσῃ σὺ καὶ ὁ οἶκός σου (*hoi de eipon,
Pisteuson epi ton Kurion Iesoun, kai sōthēsē su kai ho oikos sou*) is rendered,
"They answered, 'Believe on the Lord Jesus, and you will be saved, you and your
household.'"

[103] Augustine, Homily 29, in *Homilies on the Gospel of John* (1–40), ed. Allan
D. Fitzgerald, trans. Edmund Hill, The Works of Saint Augustine: A Translation
for the 21st Century 3/12 (Hyde Park, N.Y.: New City Press, 2009), 493; Sermon 144, *Sermons on the New Testament* (94A–147A), ed. John E. Rotelle, trans.
Edmund Hill, The Works of Saint Augustine: A Translation for the 21st Century
3/4 (Brooklyn, N.Y.: New City Press, 1992), 431.

[104] Augustine, Exposition 77.8, in *Expositions*, trans. Boulding, 98; Augustine,
Sermon 130A, in *Newly Discovered Sermons*, trans. Hill, 1.

a way in which we should not dream of believing into Paul."[105] Hill does not explain why he did not then embrace the accurate, awkward phrasing in his translation! Similar choices are made consistently by translators of the *Summa Theologiae*, where *credere in Deum* is rendered "to believe in God."[106] Recent scholarship on *Piers Plowman* does not translate the phrase *credere in Deum* at all when providing translation of Lombard in footnotes.[107]

The Twentieth and Twenty-First Centuries:
Uniqueness Lost in Translation

In the past hundred years of Christian theology, there have been a few glimmers of attention to the difference that *credere in Christum* makes. These glimmers, however, are usually relegated to outlines and footnotes.

One instance of the latter appears in a 1921 edition of *The Standard Sermons of John Wesley*, edited by the British-born First Master of Queen's College, University of Melbourne (Australia), Edward H. Sugden. What is noteworthy about Sugden's note is that he grasps and translates the phrase, but he did so from the Greek, not the Latin! In commenting that Wesley's early theology had yet to consider faith in relational, rather than merely transactional, terms, Sugden noted, "In the N.T. the verb *pisteusin* in the sense of saving faith has two constructions: St. John always speaks of saving faith as *pisteusin eis Xriston*, believing <u>into Christ</u>, i.e. believing so as to be united vitally with Christ."[108] He proceeds to elaborate on various prepositional options appearing in the Koine Greek of the New Testament in both Pauline and Johannine literature, noting that the emphasis in the phrase in

---

[105] See Edmund Hill's translation note in Augustine, Sermon 130A, in *Sermons* (94A–147A), 127, n. 15.

[106] Thomas, *Summa Theologica* IIa-IIae, q. 2, a. 2. The authoritative translation by the Fathers of the Dominican English Province, which is used throughout this chapter, remains the standard, and various scholars' efforts to tackle translations of their own have not shown signs of changing from use of the vernacular "believe in God," considering a sufficient distinction from "believe in a God."

[107] Wood, *Conscience*, 120–21, n. 38. Wood's personal interpretation is evident in her elision of "incorporated in his members" to "incorporated into his body (of believers)."

[108] Edward H. Sugden, *The Standard Sermons of John Wesley* (London: Epworth, 1921), 1:162–63, n. Recall reference to this passage in n. 5 of chapter 1 above, from which Sugden's description of union with Christ is borrowed for defining "relational" in the present work.

question is not justification by faith of a transactional nature, as is often the purview of the doctrine of salvation, but in the sense of bringing the soul into oneness with Christ's own self. The predominance of relational language, of movement, and of incorporation are enough to make one wish Sugden's words had more prominence than a mere footnote.

That same year, American editor Arthur Pruess translated the work of University of Tübingen professor Anton Koch,[109] who had referred briefly to the *credere* formula in describing *Man's Duties to God*, his title of the fourth volume in *A Handbook of Moral Theology*.[110] As the title suggests, this moral theologian takes a deontological approach to faith, and while Koch thoroughly cites his brief presentation of the formula (leaving out seemingly only Bede), he emphasizes in connection to *credere in deum* good works as a means of, rather than a response to, uniting oneself with Christ by one's own power.[111]

An instance of the glimmers' appearance in outline form is in Karl Barth's *Dogmatics in Outline*, compiled from his lectures on systematic theology in war-decimated Germany in 1946. Barth provides a mere hint at the difference that *credere in Deum* makes, with no formal presentation of the phrase itself, nor contrast to *credere Deo* and *Credere Deum*. Barth writes, while reflecting on the importance of the word "in" at the beginning of the Apostles' Creed, "In Christian faith we are concerned quite decisively with a meeting. 'I believe in'—so the Confession says; and everything depends on this 'in,' this object of faith, this *eis*, this *in* (Latin)."[112] Barth never goes further than to name the phrase *Credo in*, nor does he credit Augustine. For all his emphasis on the object of faith, with whom we meet and through whom we are "never alone," he never attends to the way in which the case of the object governs the preposition's

[109] Paul McKeever, "Seventy-five Years of Moral Theology in America," in *The Historical Development of Fundamental Moral Theology in the United States*, ed. Charles E. Curran and Richard A. McCormick, Readings in Moral Theology 11 (Mahwah, N.J.: Paulist Press, 1999), 10.

[110] Anton Koch, *A Handbook of Moral Theology*, vol. 4, *Man's Duties to God*, ed. Arthur Pruess (St. Louis: B. Herder, 1921), 15–16.

[111] Koch, *Handbook of Moral Theology*, 4:16.

[112] Karl Barth, *Dogmatics in Outline*, trans. G. T. Thomson (New York: Harper & Row, 1959), 15.

meaning and conjures a sense of movement *into* relationship and *into* Godself.[113]

While Barth gives no credit to Augustine, that does not necessarily mean that those who recently have mentioned Augustine do any better in terms of specificity. As described in the introduction to this book, the threefold formula appeared in an unnumbered footnote in the World Council of Churches Faith and Order Commission's 1991 document *Confessing the One Faith: An Ecumenical Explication of the Apostolic Faith as It Is Confessed in the Nicene-Constantinopolitan Creed (381).*[114] The note is intended as commentary on the phrase "We believe in one God." It makes mention of the threefold *credere* formula with the reference cited no more specifically (even in a revised 2010 edition) than "In the West, Augustine pointed to three aspects of the act of believing."[115] The tiny paragraph barely merits notice, and certainly makes no mention of the way in which that "pointing to" occurs in preaching and commentary across multiple works by Augustine, then was further systematized by numerous theologians, and finally was essentially lost in translation. An opportunity for a compelling catechetical moment is lost.

In the twenty-first century, the only major references to *credere in Deum* appear to have been made by a British, lay, Roman Catholic theologian and the first Latin American Pontifex Maximus. Lay Catholic theologian Stephen Bullivant, in his 2012 work *The Salvation of Atheists and Catholic Dogmatic Theology,* explicitly names all three types of *credere* in defining atheism, but specifically focuses on the contrast between *credere Deum* and *credere in Deum* to draw out whether propositional or trusting belief (or both) is quintessential to his definition.[116] He thus cites *Serm.* CXLIV and the *Summa,* without attention to other works on the formula in either Aquinas or Augustine (let alone in Bede or Lombard, though he exegetes the same James

---

[113] Barth, *Dogmatics in Outline,* 16. It is important to note that the original German might attend to this issue better, but even if it does and gets lost in translation, Thomson chooses to leave in Latin what Barth originally had in Latin, and it is not the full phrase *credo in Deum* at any point.

[114] World Council of Churches, *Confessing the One Faith: An Ecumenical Explication of the Apostolic Faith as It Is Confessed in the Nicene-Constantinopolitan Creed (381)* (Geneva: WCC Publications, 1991).

[115] World Council of Churches, *Confessing the One Faith,* 16.

[116] Stephen Bullivant, *Salvation of Atheists and Catholic Dogmatic Theology* (New York: Oxford University Press, 2012), 19.

passage we have encountered here in examining Bede's *In Septem* and Augustine's Dolbeau 19/Mainz 51/Sermon 130A).[117] Throughout the discussion, he translates *credere Deum* as "to believe *that* God exists" (emphasis original) and *credere in Deum* as "believe in God," despite the likelihood of the latter to be understood to mean the former just as easily in English. Avoiding such potential for confusion entirely, Pope Francis, in his first apostolic exhortation, *Evangelii Gaudium*, leaves the phrase untranslated in the Vatican's English translation.[118] There he refers to the *Aparecida* document on Latin American popular piety as a proclamation of the gospel that prefers symbols and action to "discursive reasoning."[119] Citing Thomas Aquinas' presentation of the formula in the *Summa*, the pope observes that in Latin America, "in the act of faith greater accent is placed on *credere in Deum* than on *credere Deum.*" What can be done in contemporary theology with this curious phrase, this *credere in Deum* that literally is "believing into God," when the Vatican leaves it untranslated from Latin, and when those who do translate it into English choose "believing in God," which renders it indistinguishable from "believing that God exists"? Contemporary theology has not gone far with it, but it is possible to lay groundwork for a constructive theological proposal.

We are at a critical moment in the history of doctrine and of the church to retrieve the full force of Augustine's emphasis on and definition of the phrase "believing into Christ" in contrast to the rest of the formula. Data-driven research reveals that people are awakening to and speaking up (both in their absence and in their actions) about harms done in and by churches and by allegedly Christian individuals (or in the name of Christianity).[120] Many in the church genuinely want to respond by offering restitution, making amends, restoring relationships, and transforming Christianity but may lack a theological foundation upon which to do so that is both anciently rooted and forward-thinking, that can sustain such work over the long period of

---

[117] Bullivant, *Salvation of Atheists*, 20–24.

[118] Pope Francis, *Evangelii Gaudium* 124, http://w2.vatican.va/content/francesco/en/apost_exhortations/documents/papa-francesco_esortazione-ap_20131124_evangelii-gaudium.html.

[119] Francis, *Evangelii Gaudium* 124.

[120] In his work, including both *Salvation of Atheists* and *Faith and Unbelief* (Mahwah, N.J.: Paulist Press, 2013), Bullivant has drawn attention to data and examples suggesting the role of religious hypocrisy in the rise in numbers of persons identifying as atheists and nonreligious.

time required to accomplish it and result in transformed relationships in churches and communities thereafter.[121]

Even evangelism, whether defined as explicitly trying to improve negative data by "winning converts" or as bearing good news where it is sorely needed regardless of data-driven outcome, relies on various forms of propositional belief-that (God exists, Jesus is Lord, Jesus died as an atonement for sin, etc.). Some branches of self-described evangelical Protestantism who ostensibly value evangelism may talk about a relationship with Jesus, but they often do so in a way that is intensely individualistic and pivots quickly to unquestioning acceptance of specific propositions and behaviorism that bifurcates bodies from souls or even demonizes the flesh by prooftexting prohibitions from the Pastoral Epistles.

Additionally, the urgency is heightened by people who have not been as directly impacted by the church's abuses but who nevertheless question the contemporary relevance of the Christian faith and crave a greater sense of belonging than they have felt church offers, such as those who see negative nominally Christian witnesses and raise questions named in this book's introduction. This negative witness arises from individuals and communities calling themselves by Christian names while inflicting harms Christ could not possibly endorse—for example, the "Westboro Baptist Church," who wrongly allege that Christ hates LGBTQIA+ persons and their allies.[122] Such examples demonstrate the difference between a bobbleheaded nod of assent to propositions or tenets about God and clinging in relationship to God through Jesus Christ in a way that transforms every other relationship in care for others.

Some Christians in name only are interested in being transformed to Christians in life and deed, to recall Bede—for example, white American church members appalled by police brutality against Black persons, who are increasingly recognizing their complicity in or outright perpetuation of systemic racism and racist abuse.[123] They want

---

[121] David Crary, "More U.S. Churches Are Committing to Racism-Linked Reparations," Associated Press, December 13, 2020, https://apnews.com/article/race-and-ethnicity-new-york-slavery-minnesota-native-americans-4c7dbcae990bd11dee5a5710c63ece25.

[122] See Rebecca Barrett-Fox, *God Hates: Westboro Baptist Church, American Nationalism, and the Religious Right* (Lawrence: University Press of Kansas, 2016).

[123] Michael Balsamo and Ashraf Khalil, "Vandals Hit Black Churches during Weekend Pro-Trump Rallies," Associated Press, December 13, 2020,

to change their practices and treatment of others and experience transformation that helps them see and care for those whom they have overlooked and harmed.[124] If transformed understanding of (in this case) racial relationships is combined with transformed understanding of Christian belief as relational and of what is entailed in "believing into Christ," the flourishing of both the ones harmed and the ones who have perpetrated harm is facilitated fully.

Flourishing from this perspective is precisely participation in divine life and becoming not superior, nor "holier than thou," but more wholly Christlike. This element is Christianity's greatest contribution to universal concepts of flourishing, and the time for it to be centered, comprehended, and enacted is now.

---

https://apnews.com/article/election-2020-joe-biden-donald-trump-race -and-ethnicity-elections-dc8f6803f90f844177f324d374242cb6. The assault by white supremacists on the properties of two of the oldest historic Black churches in the nation's capital presents an opportunity for white Christians to demonstrate neighbor love.

[124] Crary, "More U.S. Churches."

4

Restoring the Relational Sense

A Point of Clarification: Who Is "We?"

Throughout this book, the majority of the uses of the first-person plural pronoun have referred to me, the author, and you, the reader, as "we" have explored the establishment, systematization, reduction, and fading of the *credere* formula. Only occasionally have I used "we" to refer to believers in general, the church universal, or, somewhat more specifically, all who might choose to embrace the awkwardness of believing-into as a result of "our" exploration. I have attempted to use sparsely "we" in the latter sense out of an acute awareness of the frequency with which the "we" of theology assumes a white, Eurocentric, heteronormative default perspective. Any layperson who has sat uncomfortably through a sermon in which the preacher starts, "We all know what it's like to . . ." knows how alienating a "we" can be, and we theologians who have a hand in training said preachers have a call to model a better way. Recalling the vision of deification I described in chapter 1 (daring to use "we" in multiple ways) requires me to join a host of theologians who seek to decenter that default in theology:

> Another's flesh—whether it looks like, moves like, and loves like mine or not—is as valuable to me as is my own, and I will protect and cherish it, because all together we are fused into Christ's flesh. Sacraments play a key role in furthering and sustaining this relationship, of course, yet are themselves amplified as we imagine what peace and nonviolent action become possible when we understand one another's bodies and lives as connected to our own in this way.[1]

---

[1]   See above, p. 16.

One such decentering theologian, Nancy Bedford, describes this task as "working to find ways for theology to disarticulate its complicities with the violence of white racism," which demands my recognition of my privilege, derived from the dominant markers with which I identify (or can be presumed to identify by others), chiefly, white privilege.[2] As Bedford notes, "The violence of white racism and white privilege works against flourishing and joy."[3]

As certainly as there are some aspects of my identity that grant me privilege in church, academy, and world, so too, there are others that cause me to experience marginalization therein. I have experienced both, likely as Augustine did in negotiating the aforementioned tension between his Roman and North African identities. So, it is important to note that decentering the dominant default does not mean replacing it with a different dominance of my own particularity, nor of insisting that my offering applies to everyone, much as I might desire the flourishing of all, when I cannot claim everyone's particular experience, nor even that my experience as a (fill in the identity marker here) speaks for all persons who so identify. What epistemic humility dictates for "us" going forward, then, is that I endeavor to imagine and account for the ways in which what I describe may vary and invite you, the reader, to imagine and hold me to account for whatever is necessary for the vision to include you and be conducive to your flourishing. For the remainder of this book, then, "we" refers to the body of bodies gathered in all our particularity throughout the world who hold in common the yearning for ever more relational faith for human flourishing, bearing the charity and patience toward one another to stick together and see it through, with the help of Holy Spirit Glue.

Reception and Restoration

There arose near the conclusion of the last chapter the question "What can be done in contemporary theology with this curious phrase, this *credere in Deum* that literally is 'believing into God,' when the Vatican leaves it untranslated from Latin, and when those who do translate it into English choose 'believing in God,' which renders it indistinguishable from 'believing that God exists'?" In order to imagine what

---

[2]   Nancy Bedford, "Theology, Violence, and White Spaces," in *Envisioning the Good Life*, ed. Matthew Croasmun, Zoran Grozdanov, and Ryan McAnnally-Linz (Eugene, Ore.: Cascade, 2017), 156.
[3]   Bedford, "Theology, Violence," 156.

Christians might be willing to do with an innovation by restoration, it is helpful to consider how the formula might have been understood and embraced before becoming lost.

Though the original texts in which the formula is established by Augustine are aurally focused sermons, reception theory is helpful in examining reader response over time. This theoretical approach allows for a consideration of choices made by editors and translators and concerns about power that might have motivated them, such as worries that appearances of concupiscence or incoherence might threaten a respectable place for Christianity in the public square. Amid such concerns, terminology about "going into Christ," "clinging to him," and being "incorporated in his members" would be considered better off buried in Augustine, Bede, and Lombard than exposed to public scrutiny.

Creative contemplation of how Christian literature was received by original hearers and readers, as well as those hearers' and readers' impact on that literature as it was handed down through centuries, enables us to imagine how the relational sense of belief-into might have faded from common parlance and practice. Having reconstructed and responsibly imagined the reception history of the texts related to the formula and responses to these texts in their original context and over time (in the last chapter), it is now time to consider that reception history and responses in relation to their effect on the translation and tradition of *credere in* + accusative.[4] It is an effort employing something akin to the contested concept of *Rezeption* introduced by Hans Robert Juss to literary criticism in the late 1960s and Wolfgang Iser's tensely related *Wirkung* theory, which "refers to active involvement of readers, in response to the sentences of a text, in the construction of the illusion which is a literary work of art."[5]

More recently, theorists of ecumenical ecclesiology have concerned themselves with reception of and reader response to Christian

[4]   Jennifer Riddle Harding, "Reader Response Criticism and Stylistics," in *The Routledge Handbook of Stylistics*, ed. Michael Burke (New York: Routledge, 2014), 76.

[5]   Linda L. Gaither, *To Receive a Text: Literary Reception Theory as a Key to Ecumenical Reception* (New York: Peter Lang, 1997), 14. There is some irony in even briefly mentioning this school of criticism and in particular this theory, as critics who contend that Iser has been misread point to the losses in translation of his theoretical terminology, including *Wirkung*, to English from the original German (16).

texts and teachings. Commenting on the response by local councils of the early church to decisions made by representatives of the entire church, William G. Rusch, a scholar of the early church and contemporary ecumenism, notes, "In all these ante-Nicene synods, the role of formal juridical acts seems relatively minor. Seen as a whole, *reception* is conceived as a spiritual and theological process of confirmation and completion."[6] Reception and re-reception occurred in local congregations as they reviewed and responded to conciliar decisions, sometimes with documents of their own. This idea is supported by Yves Congar's identification of "'an array of actual receptions' among the historical 'facts' of the life of the Church."[7] Also occurring outside of councils, reception in the patristic church even after Nicaea frequently happened through liturgy, often emerging on the local level and then shared far and wide among local churches.[8] Rusch offers, as an example, reception of the *epiclesis*, invoking the Holy Spirit in the eucharistic liturgy of the East in the fourth century.[9]

It is possible to consider, as another example, the preaching of Augustine in the church at Hippo and the transmission of his sermons, in which the original hearers of Augustine function as the original "receivers" and sharers passing along the concepts of *credere in eum* before they are further systematized and eventually reduced and faded. In presenting the *Newly Discovered Sermons*, editor John E. Rotelle observes that later medieval copyists would have different priorities in preserving the works of Augustine than had he and his immediate successors who cared for his library.[10] Sermons addressing concerns germane to the local churches of North Africa in Augustine's day would seem to the Scholastics too

---

[6]   William G. Rusch, *Ecumenical Reception: Its Challenge and Opportunity* (Grand Rapids: Eerdmans, 2007), 18 (emphasis original).

[7]   Gaither, *To Receive a Text*, 9. She refers to Ives Congar's "Reception as an Ecclesiological Reality," trans. John Griffiths, in *Election and Consensus in the Church*, ed. G. Alberigo and A. Weiler (New York: Herder & Herder, 1972), 57–58, in which Congar identifies as examples "non-reception (the *filioque* clause in the Eastern Church) . . . delayed reception (Chalcedon) . . . re-reception (a new reading finds fresh application for an historical document) . . . and even reversals (doctrines or practices received for a fairly long time cease to be applied)."

[8]   Rusch, *Ecumenical Reception*, 21.

[9]   Rusch, *Ecumenical Reception*, 21.

[10]   Augustine, *Newly Discovered Sermons*, ed. John E. Rotelle, trans. Edmund Hill, The Works of Saint Augustine: A Translation for the 21st Century 3/11 (Brooklyn, N.Y.: New City Press, 1997), 13.

parochial and time-bound to have continued relevance demanding their preservation.

Rusch identifies a transition in emphasis, between the days of the early church and the Middle Ages, from a shared to an increasingly hierarchical process and meaning of reception.[11] He perceives reception initially to be something that "the Church simply lived out," with the handing on of decisions, texts, and traditions from across generations and locations considered the job of all members of the church as a community of local bodies in fellowship, under the guidance of the Holy Spirit.[12] That reality changed, as a "sharp distinction" arose between the active, teaching part of the church and the passive, learning part of the church in the Middle Ages.[13] The inspiration of the Holy Spirit was relegated to the consensus reached by approved persons designated to represent the masses, and reception by local church members merely consisted of accepting the decision. Rusch colorfully describes the difference as the church's rendering its organically "lived out" reception by a fellowship of local communities a thing of the past and becoming instead in the Middle Ages "a universal corporation in which clergy and laity expressed their opinions on important issues."[14] Note the difference between the potentially messy, communal, implicitly embodied notion of living something out and the sanitized, intellectual act of expressing opinions on issues. This shifting perception of reception as part of "constitutional law" in such documents as the twelfth-century *Decretum Gratiani*, foundational to canon law, ironically would appeal for warrant to Augustine's writings.[15] Changing the purposes for which Augustine's writings were used could certainly change the emphases with which they were transmitted and received.[16] It is impossible to know now, however, just how strange the unique Latin grammatical construction, when spoken as *credere in eum, credere in illum, credere in Christum*, or *credere in Deum*, would have seemed on the ear of Latin-speaking hearers of Scripture thus expounded by Augustine.

The reasons for avoiding the admittedly awkward translation, "believing into him/Christ/God," and its relational sense and imagery

---

11   Rusch, *Ecumenical Reception*, 22.
12   Rusch, *Ecumenical Reception*, 22.
13   Rusch, *Ecumenical Reception*, 23.
14   Rusch, *Ecumenical Reception*, 23.
15   Rusch, *Ecumenical Reception*, 23.
16   Rusch, *Ecumenical Reception*, 23.

throughout centuries of Christian tradition could include a perceived need to secure a less vulnerable, more clearly rational and respectable place for the Christian faith in the public square. This aim would not be well met by vulnerable terminology of loving, cherishing, and going into a Christ who comes into believers, much less by that of believers who cling to him. Attendant notions of class would further complicate matters, as bodies that were treated with less respect, as property, being united to the divine-human One and thus all united into him would be downright undignified. The suggestion that bodies of all colors, shapes, sizes, origins, and abilities matter equally to Jesus certainly runs afoul of imperial priorities. Terminology of "thinking with assent," however, seems perfectly rational and respectable. This perceived need for rational respectability for the sake of survival sprang up throughout history, starting in the early church.[17] The demand for rational coherence in Christian thinking might have made it difficult to reconcile the bodily language (even if serving a figurative purpose) of Augustine's later works with his nearly opposite treatment of the body in his earlier, more ethereal works, which were so influenced by Platonism.[18] Even in *City of God*, where the pilgrimage of the church to the heavenly city is not depicted as bodily escape, there is nevertheless language equating evil with the carnal and good with the spiritual, perhaps sufficient to raise this concern for coherence.[19] Yet the *credere deum . . . credere in Deum* formula persisted

---

[17]   William G. Rusch, *The Trinitarian Controversy* (Philadelphia: Fortress, 1980), 16. "The Apologists, Clement, and Origen desired to explain Christianity to their pagan neighbors to prove that it was intellectually respectable and not injurious to the Roman Empire." Rusch notes additionally the pure curiosity of such figures that caused them "to probe the implications of their own faith and to articulate it in as cogent a manner as possible." Augustine would of course have to address similar concerns about impacts on the Roman Empire in *City of God*, after the invasion of the Visigoths.

[18]   This is not to suggest that Augustine ever endorses lust or concupiscence in his use of imagery pertaining to the body, even when using it to conjure the all-consuming nature of *cupiditas* in order to direct his hearers to aspire to a form of *caritas* of that same degree of intensity. His two books *On Marriage and Concupiscence* in the years 419 and 420 make that clear.

[19]   For example, Babcock's appropriate if unfortunate choice in translating *City of God* XV.1, 139. This is just one of many examples that give rise to charges of dualistic opposition of flesh and spirit in Augustine's works, whether fairly or not: "And that is why each one of us, since he comes from a condemned stock, is of necessity first evil and carnal due to Adam, but, if he advances by being reborn in Christ, will afterwards be good and spiritual."

through the medieval period and even into the Lutheran Scholastics. Of course, by then it was already scrubbed of relational, and especially bodily, imagery. One problem with the Lutheran Scholastics' having emphasized "trust" is that "trust in" is not enough. It still can conjure transactional, rather than relational, meaning, as goods held in trust can be withdrawn, unlike bodies fused together, which must cast in their lot together, move together, and care for one another.[20]

As old as the formula itself is the possibility that the bodily imagery and attendant notion of relational belief that involves the whole person would run up against the fear of concupiscence and (resistance to gnostic rejection of the body notwithstanding) the church's resulting devaluing of the body. Resistance to the bodily language in Augustine's descriptions is built into their original milieu. While Augustine was arriving at his mature understanding of the body, there remained numerous contemporary voices that sharply disagreed. "His gradual acceptance of the originally created goodness of the human body and its sexual nature" in his mature thought, which coincides with all of the writings that feature believing into Christ, sets him apart from the "most vocal contemporary voices," such as Jerome and Gregory of Nyssa.[21] Already his language goes against the grain of what is expected going forward. Perhaps these voices already influenced interpretative choices Bede made, even before he was trying to translate the Creed into English. Considering this context, it is more surprising that Lombard retained (or recovered) the bodily language at all.

It is important to note that, at the time of Thomas Aquinas, "the will" that he made more central did also function as the seat of the affections. However, a shift in the location of the affections theologically from faith to love began to become evident in Thomas' commentary on Romans, in which he described believing into God as a movement more of charity than of faith, almost in agreement with the objector from his commentary on Lombard.[22]

[20] Lacking the connotation that *credere in* + accusative offers of incorporation of our very selves, it brings us no closer to Christ than *credere* + dative and is not unique to Christianity, let alone constitutive of it. It still permits a "wait and see" attitude to validate whether trust was in fact warranted.

[21] David G. Hunter, "Augustine on the Body," in *The Blackwell Companion to Augustine*, ed. Mark Vessey (Oxford: Blackwell, 2012), 354.

[22] Thomas Aquinas, *Super Epistolam B. Pauli ad Romanos lectura a capite I lectione VI ad caput IV: Nam credere in Deum, demonstrat ordinem fidei ad finem, qui est per charitatem; nam credere in Deum, est credendo in Deum ire,*

The more the division of affection and intellect becomes an ety-mological reality, the more one may be tempted to ask: Does empha-sizing the relational mean we are abandoning the propositional? By no means—the propositional simply ceases to be treated as the con-stitutive element of Christianity and instead becomes a means to the end of the relational sense of belief that is constitutive. The impact of believing-into on the content of the Christian faith is not so much to change its propositions in any way as it is to change the purpose of those propositions. To borrow language from analytic philosophy, the "knowledge by description" of the three persons is purely for the pur-pose of an introduction of each human person to the persons who dwell in unity, in order that the person may pursue "knowledge by acquain-tance" through belief into Christ.[23] Belief-in that can be easily confused with "assent to the existence of" does not offer as rich an understanding as belief-into, with which one can imagine placing one's hand into the hand of the Parent, Son, and Holy Spirit, in greeting and fellowship. An introduction to the Trinity that begins with such a greeting implies an invitation to fellowship that ignites an interest in entering into further relationship with this God and with the body of believers, who offer the locus for such entry through baptism and the opportunity for mainte-nance of this fellowship through the Eucharist.

In light of the previous considerations, it is little wonder that, outside of the church by the twentieth century, epistemological examinations of belief treat it as a propositional attitude and deter-mine whether or not theism is justified or rational based solely on whether or not God can be proven to exist. None of the prominent analytic philosophers who took up the subject, such as those named in the introduction, described acquaintance with the *credere* for-mula from Augustine or any other source. To be clear, only Mitch-ell, out of all these philosophers, set out with a focus on Christian theism, the rest considering nothing more specific than theism. So, to some extent an underlying question is whether and what the relational sense of belief-into, so specific to Christ, can contribute beyond its own peculiarity. To this challenge, it is not out of bounds

---

quod charitas facit. "For to believe into God refers to an order of faith toward an end, which is done by charity; for to believe into God is by believing to go into God, which charity does."

[23]   H. H. Price, *Belief* (New York: Humanities Press, 1969), 76–77. Price's work was considered among that of other philosophers in the introduction.

to answer that there need not be a contribution beyond Christianity of something so peculiar to it.

Such a statement, however, might give the lie to supersessionism and bears qualification. In no way does the peculiarity of *credere in eum* give license to believers-into to denigrate or claim superiority in any way to Jewish, Muslim, or any other non-Christian persons and practices. On the contrary, one who believes into Christ is in such constant relationship with the Trinity that disagreements and even adjustments to one's understanding of propositions about God, including the questions and objections of believers in other gods or practitioners of other ways, are not perceived as threats that lead to defensive denigration or claims of superiority.[24] Instead, the valuing of the body within this concept contributes to human flourishing as it was conceived at the beginning of this book: our enjoying the wholeness of existence as people connected in life-giving relationship with one another.

While Christianity may connect this "believing into" narrative to a cross-centered table, an image to be developed further shortly, it bears it in graceful dialogue and fellowship with adherents of other religions, all the more gracefully because it does not fear being untethered from Christ if the believer-into encounters different theological claims. While it is utterly inappropriate to perceive adherents of other faiths (or persons claiming no faith) as "enemies," the fact that relationship with the divine in the person and after the pattern of Jesus of Nazareth necessitates love even of enemies illustrates the priority of love across difference. Thus, the peculiarity of *credere in eum* as believing into Christ contributes an example of something other than despairing of a lack of assent and offers corrections to Christianity as mere *credere Deum* that might be welcome relief to those who despair due to doubting propositions that seem to them irrational.

What Are We Restoring?

In restoring the relational sense of belief, it is vital to recognize that "believing into Christ" produces simultaneously assurance and humility. Being incorporated in Christ's members offers assurance that we

---

[24] Recent multidisciplinary research on entrenchment of deeply held propositions, embedded theologies, and the like reveals that the scientific processes involved in facing challenges to such propositions are similar to the processes involved in being chased by a bear. See Kate Murphy, *You're Not Listening: What You're Missing and Why It Matters* (New York: Celadon Books, 2020), 78–79.

cannot be cut off from Christ. Because our limbs now move in the directions that Christ's limbs always have moved, we humble ourselves and are humbled as Christ humbled himself and was humbled. This assurance and humility result in the human partners' eagerness to shed privilege and willingness to suffer with the suffering. Here again the identity of "we" deserves clarification. "Suffering with the suffering" can seem to exclude the agency of the already suffering, restricting the "we" to describing people of privilege who can choose whether to suffer. It demands a change in the description of the direction Christ's limbs (to which the believer-into is now glued) always have moved from the cliché "least, last, lost, and left out," rather to whatever persons we—regardless of our presence or absence of privilege—perceive as "other," whether due to different cultural or racial identity from our own, lower or higher social status than ours, or our perceived profane/sacred dichotomies.

We now perceive Christ's embrace especially of the "other" as a sharing in all brokenness, a being affected by anyone's lack or oppression. The purely propositional sense, by contrast, results in going through the motions without actually going where Christ goes, following Christ at a distance by observation but not accepting invitation to the life of action that he offers. The propositional sense seeks to control the believer's own ultimate destination while also controlling who else gets to enter the current location. It misses the movement of the relational sense, which, one might counterargue, by being a movement "into," could have this kind of gatekeeping in mind, of entering a destination to dwell forever, in the words of several beloved psalms. Nevertheless, we who embrace *credere in Christum*, by believing to go into Christ and be incorporated in his members, are not entering a place, but a person, a body, a set of limbs already on the move, incapable of being stopped and static. In the words of a twentieth-century hymn, "The church is not a building, the church is not a steeple, the church is not a resting-place, the church is a people."[25]

It is true that the practice of full immersion baptism of the naked baptizand in the early church does not take place frequently in the contemporary Western church.[26] In Augustine's church, and through-

[25]   Richard K. Avery and Donald S. Marsh, *We Are the Church* (Carol Stream, Ill.: Hope, 1972), 1.

[26]   Lawrence Hull Stookey, *Baptism: Christ's Act in the Church* (Nashville: Abingdon, 1982), 103.

out the African churches of his day, the baptizands, though naked, were not likely exposed to the view of the entire congregation in that state of undress. According to archeological evidence uncovered at the *Basilica Pacis*, "The small size of the room indicates that only the candidate, bishop, assisting deacon (or deaconess), and perhaps one or two sponsors could have been present at the ritual immersion."[27] By the time the group of newly baptized believers-into was anointed and presented to the congregation, they would be newly, fully robed.[28] Nevertheless, the surrender of self that the practice symbolized—the frank manner of stripping off the old nature by renouncing sin and confessing faith, of returning to the original innocence of Adam and Eve, and of identifying with the incarnation of Christ who entered the world naked[29]—might be approximated, if not replicated, today by approaching catechumenal formation and the sacraments with translations of the creeds using "belief *into* God" and expanding the understanding of creeds and practices themselves. Then an understanding of the propositions of any major creed as lines of an ode to a living, loving God whom baptizands and believers-into cherish with all their heart, mind, soul, and strength replaces rote memorization and recitation of facts to which a dutiful individual renders assent in order to join and remain in an organization. It seems a bit much to ask a grammatical structure to balance off, for example, the preponderance of attention accorded to the Son in comparison to the Holy Spirit (and especially to the Father) in the Apostles' Creed. Belief-into encourages the believer to pause at the beginning of the creed and to commit (or recommit) to relationship with the One it describes. Centering the relational with God could transform broken relationships within the body of Christ and the often graceless way that body moves in the world.

---

[27]   J. Patout Burns and Robin M. Jensen, *Christianity in Roman Africa: The Development of Its Practices and Beliefs* (Grand Rapids: Eerdmans, 2014), 303: "Presumably the candidates were kept waiting in the outer room and brought in one by one. Once they had been immersed, they exited into the other room, perhaps waiting as a group for their post-baptismal anointing. After they were all baptized, robed, and anointed, they joined the community for the first time in their prayers and sacred meal. To do this, they would have been escorted through the door at the opposite end of the chapel in which they had been anointed, and the waiting congregation would have immediately welcomed them."

[28]   Burns and Jensen, *Christianity in Roman Africa*, 303.

[29]   Stookey, *Baptism*, 107–8.

How Can We Restore It?

A first step toward restoring the relational understanding of believing into God for contemporary catechumens preparing to step (whether literally or figuratively) into the water might be simply to teach them what this process first entailed and why. Believing-into, emphasized as part of the approach to the creed into which two of Augustine's sermons (mentioned in greater detail below) provide insight, could restore the heartfelt reverence with which the Symbol was received and given, a process transformative of the individual in relationship to Christ and the communal body. Then a major advantage they may appreciate is that the contemporary way of seeing and reciting the creed is already formulated for the pronunciation of the restored awkward language by the catechumens and the whole worshiping body, not just the clergyperson. Thus, all together in baptism and baptismal reaffirmations, they now proclaim:

> The Apostles' Creed (with restored language in bold)

> I believe **into** God, the Father almighty,
>   creator of heaven and earth.
> I believe **into** Jesus Christ, God's only Son, our Lord,
>   who was conceived by the Holy Spirit,
>   born of the Virgin Mary,
>   suffered under Pontius Pilate,
>   was crucified, died and was buried;
>   he descended to the dead.
>   On the third day he rose again;
>   he ascended into heaven,
>   he is seated at the right hand of the Father,
>   and he will come again to judge the living and the dead.
> I believe **into** the Holy Spirit,
>   the holy catholic Church,
>   the communion of saints,
>   the forgiveness of sins,
>   the resurrection of the body,
>   and the life everlasting.

This small adjustment begins the restoration process, not turning the propositions out on their ear but rather tuning the believers' ears to recognize the lyrics and tune of the song describing the one loved, cherished, gone into, incorporated in, united to, and clung to by the members.[30] The WCC Faith and Order document *Confessing the One Faith* notes that the Apostles' Creed "uses 'credere in' [*sic*] only in relation to the three persons of the Trinity and not with reference to the Church."[31] Yet it is this church, formed by the Holy Spirit, that bears responsibility to help believers become believers-into by instructing them in all that has gone before with regard to *Quid est ergo credere in Deum* ("What is it therefore to believe into God"). As the WCC Faith and Order already has noted the formula's existence (or a version thereof) in that brief commentary, a global ecumenical effort is necessary to bring about the change that will result in more robust relationship with Christ and among Christ members in the body.

Even as such a process is taking place, denominational bodies can attend to their own catechisms and faith formation curricula, shaping them to include the formula and a basic understanding of how *credere in Deum* operates in sacraments and creeds. Authors of scholarly literature for lay and academic audiences may take up believing-into like a lens through which to view events in church history and various loci of systematic theology. Rather than wait for such studies

---

[30]   Wilfred Cantwell Smith, *Faith and Belief* (Princeton, N.J.: Princeton University Press, 1979), 76–77; 254, nn. 25–26. Smith made an argument in favor of the etymology of *credo* as rooted in श्राद्ध *srāddha*, a Sanskrit word related to things done in faith that, together with what he considered to be *credo*'s structural origin (as compound of Latin *cor*, "heart," and *do*, "to put/place"), he claimed calls for translation of *credere* as "to set one's heart on." As attractive as its potential to undergird relational belief may be, this "received" etymology and translation was scrutinized and found wanting even in Smith's time. It is further challenged by usage, both outside Christian literature and even in Augustine's own designation, of its cognitive denotations, such as in *credere eum* and *credere eo*. Smith rejected propositional belief even in the Apostles' and Nicene Creed, to which Pojman responded that, even if one allowed Smith's assessment, other creeds such as the Athanasian are clearly aimed at making propositional belief "a necessary condition for salvation." Restoration of belief-into does not require the rejection of propositional belief but views it as important knowledge by description that helps believers gain knowledge by acquaintance of the God into whom they believe.

[31]   World Council of Churches, *Confessing the One Faith: An Ecumenical Explication of the Apostolic Faith as It Is Confessed in the Nicene-Constantinopolitan Creed (381)* (Geneva: WCC Publications, 1991), 16. The English text of the Apostles' Creed as it appears on the previous page of this book is found on pp. 13–14 of the WCC publication.

and processes to be complete, however, local congregations—where liturgy once was the lifeblood of reception and transformation in the body of Christ[32]—can work on incorporating *credere in eum* into prayers, songs, and sermons, especially if popularly accessible works about its meaning, reception, and operation are made available.

The questions, responses, and insights from laypersons and clergy of local churches would then contribute to the understanding and continued sharing of how those who believe into God through Christ are able "by believing to love, by believing to cherish, by believing to go into him and be incorporated in his members." It would continue the work that the World Council of Churches has been doing for the past century, of restoring reception to its initial status as the work of the whole church.[33]

Scholars connected to local churches can serve by guiding processes of determining how to express the uniqueness in languages other than English and in considering how best to represent occurrences of belief-into in future translations and versions of Scripture and other early church literature. Acknowledging that belief-into spans across the Hebrew Bible and New Testament, scholars and other leaders of the interfaith community could steer reception away from antisemitism and other perils by joining together and enhancing what the WCC Faith and Order demonstrated in *Confessing the One Faith*. They balance attention to the ways in which "Jesus affirmed the faith of Israel concerning the one God . . . (and) endorsed the 'Hear O Israel' as the first and greatest commandment and the way to eternal life" with acknowledgment that "the New Testament also makes clear that this God is in a unique relationship with Jesus Christ . . . (and) . . . also links the Spirit—'who proceeds from the Father'—with the Son."[34] Those who are glued into that relationship by Christ cannot then gloss the descriptions of "the Jews" in the New Testament and early Christian literature with the reality of the Jewish experience of and covenant relationship with God. As *Confessing the One Faith* provides paragraphs of support for the Jewishness of Jesus and concrete correction to and prevention of antisemitism as it relates to the Nicene Creed's phrase "under Pontius Pilate," so, too, believers-into

---

[32]   Rusch, *Ecumenical Reception*, 21.
[33]   Rusch, *Ecumenical Reception*, 21.
[34]   World Council of Churches, *Confessing the One Faith*, 20. The "Hear O Israel" here mentioned is the foundational prayer in Judaism known as the *Shema*.

are called to recognize the Glue that binds them in human and divine relationship as equipping all together to seek liberation and justice.[35]

In order for this whole constructive proposal to gain traction, participation in the body of Christ will have to transcend the hierarchy of defined roles such as laypeople, clergy, and scholars. Simply changing language—even in those areas of the body of Christ where reception doesn't involve resistance or simple rejection—is not going to transform the functions of the body entirely on its own. Efforts at advocacy of inclusive language for God and for most appropriate ways of naming the Trinity are but a strong start to healing the body's systemic sins of sexism, racism, subordinationism, and other means of marginalization. Just as those efforts must be joined with ethical decisions daily by those who take them seriously, so, too, it will be necessary for scholars, clergy, and laypeople, alike to model their prayers and practices on the relational aspect of belief into God.

When that "relation to the divine becomes the axis of our lives,"[36] as Volf promises, it will positively affect relationships across the body of Christ. In baptism, believers-into who exhibit the three theological virtues added by the Holy Spirit, who causes them to give birth to love of God and neighbor, could embody what they advocate by gathering together around such a table. The rising number of full-communion agreements and interdenominational dialogues toward that end worldwide raises hope for greater unity at the eucharistic table, at a time when witnesses to unity are rather scarce.[37]

[35]   World Council of Churches, *Confessing the One Faith*, 61.

[36]   Miroslav Volf, *Flourishing: Why We Need Religion in a Globalized World* (New Haven, Conn.: Yale University Press, 2015), 81. Recall from chapter 1 that Volf makes reference to *Confessions* 1.1.1.

[37]   The 1999 *Joint Declaration on the Doctrine of Justification* is a prominent example, the English translation of which is available: The Lutheran World Federation and the Pontifical Council for Promoting Christian Unity, *Joint Declaration on the Doctrine of Justification* (Grand Rapids: Eerdmans, 2000). Originally an agreement between The Lutheran World Federation and the Roman Catholic Church, it has since received affirmation from the World Methodist Council, Anglican Communion, and World Communion of Reformed Churches. Multiple member churches of these larger bodies have since entered into full communion with one another or are in dialogue about doing so. Other dialogues that have been ongoing with interest in such agreements include those between the Lutheran World Federation and the Ecumenical Patriarchate, the first soteriological statement being the Lutheran-Orthodox Joint Commission's "Understanding of Salvation in the Light of the Ecumenical Councils," in 1995. See Risto Saarinen, "Salvation in the Lutheran-Orthodox Dialogue: A Comparative Perspective," *Pro Ecclesia* 5, no. 2 (1996): 202–13.

Why Restore It?

Rarely in contemporary popular discourse is faith discussed in such first-person "I/We believe" statements as the Apostles' Creed; however, this discourse has been affected negatively by the loss in translation of the humility and conspicuous sanctity that the relational sense of belief-into contributes to Christian witness. Throughout the formation of the Christian canonical heritage, many Christian saints suffered and surrendered their lives as the penalty of adhering to Christ in confession and action.[38] They did so predominantly without arrogance or seeking to harm others, even their persecutors and executioners. Incorporation into the members of Christ who humbly had submitted to suffering and death resulted in their surrendering in a similarly humble and bold manner, speaking truth to power with both courage and grace.

At the dawn of the twenty-first century, however, while persecution continues to be a reality worldwide, there is evidence of vast decline in the proportion of persons identifying as Christian by assent to propositions who also actively participate in practices of the Christian faith, such as worship attendance, sacraments, prayer, fasting, acts of charity, and testimony.[39] These practices matter to the present project, as deifying means of grace that contribute to growth in relationship with God, with self, and with fellow worshipers, as well as with the world, by preparing participants to recognize opportunities to let faith work in neighbor love. While World Values Survey data reveal a decline overall in the number of respondents reporting religion in general as "very important" in their lives,[40] recent Pew research reveals that Christians are the single largest religious

[38]   Horace Six-Means, "Saints and Teachers: Canons of Persons," in *Canonical Theism: A Proposal for Theology and the Church*, ed. William J. Abraham, Jason E. Vickers, and Natalie B. Van Kirk (Grand Rapids: Eerdmans, 2008), 97–118.

[39]   Diana Butler Bass, *Christianity after Religion: The End of Church and the Birth of a New Spiritual Awakening* (New York: HarperOne, 2012), 16. Butler Bass had been dismissive of clergy complaints of decline that emerged in her research of the church and Christian life in the United States (due to tendencies of clergy to exaggerate apparent trends to fit certain narratives), until a preponderance of survey data pointed to said decline, collected from a broad swath of sources—academic, journalistic, denominational, and theological.

[40]   R. Inglehart et al., eds., World Values Survey: Round Six—Country-Pooled Datafile (Madrid: JD Systems Institute and C. Haerpfer, 2014), https://www.worldvaluessurvey.org/WVSDocumentationWV6.jsp; C. Haerpfer et al., eds., World Values Survey: Round Seven—Country-Pooled Datafile (Madrid

group worldwide and—partly as a result—are most likely to live in a nation where they may face harassment, even (or, it seems, especially) in majority Christian nations, where division along the lines of different traditions of Christianity (including those arising from racial and cultural differences) may result in persecution.[41] Even in nations where Christianity is reported as being on the rise, the number of Christians reporting regular practice of Christian faith is far lower than the number identifying as Christians through assent to the existence of God and what researchers consider to be other Christian propositional beliefs. In a recent study indicating that a higher number of Roman Catholic Christians than Orthodox Christians in Europe report regular practice, the highest rate of practice in Europe barely rises above 50 percent.[42] In Latin America, studies revealing a larger "commitment gap" and lower likelihood to "share faith" among Roman Catholics than among Protestants presents percentages that suggest fewer than half of either group regularly practice the faith to whose propositional tenets they give assent.[43] These distinctions are not intended to suggest that one tradition (Roman Catholic, Orthodox, or Protestant) is superior to another, in terms of commitment to practice, but, rather, that regardless of tradition, the highest proportion still only reports around 50 percent participation.

The potential to confront disunity with restoration of belief-into, as it pertains to communal faith, calls us to adapt Volf's metaphor of "relation to the divine" as "the axis of our lives" to imagine that axis as a cross at the center of a great, round Communion Table. Rejecting *credere in eum* in favor of mere *credere ei* and *credere eum* may render sacraments nothing but going through motions and render

and Vienna: JD Systems Institute & WVSA Secretariat, 2020), http://www.worldvaluessurvey.org/WVSDocumentationWV7.jsp.

[41]   Katayoun Kishi, "Christians Faced Widespread Harassment in 2015, but Mostly in Christian-majority Countries," *Fact Tank* (blog), June 9, 2017, http://www.pewresearch.org/fact-tank/2017/06/09/christians-faced-widespread-harassment-in-2015-but-mostly-in-christian-majority-countries/.

[42]   Arayana Monique Salazar, "Orthodox Christians in Europe More Likely to Believe than Practice Their Religion," *Fact Tank* (blog), May 7, 2017, http://www.pewresearch.org/fact-tank/2017/05/30/orthodox-christians-in-europe-more-likely-to-believe-than-practice-their-religion/.

[43]   Pew Research Center, "Religion in Latin America: Protestants More Likely to Share Faith," November 10, 2014, http://www.pewforum.org/2014/11/13/religion-in-latin-america/pf_14-11-13_latinamericasurveyprotestants/; "Latin America: The Commitment Gap," November 10, 2014, http://www.pewforum.org/2014/11/13/religion-in-latin-america/pf_14-11-13_latinamericasurveycommittment/.

those motions less effective spiritually than if the believers never had gone through the motions at all. Consider with Bede those who call themselves Christians and are known as good churchgoers, with the creeds memorized and never missing mass, but who are so entirely self-centered and curved inward that their aloof rejection of fellow members or the poor seeker sullies the Christian witness. Many seekers who might otherwise have sought to be incorporated in Christ's members, upon being judged or rejected, then want nothing to do with the body and its apparently inefficacious sacraments.

Credere in eum turns this parable on its head, as the "bad" ones that Augustine foresaw alongside the "good" ones in the *corpus permixtum* are in fact the ones who lack the love of God and neighbor and concern themselves with their neighbors only for the purpose of judging them. Their purely propositional, inward curve has left them unable to allow the Holy Spirit to conceive and bring this love to birth in them. Their penchant for rejection of difference and unwillingness to suffer with others is not new, but it is not constitutive of Christianity. "What the church rejects," notes American systematic theologian Kendall Soulen, with regard to division dating back to the earliest "mixed body" of Jewish and Gentile Christians, "is not the difference of Jew or Gentile, male and female, but rather the idea that these differences essentially entail curse, opposition, and antithesis."[44] Recognition that the picture of participation in practices is bleak across traditions belies the trope that one tradition represents "true" Christianity better than another, such as Protestant Christians in the United States have claimed against Roman Catholics throughout the nation's history.[45]

This trope, which was particularly prominent after World War II, when respected Protestant periodical *Christian Century* published a thirteen-part series of articles entitled "Can Protestantism Win America?" out of editor Charles Clayton Morrison's fear that allegedly antidemocratic, papal Roman Catholicism was on the rise, has been an undercurrent throughout U.S. history.[46] This worry that

[44]   R. Kendall Soulen, *The God of Israel and Christian Theology* (Minneapolis: Fortress, 1996), 170.

[45]   John Fea, *Believe Me: The Evangelical Road to Donald Trump* (Grand Rapids: Eerdmans, 2018), 56.

[46]   Fea, *Believe Me*, 93–94. By the mid-eighteenth century, Roman Catholicism had grown and spread up and down the eastern seaboard and the fear thereof along with it, which was politicized as it became associated with French despotism during the French and Indian War. Fea gathers a wide array of textual

a diminishment of dominance was imminent is but one of the many fears that have plagued American Protestants, from the time of the founding of the Massachusetts Bay Colony in rigidly propositional, self-proclaimed "orthodox" belief (all the while practicing a mix of Christianity, magic, and folk practices)[47] to what historian John Fea describes as the twenty-first century "court evangelicals," grappling for perceived political power by proximity to the forty-fifth president of the United States.[48]

The election of that president, who at the time of his campaign, and consistently thereafter, exhibited character and practices inimical to everything white evangelical Protestant voters had reportedly held dear, came as a result of 81 percent of those voters' choosing a "politics of fear, the pursuit of worldly power, and a nostalgic longing for an American past that may never have existed in the first place."[49] Rather than "faith working through love," these voters—whose nostalgia is for a past that certainly did not exist as they picture it—have practiced a rigidly propositional faith that expects a strongman, a brute, to protect them and their so-called religious liberty, their own flourishing at the expense of others.[50] They seek this protection at great cost to the rest of the world, to many of their own fellow citizens, and even to fellow Christian believers, from whom they seek to distance themselves by policies that are rooted in racism, nativism, xenophobia, intolerance, and American exceptionalism.[51] The attitude of bold surrender that results from the relational sense of belief-into directly opposes this distancing.

Rather, bold surrender urges us to draw near, protecting and cherishing persons whose flesh does not look, move, or love like ours, because it either is as fused to Christ's members as ours is, or because it now is as dear to us as it is to Christ, who loves all, not just his own

---

evidence, including such statements as "Monarchy in every instance is the Popery of government," written by Thomas Paine in *Common Sense*.

[47]   Fea, *Believe Me*, 88.

[48]   Fea, *Believe Me*, 15. Fea has coined this term to describe the evangelical faith leaders who have sought "'unprecedented access' to the White House" and in turn extol Donald Trump's leadership prowess on a par with the flattery of the monarch by medieval courtiers and the clergy who moved among them during the Middle Ages in Europe.

[49]   Fea, *Believe Me*, 13.

[50]   Fea, *Believe Me*, 133.

[51]   Fea, *Believe Me*, 12.

followers. Such bold surrender could bring about the alternative that appears unappealing to the 81 percent, what James Davison Hunter calls "faithful presence."[52] This presence provides a powerful opportunity for the world to witness Christian faith in action, rather than understandably gain the perception that Christianity endorses white supremacy, builds exclusive walls, and excuses unapologetic bragging about sexual assault, because its chief proponent and perpetrator assures followers, "Believe me."[53]

Words of the One Worth Believing, Believing In, and Believing Into

Rather than "believe me," the words I heard or read repeatedly in the days and weeks following the 2016 United States General Election were "I can't believe it." I had begun to hear from several of the people who had asked me questions throughout my previous years of pastoral ministry that I described in the introduction and that had led me to the research I was now conducting on "believing-into." Together with new questioners, they were expressing to me their disbelief, confusion, and even a sense of betrayal about the fact that a person who demonstrated character so blatantly out of step with all of the Christlike qualities prominent Christian leaders had insisted for decades mattered most had managed to ascend to the presidency of the United States, in no small part due to the support and endorsement of many so-called Christians. My questioners included sexual assault survivors, people of color, LGBTQIA+ individuals and their allies, disabled persons, undocumented persons and their families, and others who had come under attack from the mouth of the president-elect during the campaign. I reminded my previous interlocutors (and newly informed those with whom I had not yet had such conversations) that there is a difference between believing Christ, believing in Christ, and believing *into* Christ. In some instances, I turned to Scripture passages I was then newly exploring to explain the contrast in richer depth.

The scriptural texts containing the distinctive *credere in* + accusative are far more numerous than those that have been considered thus far in this book.[54] A few brief examples provide opportunity to

---

[52] Fea, *Believe Me*, 8, 11, 99, 188, 190ff.
[53] Fea, *Believe Me*, 18.
[54] See the appendix for a table of major examples.

consider the operations of *credere*.[55] Augustine's sermons and commentary thus far have led to consideration of Psalms 77 and 130, John 6:29, and John 16:9, and (in the course of a sermon on John 6, ostensibly) James 2, all supported by various prooftexts. Three more pericopes are helpful in considering *credere* here.[56]

The important though incipient nature of *credere* + dative is evident as Jesus pronounces the phrase regarding the good news after his own baptism and temptation:

> "*Impletum est tempus, et appropinquavit regnum Dei; paenitemini et credite evangelio.*"

> "The time is fulfilled, and the kingdom of God has drawn near; repent and believe the good news."

Clearly, Jesus is at the mere beginning of his ministry and message here, yet already he offers a statement of propositional belief about the timing and proximity of the kingdom of God. To respond to his command requires his hearers to believe that the kingdom is near and at hand. While there is an implicit invitation to turn away from self in repentance and believe it, there is not the relational invitation to "follow me" attached.

Jesus has words of warning against impeding humble believers of the good news who do follow and with childlike faith believe into him, in Matthew 18:6:

> *Qui autem scandalizaverit unum de pusillis istis, qui in me credunt, expedit ei, ut suspendatur mola asinaria in collo eius et demergatur in profundum maris.*

> But if anyone causes to stumble (tempts to evil, offends, scandalizes) one of these little ones, who believe into me, it would be

---

[55] While a large-scale "exercise in the theological interpretation of Scripture," such as R. Kendall Soulen is carrying out with regard to the "appropriate ways of naming the persons of the Trinity" in *The Divine Name(s) and the Holy Trinity*, is far beyond the scope of the present project, embarking on such a work with regard to *believing into God/Christ* as it appears throughout the Vulgate bears consideration as a future research project, particularly if it can springboard from the catechetical or liturgical efforts for which I call here. See R. Kendall Soulen, *The Divine Name(s) and the Holy Trinity*, vol. 1, *Distinguishing the Voices* (Louisville: Westminster John Knox, 2011), 127ff.

[56] Vulgate, http://www.vatican.va/archive/bible/nova_vulgata/documents/nova-vulgata_novum-testamentum_lt.html (translations mine).

better for that one, if a millstone were hung up on their neck and
they were plunged into the depth of the sea.

This statement's final metaphor, which may be intended to describe
punishment of the offender or the lack of efficacy of such efforts and
the degree to which they would be thwarted (i.e., the offender would
be stopped dead), allows for the possibility of understanding believing
into Christ as the strongest relationship to him. It elicits punishment
for any who attempt to break its bond (in the first interpretation), or it
exposes them as failures who succeed only in curving themselves away
from God, figuratively to the farthest depths.

After her interaction with Jesus at the well, the Samaritan woman
described in John 4 demonstrates a shift from innate belief-that to
believing-into that the text does not explicitly name but that features prominently in the *credere in eum* of her neighbors. She returns
from the well to her city after the disciples' return has interrupted the
dialogue between her and Jesus, in which he has identified himself
to her as the Messiah, about whose coming she had expressed certainty (4:25-28a). She now tempers that certainty with humility as she
reports to "the people" that she has met a man who told her everything she has ever done and then overtly wonders about his messianic
identity. She adjures them to come and see him, asking rather than
proclaiming, "He cannot be the Messiah, can he?"

After a narrative shift to Jesus and the disciples, the Gospel-writer
returns attention to the woman and the people:

> *Ex civitate autem illa multi crediderunt <u>in eum</u> Samaritano-*
> *rum propter verbum mulieris testimonium perhibentis:* Dixit
> mihi omnia, quaecumque feci! *Cum venissent ergo ad illum*
> *Samaritani, rogaverunt eum, ut apud ipsos maneret; et mansit*
> *ibi duos dies. Et multo plures <u>crediderunt</u> propter sermonem eius;*
> *et mulieri dicebant:* Iam non propter tuam loquelam credimus;
> ipsi enim audivimus et scimus quia hic est vere Salvator mundi!

> And many of the Samaritans from that city <u>believed into</u> him
> because of the woman's given testimony, "He told me all that
> ever I have done!" So when the Samaritans came to him, they
> asked him to stay among them; and he stayed there two days.
> And many more <u>believed</u> because of his word. They said to the
> woman, "It is no longer because of your speech that we <u>believe</u>,

> for we have heard for ourselves, and <u>we know that</u> this is truly
> the Savior of the world!"

Both the narrator and the neighbors credit her testimony with causing them to believe into him. By context the remaining two occurrences of the verb *credere* may be understood as implying but eliding the *in eum*. One aspect of *credere in eum* that becomes clear here is that the *ordo credentis* (order of believing) is not set in stone. In the woman's case, the modicum of belief in God's existence with which she came to the conversation changed to believing him and then to believing into him sufficiently to want to go and bring others to him. For their part the people first believed into him upon hearing her testimony and only then sought him out and eventually believed him and believed that he was who she said he was.

Augustine also sees in the two days during which Christ stayed among them a figure for the two loves of God and neighbor.[57] Then hearing his word (*sermonem*) gives the people strong belief-that—to the point of knowledge-that—he is "truly the Savior of the world!" This passage, in which a woman is the first evangelist to guide an entire city to *credere in Christum*, also points toward another important aspect of *credere in eum* that we have encountered before and will encounter again: its personal nature is inextricably communal. The Christian faith is not about individuals apart from their reality as incorporated members of Christ's body. At the same time, because they are incorporated members of Christ's body, every individual does matter, and the matter of their flesh, their body, must be cherished and cared for. There is no point at which the woman's situation or status affects her receiving and credibly sharing the good news borne by the One who has told her, "Woman, believe me, the hour is coming, . . . and is now here, when the true worshipers will worship the Father in spirit and truth, for the Father seeks such as these to worship him" (4:21). For my conversation partners, the contrast could not have been starker between the believing-into inspired by the One saying, "Woman, believe me" in this passage and the one who would soon be saying, "Believe me, I love women," while claiming the reason he could not

---

[57]   Augustine, Homily 15.33, in *Homilies on the Gospel of John* (1–40), ed. Allan D. Fitzgerald, trans. Edmund Hill, The Works of Saint Augustine: A Translation for the 21st Century 3/12 (Hyde Park, N.Y.: New City Press, 2009), 296: "He stays with them two days, that is, he gives them the two commandments of charity."

have sexually assaulted one of them was (not that he does not sexually assault women because it's wrong but) that her beauty and status were not up to his standards.[58]

It is not as if there is a lack of theological work on healthy sexuality as divine gift and its role in human flourishing for such a leader to have learned from with the assistance of the court evangelicals. There are, in fact, numerous theologians whose work gives rise to human flourishing in myriad ways, to whom the believing-into lens could serve as a useful tool in further honing their focus on these flourishing aspects for the sake of any who may take them up as a kind of catechesis for the twenty-first century.

Theologians Leading the Way

On healthy sexuality as divine gift, for example, there is the work of Sarah Coakley. Still in progress, her four-part systematic theology begins with a volume entitled, *God, Sexuality, and the Self.*[59] By means of the *theologie totale* described therein, she promises to bridge many of the gaps we already have identified in this book and more.[60] In her more recent work *The New Asceticism: Sexuality, Gender and the Quest for God*, several confluences with the present work emerge, as Coakley emphasizes the value of a "web of interactive, everyday Christian practices" involving both embodied and contemplative action, such as one finds in the Benedictine Rule:

> More or less subliminally, and with a loosening of previous moral judgmentalism, the "inner" meanings of belief start to make their impact. "Christ" ceases to be merely an external model to be imitated, but recognized in the poor, the stranger at the gate; creeds cease to be merely tools of judgment, but rather rules of life into which to enter and flourish; "beliefs" cease to be merely charters of orthodoxy dictating right

[58]   In June of 2019, writer E. Jean Carroll publicly accused Donald J. Trump of having sexually assaulted her in a department store more than twenty years earlier, his denials of which centered primarily on, not his faith nor his morals, but his assertion that she was not the type of woman whose looks would attract him. "Trump Says Woman Who Accused Him of Sexual Assault Is Not His 'Type,'" Associated Press, June 25, 2019, https://www.pbs.org/newshour/politics/trump-says-woman-who-accused-him-of-sexual-assault-is-not-his-type.

[59]   Sarah Coakley, *God, Sexuality, and the Self: An Essay "On the Trinity"* (New York: Cambridge University Press, 2013).

[60]   Coakley, *God, Sexuality*, 91–92.

practice: instead (and conversely) "practices" start to infuse "beliefs" with richer meaning.[61]

Coakley's description of creeds as rules of life that are instrumental in flourishing dovetails well with my call for a change in translation of related creeds (Apostles' and Nicene[62]), such that they begin not with "I/We believe in God" but instead "I/We believe *into* God" in order to restore the relational understanding of belief into Christ.

As we have suggested previously, creeds, more than mere lists of propositions about the Christian faith, describe the One into whom the members of the body believe, in such a way as to make it possible that each believer's spirit "entrusts itself to the Holy Spirit." Thus the believer-into is able "to cling by faith to God." Two ancient creeds, the Apostles' Creed—originating from baptism and still used in that sacrament's rite today—and the Nicene Creed—part of the eucharistic liturgy—present opportunities today to convey *credere in eum* and clinging to God in boundary-dissolving relationship rather than rote obedience. The WCC Faith and Order commission carefully adopted the latter of these two creeds for study as "the theological basis and methodological tool for the explication of the apostolic faith" in 1982.[63]

Drawn from the Nicene Creed, "apostolicity" is one of the four marks of the church, and theologian Patrick S. Cheng defines the early church as "an *external community of radical love* . . . that dissolved traditional boundaries that kept people apart such as biological relationships, social class, and physical attributes."[64] Cheng examines "within the context of queer experience" in *Radical Love: An Introduction to Queer Theology* each of the four marks for its role in dissolving "the traditional boundaries that separate us."[65]

> . . . radical love is defined as a love that is so extreme that it dissolves existing boundaries. Not only is God love, but is a love

---

[61]   Sarah Coakley, *The New Asceticism: Sexuality, Gender and the Quest for God* (London: Bloomsbury, 2015).

[62]   "Nicene" is here used as shorthand for the Nicene-Constantinopolitan Creed.

[63]   Geoffrey Wainwright, *Methodists in Dialogue* (Nashville: Kingswood Books, 1995), 18.

[64]   Patrick S. Cheng, *Radical Love: An Introduction to Queer Theology* (New York: Seabury, 2011), 106 (emphasis original).

[65]   Cheng, *Radical Love*, 107.

that is described in terms of extreme wealth and superabundance. In other words, not only is God defined as radical love itself, but God's very being consists of the continuous sending forth of this radical love to others.[66]

Not to be confused with the extreme monetary wealth enjoyed, promised, and propagated by prosperity gospel preachers, such as many of the court evangelicals,[67] this "extreme wealth and superabundance" is for Cheng rooted in Ephesians 1:18 and Romans 5:20. With appeals to examples from marital and sexual relationships (appropriate, as some archaeological evidence of the early church's effacement of social boundaries in North Africa comes from married couples' burial markers),[68] Cheng describes the four marks drawn from the Nicene Creed in terms of generosity, hospitality, unity in difference, and sending forth to create community by means that include increasingly available technology.[69] The lens of believing-into could further magnify these emphases on movement of bodies and of the body of Christ.

Movement, whether across virtual space, into waters, or toward a table, is not automatically associated with the creeds, despite the physical sensations and metaphysical implications of the sacraments with which the creeds are associated. It may be useful to consider how the conversation sounded in the ears of early believers-into, for the Apostles' Creed most likely began as an oral exchange in the process of the baptizand's entry into the baptismal waters. Imagine that a bishop addresses a *competente*, one of the "seekers" who, having pursued as much as three years of catechesis, has registered at the beginning of Lent for this Easter baptism, having "received" orally the *Symbolum* (Creed), to "give back" in this sacrament.[70] Standing in the water, they speak:

Bishop: Do you believe into God the Father Almighty?

Competente: I believe. (The Bishop administers water.)

---

[66] Cheng, *Radical Love*, 44.

[67] Fea, *Believe Me*, 142–43, 146, with reference to the work of Kate Bowler on the prosperity gospel and its impact on historical Pentecostalism.

[68] Burns and Jensen, *Christianity in Roman Africa*, 409.

[69] Cheng, *Radical Love*, 107–11.

[70] Augustine, Sermon 216.1, in *Sermons on the Liturgical Seasons* (184–229Z), ed. John E. Rotelle, trans. Edmund Hill, The Works of Saint Augustine: A Translation for the 21st Century 3/6 (Brooklyn, N.Y.: New City Press, 1993), 174, nn. 1–2.

> Bishop: Do you believe into Jesus Christ, the Son of God, who was born of the Holy Spirit and the Virgin Mary, who was crucified under Pontius Pilate, and died, and rose on the third day living from the dead, and ascended into heaven, and sat down at the right hand of the Father, the one coming to judge the living and the dead?
>
> Competente: I believe. (The Bishop administers water.)
>
> Bishop: Do you believe into the Holy Spirit and the Holy Church and the resurrection of the flesh?
>
> Competente: I believe. (The Bishop administers water.)[71]

Contemporary Christians may struggle to imagine the kind of threat to the body of Christ that necessitated such secrecy as to have kept the catechumens from so much as hearing the words of the Creed (or anything other than the Scriptures and sermon, for that matter).[72] Only once they expressed the serious intention of entering their names for baptism in forty-six days would their catechists eventually hand "the symbol" over to them after a brief sermon from the bishop.[73] It is equally difficult for many contemporary Christians to imagine not seeing it, but having to "learn it thoroughly by hearing it, and not write it down either when (they) have it by heart," as the bishop of Hippo said in his sermon "At the Handing Over of the Creed."[74] In the ensuing sermon "At the Giving Back of the Creed," Augustine uses similar language about "the Symbol of the most sacred mystery," advising those who have "received and given back" the creed they received, to "always retain in mind and heart, what you should recite in bed, think about in the streets, and not forget over your meals; in which even when your bodies are asleep your hearts should be awake."[75] With this admonishment the newly baptized would move into the sanctuary to join the rest of the body at the eucharistic table. Some traditions today are more deliberate about such admonitions and movements than others, surely, but all could use reminders of this physical sense of movement with water and table.

[71] Adapted from the version of *The Apostolic Tradition* excerpt in Stookey, *Baptism*, 104.
[72] Stookey, *Baptism*, 103.
[73] Augustine, Sermon 212.2, in *Sermons* (184–229Z), trans. Hill, 138, n. 1.
[74] Augustine, Sermon 212.2, in *Sermons* (184–229Z), trans. Hill, 138.
[75] Augustine, Sermon 215.1, in *Sermons* (184–229Z), trans. Hill, 160.

It is at that table that the most inclusive Symbol, the Nicene Creed, is most frequently confessed as an important component of the Mass (also known as Service of Word and Table, among other names). The fact that this creed's original language is Greek does not cause quite as many difficulties as does the difference in structures between the manuscript and the standard translation.[76] Applying a restoration of believing-into along with one additional *credimus* demonstrates again the usefulness of believing-into for combatting heresy, and it also suggests ways of addressing belief in(to) deities other than the Trinity:

The Nicene Creed (with restored language in bold)

We believe **into** one God,
We believe into the Father, the Almighty,
    maker of heaven and earth,
    of all that is, seen and unseen.
We believe **into** one Lord, Jesus Christ,
    the only Son of God,
    eternally begotten of the Father,
    God from God, Light from Light,
    true God from true God,
    begotten, not made,
    of one Being with the Father.
    Through him all things were made.
For us and for our salvation
    he came down from heaven:
by the power of the Holy Spirit
    he became incarnate from the Virgin Mary,
    and was made man.
For our sake he was crucified under Pontius Pilate;
    he suffered death and was buried.
On the third day he rose again
    in accordance with the Scriptures;
he ascended into heaven
    and is seated at the right hand of the Father.

---

[76] World Council of Churches, *Confessing the One Faith*, 10–12. The following English text of the Nicene Creed is found on pp. 11–12.

He will come again in glory to judge the living and the dead,
   and his kingdom will have no end.
We believe **into** the Holy Spirit, the Lord, the giver of life,
   who proceeds from the Father and the Son.
   With the Father and the Son he is worshiped and glorified.
   He has spoken through the Prophets.
In one holy catholic and apostolic Church.
We acknowledge one baptism for the forgiveness of sins.
We look for the resurrection of the dead,
   and the life of the world to come. Amen.

The Greek text displays the confessional verb *Pisteuomen* (from *pisteuō*), "we believe," only once, as the first word of the entire Creed. Thereafter each clause for the Son and the Spirit simply starts with καὶ εἰς (*kai eis*), "and into," followed by an accusative object. While the phrase "one holy catholic and apostolic Church" is also in accusative case, its line does not begin with "and," so perhaps the council expected that lack of conjunction to subtly designate that we do not believe in the church the same way that we believe into the Trinity. The choice whether to place a verb in translation before that phrase is possibly more arbitrary than its placement before each person of the Trinity. Regardless, we can affirm the appropriateness of a form of *credere* + accusative being an interpretation of the confession regarding the church within the clause on the Spirit who brought it to life and continues to conceive love of God and neighbor in it.

Note that a minor adjustment of the creeds gives believing-into the potential to thwart subordinationism, just as it once was offered as a tool to overcome Sabellianism. Since the beginning, the "one God" was not alone but enjoyed intra-Trinitarian relationship. So presenting the creed with only one occurrence of the verb "we believe" and applying it only to the phrase "one God," but not equally to each of the three persons, disproportionately connects the Father to the unity and runs the risk of leaving *competentes* thinking that the one God into whom Christians believe is the Father, and the others—the Son and the Spirit—are less than divine or are lesser deities into whom we also believe. Offsetting the "one God" as a single, primary line, then applying the verb equally to each of the three persons, encourages a greater understanding of the equality of the three persons. It paves the way for this ecumenical creed to do its work of helping *competentes* be clear on what believing into God is, so that they will be able to understand the Trinity, because they can know God intimately. Seeing that the curvature or bond of love between the Father and Son is the Glue that Christ applies to incorporate believers-into in his members enables believers to recognize the Father and the Son in right, nonhierarchical relationship to each other's distinct persons, because they are in right relationship with the Father and the Son themselves.[77] They are in constant communion with the Holy Spirit as well, for the Spirit is the Glue that transforms them into members of the body of Christ. The Glue holds together the body's members and empowers them to practice mercy toward one another and to move together in works of mercy in the world.

This notion demonstrates a feature of antiquity that cannot be assumed in contemporary Christianity, that of individual faith as inseparable from communal faith. Yet it remains the contemporary objective, according to the Faith and Order Commission of the World Council of Churches:

> Administered in obedience to our Lord, baptism is a sign and seal of our common discipleship. Through baptism, Christians are brought into union with Christ, with each other and with the Church of every time and place. Our common baptism, which unites us to Christ in faith, is thus a basic bond of unity. We are one people and are called to confess and serve one Lord in each place and in all the world. The union with Christ which we share through baptism has important implications for Christian unity. "There is . . . one baptism, one God and Father of us all . . ." (Eph. 4:4-6).[78]

This passage, from the explication of baptism as "incorporation into the Body of Christ," describes well the communal nature of saving faith as the early church understood it.

The Faith and Order Commission proves the continued contemporary relevance of this concern for birth and growth in noting that baptism "is related not only to momentary experience, but to life-long

---

[77] Augustine, *Tract. Ev. Jo. XXIX*, 7.
[78] World Council of Churches, *Baptism, Eucharist and Ministry* (Geneva: WCC Publications, 1982), 2 (hereafter *BEM*).

growth into Christ."[79] The deifying relationship that results engenders new, more just purpose, as the baptized believers into Christ live wholly for Christ, Christ's body, and the world, in future anticipation of and also present contribution to the new creation.[80] While this emphasis on living wholly for Christ is not intended to obscure the strong traditional symbolism of dying with Christ in baptism (especially emphasized in full-immersion baptism), it does make possible a soteriological reorientation for anyone deprived of Christianity's contributions to flourishing due to the centrality of violence and death in traditional atonement theories.

The greatest contemporary contribution to such reorientation is found in the work of theologian Delores Williams. In "Black Women's Surrogacy Experience and the Christian Notion of Redemption," she identifies the source of Christian redemption as the "*ministerial vision*" of Christ, rather than his gruesome death on the cross.[81] The latter, regardless of the atonement theory preferred by members of a particular tradition (and she arrives at her proposal only after an exhaustive genealogy of atonement theories throughout the ages), underwrites a harmful notion of "surrogacy" that has proven death-dealing to Black women for centuries.[82] She arrives at the "ministerial vision" of Christ's ante-mortem life as the defining element of his person and work, with Christ as God's Son who comes to show humans life in its abundance, working to raise the dead, cast out demons, and transform traditions.[83]

> The resurrection of Jesus and the flourishing of God's spirit [*sic*] in the world as the result of resurrection represent the life of the ministerial vision gaining victory over the evil attempt to kill it. Thus, to respond meaningfully to black [*sic*] women's historic experience of surrogacy-oppression, the theologian must show

[79] World Council of Churches, *BEM*, 3. With reference to Rom 8:18-24; 1 Cor 15:22-28, 49-57.

[80] World Council of Churches, *BEM*, 3.

[81] Delores S. Williams, "Black Women's Surrogacy Experience and the Christian Notion of Redemption," in *Cross Examinations: Readings on the Meaning of the Cross Today*, ed. Marit Trelstad (Minneapolis: Fortress, 2006), 31 (emphasis original).

[82] Williams, "Black Women's Surrogacy," 19–20. Williams indicates that surrogacy sets Black women's experience of oppression apart from the forms of oppression that have plagued other marginalized groups of women in America, and Williams identifies two types, antebellum "coerced surrogacy" and postbellum "voluntary surrogacy."

[83] Williams, "Black Women's Surrogacy," 30.

that redemption of humans can have nothing to do with any kind of surrogate role Jesus was reputed to have played in a bloody act that supposedly gained victory over sin and/or evil. . . . Hence, the kingdom-of-God theme in the ministerial vision of Jesus does not point to death; that is, it is not something one has to die to get to. Rather, the kingdom of God is a metaphor of hope God gives those attempting to right the relations between self and self, between self and others, between self and God as prescribed in the Sermon on the Mount and the golden rule.[84]

Williams focuses on Christ's ante-mortem life primarily, and his resurrection life as sign of God's defeat of what the cross *does* represent—not the manifestation of God's love in the "death of God's innocent child" at the hands of "cruel, imperialistic, patriarchal power," but the evil effort to kill off Christ's ministerial vision.[85] Once the church becomes a location of ministerial vision for African American women, the powers that be can follow the womanist lead and train their congregations to treat Black women not as objects for sacrifice, but as subjects who demonstrate with one voice "how to live peacefully, productively, and abundantly in relationship."[86]

Given that Williams, in her landmark work *Sisters in the Wilderness: The Challenge of Womanist God Talk*, had strongly criticized the exclusive patriarchy of many "African-American denominational churches" (which she distinguishes from "the black church invisible" that "does not exist as an institution"), it may seem an insurmountable task to reorient long-cherished, traditional understandings and practices of existing churches.[87] Williams named a few African American denominational churches that were making the effort in at least some areas of her concern,[88] but then she turned outside the "mainstream" for a case study in the transformation for which she called, to the "Universal Hagar's Spiritual Church."[89]

Transforming traditions might seem just as tall an order as the other two actions Williams names in connection with ministerial vision,

---

[84]   Williams, "Black Women's Surrogacy," 30–31.
[85]   Williams, "Black Women's Surrogacy," 30.
[86]   Williams, "Black Women's Surrogacy," 32.
[87]   Delores Williams, *Sisters in the Wilderness: The Challenge of Womanist God-Talk* (Maryknoll, N.Y.: Orbis, 1993), 204–6.
[88]   Williams, *Sisters*, 209.
[89]   Williams, *Sisters*, 219ff.

casting out demons and raising the dead (both of which she contextualizes for today). However, belief-into demands that the body of Christ be always on the move, which requires regular re-visioning of traditions, lest they become merely going through the motions. Where is introduction of such a reorientation even possible?

Baptism is a fitting locus for relational training in the art of living out and living out of the ministerial vision, as it displays for a given congregation a sign of the process of Christ's application of Glue that binds together the limbs of the new believer-into and Christ's own limbs. In so doing it continues to remind the already-baptized witnesses that their limbs, too, go where Christ's go and now will reach out to the one(s) newly baptized. The congregation's immediate connection by means of the Glue gives them the responsibility of facilitating relationship with Christ and one another for the newest ones incorporated in Christ's members, such that they know and move in the direction Christ leads them all, here and now. When the congregation is so boldly surrendered to this responsibility that they continue coming together and looking forward to the next opportunity to welcome new believers into Christ, then believing-into also appears to involve believing into one another. As *credere in eum* was reserved by Augustine solely to describe faith relationship with God and not with or among humans, so believing-into applies here solely because it is a believing into the whole body of Christ—including those who have, by believing, gone into him in the past, present, and future.

The baptizand, regardless of age, is not the "future of the church," as is often stated in baptismal ceremonies (especially when referring to infants and children, for which we may include here dedication ceremonies in traditions that do not practice infant baptism), but a present believer-into already being incorporated in Christ's members. The vows, whether taken by the baptizand or by sponsors or parents on their behalf (and ideally reaffirmed by the whole congregation), become promises not only to God but to one another that we will care continually for one another's bodies—regardless of their differences in condition, age, color, identity, or ability—as one and the same body. But how is it possible for an infant to care for anyone else's body? An infant reminds the congregation that life is always beginning anew, and the presence of an infant (yes, even when crying so loudly that the sermon becomes difficult to hear) is a blessing. The touch of an infant can itself be transformative. During the time of blessing the infant with a presentation to the congregation (after baptism or dedication), many congregations have clergy or another congregational leader carry the infant down the aisle or around the space, reminding everyone in attendance of the importance of nurturing this child in the faith as they grow. The body of Christ is called to be the kind of community in which passing the child from person to person is a source of joy for both the child and the congregation. The presence of others—regardless of whether there is physical touch (with consent, or parental consent in this case)—can be comforting in body and soul. Thus, by their very presence, every newly glued-in believer-into contributes to the mutual care for the body, including anyone whose body does not conform to expected standards of capacity to care for self or others.

This transformation of tradition requires us to perceive baptism as a community event that, though punctiliar, begins a lifelong relationship and a building momentum to move as the body of Christ. Emphasizing that lifelong aspect of growth, the Faith and Order Commission argues against keeping even the youngest members of Christ's body from also participating in Eucharist, for "baptism, as incorporation into the body of Christ, points by its very nature to the Eucharistic sharing of Christ's body and blood."[90]

Believers eat of the bread and drink of the cup not in order to satisfy bodily hunger, but in order to be united to the body of Christ's humility.[91] Just as Jesus applies the Glue of the Holy Spirit to incorporate the believers-into in his members through baptism, through the Eucharist, he goes into the believers-into, in a reciprocal movement of relationship (it matters not whether we subscribe to transubstantiation, consubstantiation, or neither, as even Augustine did not specify how this movement of Christ results in his being united with the believer-into, other than "in some way").[92]

This sacrament both conveys the gift of divine mercy and shapes and forms believers-into as the body of Christ. The Christ, who entered history through the incarnation, now enters the believers-into who share his humanity and have gone into the baptismal waters as "the entire congregation welcome(s) the new Christians to the Table of the Lord."[93]

[90]   World Council of Churches, *BEM*, 4.

[91]   World Council of Churches, *BEM*, 447 (25.17). Those who come to him and drink of the inner fountain from which he drinks are humble and do his will, not their own.

[92]   Augustine, *Serm.* CXLIV.2 (PL 38:788).

[93]   Stookey, *Baptism*, 104. With reference to *The Apostolic Tradition* attributed to Hippolytus.

As Christ applied the Glue in baptism to keep believers from curving back inward on themselves, so Christ sends the Spirit to fill believers-into as they take in bread and wine in order for them to reach the full height of Christ, who does not curve inward but who does stoop in humility. Christ, in the *anamnesis* (memorial)[94] of the Eucharist (thanksgiving—particularly to that One who sent him[95]) heals human affections in order that believers-into may take on the same stooping posture of humble love. It is not self-confidence but divine assurance of God's pardoning initiative that both adds hope and love to believers' faith and frees them from pride. It is remarkable how easily the pride swells again when the Eucharist is treated as obligation, rather than a feast by the body of Christ. In terms of Augustine's formula, one who has been baptized, for example as an infant, and somehow or other not yet experienced faith beyond *credere eum or credere ei*, may by participating in the Eucharist come to *credere in eum*.

Yet, in many Protestant denominations, the opportunities to participate in the Eucharist have grown rare and the interest in increasing their availability also wanes. A little lesson in *credere in eum* operating in the Eucharist—if not persuading them to seek Christ for the sake of Christ—at least might remind many Christians of the humble strength operating in the Eucharist and increase their desire for it.

Along with the lack of frequency, the lack of liturgy is also a problem. The *anamnesis* has grown as inappropriately anemic in many contemporary Protestant churches as it has become overly bleak in some congregations of more ancient traditions (both East and West).[96] In order to be fully filled with and united to Christ, the eucharistic liturgy and eucharistic theology of believers into Christ "should seek to set forth the full range of the church's experiences of and affirmations about Jesus Christ: humble incarnation, ministry of teaching

---

[94]   World Council of Churches, *BEM*, 9: "The Eucharist is the memorial of the crucified and risen Christ, i.e. the living and effective sign of his sacrifice, accomplished once and for all on the cross and still operative on behalf of all humankind. The biblical idea of memorial as applied to the Eucharist refers to this present efficacy of God's work when it is celebrated by God's people in a liturgy. Christ himself with all that he has accomplished for us and for all creation (in his incarnation, servant-hood, ministry, teaching, suffering, sacrifice, resurrection, ascension and sending of the Spirit) is present in this anamnesis, granting us communion with himself."

[95]   World Council of Churches, *BEM*, 9.

[96]   Laurence Hull Stookey, *Eucharist: Christ's Feast with the Church* (Nashville: Abingdon, 1993), 123: "The Eucharist is not a penitential rite but an act of Thanksgiving."

and healing, sacrificial death, transforming resurrection, presence in the church and world, and ultimate reign of righteousness."[97] A sign that attention to the formula might bring about the unity that would best display this righteousness to the world is the return of the *epiclesis* long preserved by the East to many eucharistic liturgies in the West in the twentieth century.[98] In many places it includes the invocation of the Holy Spirit not only upon the elements but also on the congregation, that they "may truly be the body of Christ in the world."[99] The WCC Faith and Order Commission notes how "confidently [the church] invokes the Spirit, in order that it may be sanctified and renewed, led into all justice, truth and unity, and empowered to fulfil its mission in the world."[100]

If that Spirit is to lead the church into *all* justice, then it will be necessary to understand that to "truly be the body of Christ in the world," all the bodies in the world need full representation in the body of Christ. As alluded to above, in the discussion of baptized bodies, all glued into Christ and caring for one another's bodies, what theologian Nancy Eiesland has called an "alternative understanding of embodiment" is necessary:

> This alternative understanding of embodiment suggests that embodiment is a social accomplishment, achieved through attentiveness to the needs, limits, and bounty of the body in relation to others. It recognizes that limits are real human facts and that heroism cannot eliminate some limits. It encompasses the recognitions that disability does not mean incomplete and that difference is not dangerous.[101]

This alternative understanding calls us to reimagine everyday practices in the church, from worship to sacramental life, so each member of Christ's body has full access to all the church offers. Further, access is not the same as availability when flourishing is the goal. This fact is made clear by Eiesland's reflections on her experiences of giving and receiving Eucharist, in which it seems to congregational leadership

---

97   Stookey, *Eucharist*, 99.
98   Stookey, *Eucharist*, 102–3.
99   Stookey, *Eucharist*, 103.
100   World Council of Churches, *BEM*, 11.
101   Nancy Eiesland, *The Disabled God: Toward a Liberatory Theology of Disability* (Nashville: Abingdon, 1994), 47.

sufficient to inform her that she need not maneuver forward with her assistive device, as she would be brought elements at her seat after all others had received theirs:

> My presence in the service using either a wheelchair or crutches made problematical the "normal" bodily practice of the Eucharist in the congregation. Yet rather than focusing on the congregation's practices that excluded my body and asking, "How do we alter the bodily practice of the Eucharist in order that this individual and others with disabilities would have full access to the ordinary practices of the church?" the decision makers would center the (unstated) problem on my disabled body, asking, "How should we accommodate this person with a disability in our practice of Eucharist?" Hence receiving the Eucharist was transformed for me from a corporate to a solitary experience; from a sacralization of Christ's broken body to a stigmatization of my disabled body.[102]

Each time the body of Christ gathers at the Communion table, it remembers the mercy of God in sending Christ to the Earth, who by the Spirit's power always perceived the deep yet unexpressed need of forgiveness of sin in each person who came or was brought to him with what appeared to be needs for physical or mental healing.

Christ's priority was never to conform bodies to societal expectations or norms, and he frequently seemed to heal ills with some reluctance, as if for the purpose of restoring and sending them to a society that would not otherwise receive them. How, then, have we come to construct worship spaces and entire church buildings that are inaccessible and exempt from any relatively recent requirements by governments to modify them for greater accessibility? How has the body of One who clearly wants all bodies, of all kinds, as well as all minds, equally glued into his own members grown so parsimonious in practices of hospitality, nurture, and anointing for leadership of persons with perceived disabilities?

At this table, whether partaking for the first time or on a continual basis, participants may experience the difference between believing in and believing into Christ, namely that the sent One also comes into us, and we are united to him by the Holy Spirit. Yet it is as if the body of Christ has developed an intolerance for change that could make this

---

[102] Eiesland, *Disabled God*, 112.

table fully accessible, as if any disability could impede Christ's coming-into the believer-into. If that same uniting Spirit "effects good works in such a way that we collaborate well with God, for we are told, without me you can do nothing," so it is beyond time to improve the collaboration in order to ensure that "sacralization of Christ's broken body"—which retains its post-resurrection wounds in all their epistemic power—is free from "isolation" or "stigmatization" of any body. How are we to retrain the body out of its intolerance of change and into a muscle memory that reflexively, eagerly extends and expands hospitality?

Eiesland's "two-way access" theological method is helpful, by which "persons with disabilities must gain access to the social-symbolic life of the church, and the church must gain access to the social-symbolic life of people with disabilities."[103] A reciprocal gifting results. Viewed through the lens of believing-into, this gifting means that, in the same way that we who are glued to Christ are also glued to and enjoy relationship with and care for one another, so, too, we who embody access amid previously inaccessible life in the body of Christ encounter a space reflective of every body that participates, a hospitality not of the non-disabled toward the disabled, but of all bodies made one in the resurrected-wounded Christ.

Like all of the practical proposals in this book, implementation requires instruction in the *credere* formula itself that then becomes a lens through which to view the propositional content of the creeds and the doctrines that have developed from them as loci of human flourishing, rather than division, isolation, or stigmatization. Approaching the sacraments and creeds as affirming the loving placement of all one's life into God's hands in order to be incorporated in Christ's members allows believers to see themselves as integrated into those hands that always stretch with love in the direction of all humanity, oneself included. Human flourishing is brought to the fore without supplanting the centrality of the Trinity. That level of transformative instruction is not unheard of, as two theologians of recent, blessed memory provide excellent examples of catechesis that can transform the very concept thereof.

Marilyn McCord Adams was devoted to both the utmost in rational clarity in her contributions to philosophical theology and to the solving of logical problems with the understanding that these

---

[103] Eiesland, *Disabled God*, 20.

problems emerge from and in the lives of real people in relation to a real God. She revealed an anciently rooted, relevant catechetical pedagogy for the twenty-first century in a brief item entitled "And Finally . . . Really Present Relationship!"[104] Noting that "New Age spirituality, yoga, and meditation" are helping many satisfy the perennial hunger people have for life in relationship with transcendent realities and for training that facilitates that connection, she continued,

> by contrast, mainstream churches are embarrassed to admit the need for this, much less mount training programs to address it. These churches cannot survive unless they reinvent themselves as schools. Of course, pedagogy will be shaped by theology. But, at a minimum, three ingredients will be required: people who visibly embody the connection with really present Godhead, a community culture sending the message that nothing is more important than growing up into the knowledge and love of God, and a lifelong syllabus of concrete practices to frame our relationships with God and one another.[105]

Crafting that "lifelong syllabus" in relational faith that leads to human flourishing may seem daunting to all but the most thoroughly trained theologians and religious educators. Though McCord Adams came to her career in theology rather reluctantly, as detailed in an autobiographical essay entitled "Truth and Reconciliation," with the help of Anselm, she deduced that "between birth and the grave, the human assignment is to strive into God with all of our powers" in order to see that "theology is something you do with your whole self, but—in the rough and tumble of this world—you cannot wait to do it until your self is whole."[106]

Her unintentionally final work (originally planned to be the start of a trilogy), *Christ and Horrors*, addresses the "metaphysical size gap" between God and humanity and Christ's defeat of the "horrendous evils" that result, all as challenge to fellow philosophers and theologians to stop shying away from the task of addressing the real horrors

---

[104] Marilyn McCord Adams, "And Finally . . . Really Present Relationship!" *Expository Times* 126, no. 5 (2015): 260.

[105] McCord Adams, "And Finally," 260.

[106] Marilyn McCord Adams, "Truth and Reconciliation," in *Theologians in Their Own Words*, ed. Derek Nelson, Joshua M. Moritz, and Ted Peters (Minneapolis: Fortress, 2013), 21, 24.

that real people suffer in this world.[107] This bold work that built on her earlier writing on such evils came over a decade after she acknowledged her ability to offer only a partial answer to questions of why vulnerability and evil exist, saying, "My admission of ignorance leaves my eschatology underdeveloped. But in this, I keep the company of most twentieth-century theologians I have read!"[108] McCord Adams offers the invitation and example to any who are willing but uncertain how to proceed.

Trusting the process of deification, the believer-into is not ashamed to admit ignorance and boldly surrender to a call that is pursued in everyday actions of noticing and responding, rather than ignoring horrors and dealing with, or expecting others to deal with, such horrors in isolation. The main skills required for faith to work through love in this way, gleaned from McCord Adams, are (1) embodied, God-connected showing up, (2) noticing others as Jesus does, with noticing skills facilitated by growing knowledge and love of God, and (3) responding relationally in concrete ways as Jesus responds. These skills are available to everyone. As we noted at the outset, in order to contribute to the flourishing of all, the relational sense of belief must be foundational to the most basic practice of Christian faith by every believer, not just a nice aspiration for the upper echelon of super saints and deepest disciples. Believing into Christ is for everyone. Jesus implied as much in centering a child as paragon of faith practice, to be emulated and welcomed (Matt 18:2-5; Mark 9:36-37; Luke 9:47-48).

It was as a child that theologian Sallie McFague first experienced awe and a kind of "conversion," as she was struck with a sense of her own mortality on the way home from school, which she could in no way have known was beginning a process that would culminate in one of the most prolific and transformative careers in the church and academy in the twentieth and twenty-first centuries.[109] What she admires, however, is not accomplishments and accolades but the "working theology" of several storied figures (Augustine, Sojourner

---

[107] Marilyn McCord Adams, *Christ and Horrors: The Coherence of Christology* (New York: Cambridge University Press, 2006), 40, 2, 42–43.

[108] Marilyn McCord Adams, "Horrors in Theological Context," *Scottish Journal of Theology* 55, no. 4 (2002): 479.

[109] Sallie McFague, *Life Abundant: Rethinking Theology for a Planet in Peril* (Minneapolis: Fortress, 2001), 4.

Truth, Dietrich Bonhoeffer, Dorothy Day, and Martin Luther King Jr.), who, she reminds readers, were everyday people who let their beliefs impact their living in ways that made them "mini-incarnations of God's love," which may seem quaint until she makes what she calls the "outrageous" suggestion that "each of us is called to this vocation, the vocation of sainthood."[110] This outrageous call makes sense in light of the fact that McFague consistently called for recognition that "Finally, God as parent wants *all* to flourish. Divine agapic love is inclusive and hence a model of impartial justice."[111]

Like Adams, McFague demonstrated epistemic humility. She wrote each of her books, she said, in "an effort to make up for the deficiencies of the last one."[112] The result is a steady record of her own experience of, as well as commentary on, deification, which concept McFague described in numerous ways,[113] including:

> Thus salvation is deification in the sense that to be fully human is to grow into what we were created to be—the image or reflection of God. We attain this slowly through the journeys of our lives, as we learn through voluntary poverty to diminish the ego, opening ourselves to the friendship of God—divine self-emptying that we might flourish—and hence become, like God, instances of empathetic attention to all others at every level of our personal and public lives.[114]

The learning through "voluntary poverty" that she describes here, along with the other steps she identifies,[115] is akin to the bold surrender made

[110] McFague, *Life Abundant*, 3

[111] Sallie McFague, *Models of God: Theology for an Ecological, Nuclear Age* (Philadelphia: Fortress, 1987), 108 (emphasis original).

[112] McFague, *Life Abundant*, xi.

[113] In *Life Abundant*, McFague described deification as the understanding of salvation to which her version of the Christian way of thinking inevitably leads, "becoming like God. Made in God's image, we are to live into that reality by doing what God does: love the world. Jesus Christ is the incarnation of God because he did that fully—his mind, heart and will were one with God's love for the world" (13). Centering salvation in the incarnation, she named care for the planet, which is God's body, as one way in which deification occurs and makes possible our "becoming like the incarnate God" (198).

[114] Sallie McFague, *Blessed Are the Consumers: Climate Change and the Practice of Restraint* (Minneapolis: Fortress, 2013), 201.

[115] McFague, in the previous block quotation from *Blessed Are the Consumers*, was summarizing deification (which she considered associated with "salvation" in the Eastern Orthodox tradition as readily as atonement theories are in the West)

possible through reoriented catechesis, with the objective of making believing-into the default for every believer.

In identifying that objective, we come again to one of our first considerations in this book: What difference can changing a few words make? A difference in action. In one of her final publications, an essay entitled "Falling in Love with God and the World," McFague claimed that "the particular task of theologians" is at the "roots" of action and is "linguistic: suggesting different language for talking about God and ourselves—with the hope that different action might follow."[116] Aware that one does not automatically follow on the other, she nevertheless asks, "If we do not change our basic assumptions about God and ourselves from one in which God and the world are separate and distant, can we expect people to change their behaviour? If we know nothing else, do we have a choice?"[117] McFague's implied response is that such change is urgently necessary, as is daring to expect changes in behavior, for which praxis is key, as we shall address in the next chapter. Moreover, the good news is that we *can* know something else: believing *into* Christ, such that our limbs automatically move where Christ's limbs go, as we "awaken," in McFague's language, to "faith" not as propositional "belief that God 'exists'" but as "self-giving love," moved by the "intimations" thereof in the "'face' of Jesus."[118]

In this chapter, we have considered only a small, representative selection of the many contemporary theologians whose innovative works have shown confluences with the relational sense of belief that is conducive to human flourishing.[119] If the formula, and *credere in Christum* in particular, had not been reduced and faded before eventually being lost in translation, such that "believing into Christ" had prevailed

---

she already had identified as having four steps that "take on flesh and blood" in ways evident in the lives of the saints with whom she identifies throughout the book: (1) experiences of voluntary poverty; (2) attentiveness to the material needs of others; (3) development of a universal self; and (4) the application of that universal self at private and public levels (81, 188).

[116] Sallie McFague, "Falling in Love with God and the World: Some Reflections on the Doctrine of God," *Ecumenical Review* 65, no. 1 (2013): 20.

[117] McFague, "Falling in Love," 20.

[118] McFague, "Falling in Love," 29.

[119] Additional theologians to consider include (but are not limited to) William P. Alston, Catherine Keller, Thomas Jay Oord, William J. Abraham, Marcella Althaus-Reid, Christoph Schwöbel, Natalia Marandiuc, James Hal Cone, Gustavo Gutiérrez, Jon Sobrino, Ada Maria Isasi-Diaz, Karen Baker-Fletcher, Pamela Lightsey, and Eboni Marshall Turman.

as the default sense of "belief" for Christianity, their innovations might have been unnecessary. That is, instead of spending their gifts and energies recreating something akin to the vibrant sense of believing-into, they could have been expanding upon it in ways that would equip the whole body of Christ to practice the bold surrender of faith working through love, with such clinging coherence that those advancing a faith that works through fear would be an obvious aberration.[120]

My hope is that the restoration of the *credere* formula and the default understanding of Christianity as believing into Christ will provide those still at theological work (and those continuing the work of the ones who have gone on before us) a useful lens going forward to explore bodily and contemplative practice, dissolve boundaries, transform traditions, embody access, strive into God humbly, and pay empathetic attention to all others in self-giving love. In this chapter, we have suggested innovations with creeds, sacraments, and catechesis, which are all considered practices internal to the church. In the next chapter, we turn these practices inside out, depicting flourishing by believing-into as overcoming oppression and social barriers in contemporary ecclesial communities and the world they inhabit today.

---

[120] McFague, for example, in "Falling in Love," briefly engaged *Confessions* 1.2 to discuss God's presence in humans and humans' in God, reflecting well her famous panentheism (25). Her point would have benefitted from focus additionally on *credere in eum* as the act of belief-into that both makes such mutual indwelling possible and undergirds the kind of action McFague so prized.

5

Flourishing Praxis

Catechesis, Sacraments, Creeds

Praxis That Reconceives Practices

Sacraments are embodied practices. Their purpose is to unite believers with God and one another, a key component of deification. The creeds that emerge in connection with sacraments describe the participants in this holy relationship, both the visible and invisible. We should clarify the sense in which we use "praxis" here: to describe what reconceives these practices, extending them beyond the walls of church buildings, and amplifies the actions beyond what is possible through the individual lives of believers-into, now that they move together with fellow believers-into in the directions Christ always goes. Though I appreciate the contributions of classical, scholastic, and postcolonial/anticolonial theorists to the notion of praxis, I do not use it in a strictly Aristotelian, Thomistic, nor Gramscian sense. Rather, flourishing praxis is rooted in the relational sense of belief-into and facilitates deification of practitioners whose bold surrender makes them embodiments of faith working through love. The word "reconceives" used here emphasizes that deification occurs in direct proportion to our degree of openness to relationship that transforms even our foundations, including our preconceived notions. Thus what the Parent does in deification as we are incorporated in Christ with Holy Spirit Glue involves not only a rebirth but also a total reconception.

Catechesis Reconceived through Flourishing Praxis

In this framework, catechesis is no longer merely instruction on tenets in classrooms of church education wings or in parish schools. Catechesis in the church that takes initial steps to transform tradition in the ways suggested in the previous chapter—such that it now embraces believing-into and bold surrender—becomes curiosity about culture, intra-ecclesial reflective structured dialogue, awakening education for clearer communication, and training and organization for action. Members can learn (or continue learning) about the church's long history of harm and complicity in systemic sins and about efforts to end such harm, repair damage inflicted, and establish or restore relationships. This learning requires practices of listening to understand rather than to rebut, reject, or refute. It results in efforts to name people and peoples as they are, not as we have perceived them or would prefer they be, so that, all together, speaking truth to power and embodying change become possible.

Before proceeding, I must name the risk of dating my work: if I offer current or ongoing examples of the reconceptions I describe in this chapter, Dolores Williams' brave inclusion of attention to the Universal Hagar's Spiritual Church in *Sisters in the Wilderness* requires me to acknowledge the nature of change inherent in a body on the move.[1] A church that dares to practice relational faith for human flourishing will experience institutional fluidity, birth, growth, and death, which might render some examples I offer here nonexistent or irrelevant by the time my book's first printing has sold; however, the goal of examples is not that they impress with longevity, but that they make an impact with love. Lingering impact is one thing the church and world can no longer afford to measure (solely) in terms either of size of bodies or of institutional continuity. Measures of impact more in keeping with the Christ whose catechesis involved parables are the relationships formed and the lives transformed, which amounts to eternal impact even after institutions themselves evolve, change, or die.

When voices arise demanding we see that the direction we will go with Christ to heal harm in fact results from harm we ourselves (or our ancestors) have inflicted, the lesson is more difficult to face. Over centuries churches have used biblical passages and hierarchical structures to justify or deny the commission of blatant sins and crimes, such as ownership of slaves, or sexual abuse of children and adults. Confronting this kind of harm is an obviously daunting challenge. A

---

[1]   Delores Williams, *Sisters in the Wilderness: The Challenge of Womanist God-Talk* (Maryknoll, N.Y.: Orbis, 1993). The risk Williams takes in this text is clear from her naming the fact that she is stepping outside the "mainstream" of mainline and African American denominational churches: that the church she describes does not enjoy the longevity of those established churches. Of course, the presumption that older, established denominational churches will persist throughout time is more questionable than many would like to admit.

more subtle but no less insidious harm has been attempting to control people's beliefs, bodies, and behaviors through shame and guilt, an unfortunate outcome of faith that works through fear rather than through love. From entanglement with governmental authorities so that they sign statements and pass revisionist acts in an effort to craft a civil religion that demands conformity, to heteronormative purity culture teachings and endorsement of conversion therapy, self-professed good intentions have paved a hellish road of harms.

The first example, of entanglement with governmental authorities, may remind the reader of ecclesial complicity with Adolf Hitler's antisemitic "Final Solution" in Europe, but there also is enough evidence to indict United States church leaders as well.[2] Contemporary examples, discussed in the last chapter, of faith working through fear by which court evangelicals perpetuate white supremacy and a host of other systemic sins were undergirded by the National Association of Evangelicals' drafting of a revisionist historical statement asserting the nation's founding on principles of the Bible that then President Dwight D. Eisenhower signed, which preceded the addition by Congress of the phrases "under God" to the Pledge of Allegiance and "In God we trust" to currency.[3] These revisions overlooked the complicated relationship with religion exhibited by founders like John Adams and Thomas Jefferson.[4] The harms related to human sexuality are well-documented and yet still contested, such as the purity culture that "upholds abuse" across denominational lines[5] and the perpetuation of so-called "ex-gay ministries" that advance conversion therapy, over and against every evidence of its negative impacts, including, ironically, "loss of faith."[6]

[2]   Robert P. Ericksen, *Christian Complicity? Changing Views on German Churches and the Holocaust*, Joseph and Rebecca Meyerhoff Annual Lecture, November 8, 2007 (Washington, D.C.: United States Holocaust Memorial Museum, 2009).

[3]   John Fea, *Believe Me: The Evangelical Road to Donald Trump* (Grand Rapids: Eerdmans, 2018), 53–54.

[4]   John Fea, *Was America Founded as a Christian Nation? A Historical Introduction* (Louisville: Westminster John Knox, 2011), 193.

[5]   Emily Joy Allison, *#ChurchToo: How Purity Culture Upholds Abuse and How to Find Healing* (Minneapolis: Fortress, 2021). Allison's work is part of a growing body of memoirs and research exposing the harm inflicted by purity culture.

[6]   Carl G. Streed, J. Seth Anderson, Chris Babits, and Michael A. Ferguson, "Changing Medical Practice, Not Patients—Putting an End to Conversion Therapy," *New England Journal of Medicine* 381, no. 6 (2019): 500–502.

The hope is that church members who have come to understand themselves as believers-into (and who are not already painfully aware of these harms from personal experience) will humbly practice bold surrender and bravely face these hard lessons of harm done. It remains likely, however, that some believers (yes, even believers-into) will want to excuse ourselves from the hard lessons by leaning on the goodness of original intentions, difference from the denomination(s) or congregation(s) primarily responsible for the particular harm, or historical distance from the harmful acts. Still other believers may not see problems in the actions that have led to such grave harm and may be inclined to defend them. For these reasons, reconceived catechetical practices that promote a new kind of receptive listening are necessary.

While church-based structures for receptive listening, to understand and respond to community harm, have emerged occasionally from organizations such as the multifaceted Kaleidoscope Institute,[7] there also is wisdom in welcoming outside partners who willingly draw alongside the church with fresh perspective and training. Especially when we are part of a community perceived to be in the wrong, our instinct is not to learn more about the harm done and how we can respond but instead to thwart the threat, as "our brains are hardwired for this kind of vigilance, defense, and attack cycle," according to John Sarrouf, coexecutive director of Essential Partners.[8] To

---

The harmful effects of this practice, which has been endorsed over the past several decades by ostensibly church-equipping organizations such as Love Won Out, Exodus International (both now defunct), and Transforming Congregations, is documented continuously, especially as it affects LGBTQIA+ youth, by the Trevor Project (see the Trevor Project, *National Survey on LGBTQ Youth Mental Health 2019*, https://www.thetrevorproject.org/survey-2019/). "Loss of faith" appeared among the wide range of harms (including increased suicidality) reported in early, less conclusive studies surveyed by the American Psychological Association, *Report of the American Psychological Association Task Force on Appropriate Therapeutic Responses to Sexual Orientation* (Washington, D.C.: American Psychological Association, 2009), https://www.apa.org/pi/lgbt/resources/therapeutic-response.pdf.

   7   Kaleidoscope Institute, https://www.kscopeinstitute.org/history. This nonprofit corporation, founded by the Rev. Dr. Eric H. F. Law, is a subsidiary of the Episcopal Diocese of Los Angeles and offers training in "a system of practices, models, theology, and skill sets," which helps churches gain a deeper understanding and a stronger practice of ministry that engages and respects the dignity of every person.

   8   Jill DeTemple and John Sarrouf, "Disruption, Dialogue, and Swerve: Reflective Structured Dialogue in Religious Studies Classrooms," *Teaching Theology and*

counteract that cycle, Sarrouf's coauthor, religious studies scholar and award-winning educator Jill DeTemple, regularly makes use of Essential Partners' Reflective Structured Dialogue (RSD), which "models deep listening and a consistent practice of reflection" to help students stop talking past each other and start "listening to understand" and "speaking to be understood."[9]

The practice involves timed, nonobligatory, and uninterrupted sharing of story-based responses to prompts that build in intensity with each round of conversation. DeTemple has woven RSD into the fabric of her university classrooms in a way that—in my own experience—translates well to settings in both the church and the church-related academy. The key is to practice RSD regularly, such that deep listening becomes second nature and disruptive information does not crash conversation, but rather becomes an opportunity to extend hospitable curiosity to one another.[10] Instead of "We can't believe this upsetting information you're telling us," a response to disruption becomes, "Please tell us a story that will help us understand how you came to hold this position (value, perspective, etc.)" and is followed by genuinely interested listening. With its potential for "building better relationships and reducing polarization" among believers and to "build bridges among people who disagree on a wide range of topics,"[11] RSD is one of many instances of practices that make flourishing praxis possible for congregations or denominations reconceiving catechesis as listening to understand.[12]

Religion 20, no. 3 (2017): 285. Sarrouf refers to neurobiological research by Daniel J. Siegel in describing the dilemma so well addressed by the Reflective Structured Dialogue technique, which was developed from family therapy models and employed to facilitate dialogue across barriers of religious, racial, and other differences by the Public Conversation Project (now Essential Partners).

[9] Jill DeTemple, Eugene V. Gallagher, Kwok Pui Lan, and Thomas Pearson, "Reflective Structured Dialogue: A Conversation with 2018 American Academy of Religion Excellence in Teaching Award Winner Jill DeTemple," *Teaching Theology and Religion* 22, no. 3 (2019): 228.

[10] DeTemple and Sarrouf, "Disruption, Dialogue," 288. DeTemple uses a bicycling metaphor involving terms like "swerve" and "wobble" to describe the way in which RSD helps relationships and conversations to continue when disruptions occur.

[11] Katherine Gower, Llewellyn Cornelius, Raye Rawls, and Brandy B. Walker, "Reflective Structured Dialogue: A Qualitative Thematic Analysis," *Conflict Resolution Quarterly* 37, no. 3 (2020): 219.

[12] Various denominations and communities have resources available, ideally for use as a regular practice of engaging in meaningful dialogue with improved

Speaking to be understood then can be expanded to mean speaking to show that we are listening, we are beginning to understand, and we care in such a way as to respond with action. Once we have showed up in a God-connected, embodied way to learn of harms done, we are equipped to notice others as Jesus notices them, but how do we address them when we do? Receptive listening to understand, as part of a reconceived catechesis, solves the dilemma of concerns about political correctness, replacing it with what I am calling "relational reference."

The aim of political correctness is to avoid offense by using an often anonymously agreed-upon, frequently changing, "correct" terminology for individuals and groups based on identity markers for ethnicity, citizenship status, sexual orientation, gender identity, and so on.[13] At best, it is a series of compassionate gestures of good faith efforts to see people as they are. At worst, it fuels resentment and shuts down conversations as people worry that they will offend or be judged if they use the wrong terminology or name.[14]

By contrast, the aim of relational reference is to volunteer, invite, listen carefully for, and respond with the names and words (such as pronouns) that dialogic partners use to refer to themselves. It refuses to assume anything based on perception or implicit bias, and it does not hesitate to own humbly its ignorance and kindly ask when necessary, always volunteering one's own identities first. If the reconceived model of catechesis is effective, believers-into will self-identify and then be listening to learn how dialogic partners, especially those who have suffered harm at the hands of the church, refer to themselves and follow suit when building relationships with them. Words, of course, are only one part of relational faith working through love. There remains a need to reconceive sacraments as opportunities to make

---

understanding, not just when conflict mediation is necessary. In addition to the dialogue training offered by the Kaleidoscope Institute, there are numerous similar opportunities to learn effective practices from organizations such as the Dialogue Institute—originally an outreach of the *Journal of Ecumenical Studies*—housed at Temple University (https://dialogueinstitute.org/), the Multicultural Alliance (https://www.mcatexas.com/), and the Zeidler Group (https://www.zeidlergroup.org/).

[13] See Melnikova Kseniya and Guslyakova Alla, "Linguistic Features of a Politically Correct English Language Discourse," *SHS Web of Conferences* 88 (2020), https://www.shs-conferences.org/articles/shsconf/abs/2020/16/shsconf_lltforum2020_01034/shsconf_lltforum2020_01034.html.

[14] See Yascha Mounk, "Americans Strongly Dislike PC Culture," *Atlantic*, October 10, 2018, https://www.theatlantic.com/ideas/archive/2018/10/large-majorities-dislike-political-correctness/572581/.

our offerings, put our own flesh and blood on the line, and participate in the dying and rising with Christ via actions through which God cleanses our churches and our world of sin.

Sacraments Reconceived through Flourishing Praxis

In the same way that believing into Christ is not the domain of super saints and deepest disciples but is simply how to "do the work of God," so too reconceived sacraments involve everyone in action that all too conveniently otherwise gets relegated to those whom we easily label "activists." If believing-into entails to love, to cherish, to go into Christ and be incorporated in his members, then that also means going where Christ's members always go, which is to the places of worship and prayer, yes, and also to the places of struggling, sharing, healing, teaching, grieving, touching, talking, listening, forgiving, and giving. If reconceived catechesis has helped us to value equally, cherish, and wish to do good to other bodies, even those unlike ours, either because they are equally glued into Christ with ours, or because they are equally as cherished by Christ, the Creator, and the Spirit as ours, then we will be willing to risk ours to do so.

One particularly effective regional example in the United States is the Ten-Point Coalition, begun by African American clergy in Boston in the early 1990s. Rev. Eugene Rivers, Rev. Jeffrey Brown, and Rev. Ray Hammond were the main leaders of a group of approximately forty area churches who came together with their three churches and practiced a peripatetic, listening presence in the community, in response to rising murder rates and violent police response, resulting in improved relations between community, churches, and police.[15]

Another recent example is that of a congregation in Kenya who welcomed a mother and her intersex child into its fellowship, membership, and care, despite the stigmatization and criminalization of LGBTQIA+ persons in that nation. Taking their presence as a gift, Moheto United Methodist Church and its pastor, Rev. Kennedy Mwita, undertook prayerfully and attentively the study of scriptural, scientific, and all other available resources to come to an inclusive understanding of gender and sexuality. Ultimately, in a time of great division and turmoil in their global denomination over the full inclusion of LGBTQIA+

---

[15] Jenny Berrien and Christopher Winship, "Should We Have Faith in the Churches? The Ten-Point Coalition's Effect on Boston's Youth Violence," in *Guns, Crime, and Punishment in America*, ed. Bernard E. Harcourt (New York: New York University Press, 2003), 230–31.

persons, they decided to join the Reconciling Ministries Network of churches who fully affirm and commit to full inclusion.[16]

Perhaps among the most challenging opportunities to reconceive sacraments in this way are those which demand not only our physical presence of laying flesh and blood on the line, but also making an offering that requires us to put our money where our mouths are, possibly the most powerful way, within the framework of believing-into, of clinging in relationship to God through Jesus Christ in a way that transforms every other relationship in care for others. A burgeoning effort that would benefit from the participation of believers-into worldwide is that of reparations for racial oppression.

In 2020, amid nationwide protests of racism and police brutality toward persons of African descent, which rose to a fever pitch after the police killing of George Floyd in Minnesota, the state where some of the most violent atrocities against Indigenous persons in the nation's history were perpetrated, the Minnesota Council of Churches embarked upon a bold plan of "ARC": Acknowledgement, Redress (reparations, truth-telling, and education), and Closure (reconciliation).[17] The Council's action is guided in part by the landmark work of William A. Darity Jr. and A. Kirsten Mullen, *From Here to Equality: Reparations for Black Americans in the Twenty-First Century*, in which the authors assign financial value to historic harms throughout three different phases of oppression of people of African descent across the history of the United States and calculate costs for reparations.[18] The Council continues a commitment "for at least ten more years" to divest itself of white privilege by ensuring that the top leaders (board president and vice president, as well as the majority of board membership) are BIPOC, even as it commits its twenty-seven member communions to invest in reparations.[19] The Council's director

---

[16]   Heather Hahn, "First Church in Africa Becomes Reconciling," United Methodist News Service, September 9, 2019, https://www.umnews.org/en/news/first-church-in-africa-becomes-reconciling.

[17]   Minnesota Council of Churches Board of Directors, *Dismantling the Structures and Repairing the Damage of Racism in Minnesota* (September 24, 2020), http://mnchurches.webbrohd.com/blog/2020/09/28/dismantling-structures-and-repairing-damage-racism-minnesota.

[18]   William A. Darity Jr. and A. Kirsten Mullen, *From Here to Equality: Reparations for Black Americans in the Twenty-First Century* (Chapel Hill: University of North Carolina Press, 2020), 2–3.

[19]   Minnesota Council of Churches, *Dismantling*.

of racial justice, Rev. Jim Bear Jacobs, describes this investment in stark terms as he hopes it will be a line item in each church's budget, like building maintenance, because "if all the churches do is take up a special offering, there's no shift in the power dynamics that created these problems in the first place."[20] There have been denominations and dioceses therein who have made large financial commitments to reparations, but the Minnesota Council of Churches board vice president, Rev. Stacey L. Smith, deems it appropriate for their ecumenical effort to make Minnesota "the epicenter of being transformed with racial justice."[21]

While the sacramental foci in this book have been baptism and the Eucharist (the two sacraments, or ordinances in some traditions, retained in most Protestant denominations), it is important to note that this reconception of sacraments can apply to many more, if not all, of the seven sacraments of the ancient traditions, especially the sacraments of healing.[22] The truth-telling, repentant aspect of these actions can be seen as expanding publicly on the sacrament of penance and reconciliation that takes place privately between the communicant and God via the confessor. We could see an expansion of the sacrament of anointing the sick in what civil rights movement leader Rev. James M. Lawson has identified in the Black Lives Matter movement as an element of ministry to the mourning families of slain African Americans as past victims' families gather around the grieving survivors of each new victim, and together they ensure a continuation of that seemingly lost life, amplifying the cry of justice for that person.[23] Further, as increasing availability of body camera and

---

[20]   Crary, "More U.S. Churches." Rev. Bear Jacobs is a member of a Wisconsin-based Mohican tribe but takes social-justice tour participants to visit a memorial at the site of a former concentration camp where 1,600 Dakota people were held after the 1862 U.S.–Dakota Conflict, now part of Fort Snelling State Park near Minneapolis.

[21]   Crary, "More U.S. Churches." Rev. Smith is the presiding elder of the Fourth District of the African Methodist Episcopal Church, which includes Minnesota.

[22]   The autocephalous Orthodox Church in America notes that the enumeration of sacraments is a recent innovation under the influence of the Roman Catholic Church, as it is Orthodox tradition to see all acts as sacramental. See Orthodox Church in America, "The Sacraments," https://www.oca.org/questions/sevensacraments/the-sacraments.

[23]   Kathy L. Gilbert, "Lawson: Black Lives Matter a Religious Movement," United Methodist News Service, July 23, 2020, https://www.umnews.org/en/news/lawson-black-lives-matter-a-religious-movement.

bystander video and audio footage reveals the loneliness in which fatal victims of police brutality often lie dying, this prayerful enfolding of their left-behind loved ones may be seen as signifying a delayed effort at the ministering presence victims themselves have been denied in the moment of death.[24]

So as the body, the believers-into incorporated in Christ's members, finds itself on the move in the directions Christ has always gone, it shows a willingness to lay down its life for its friends, confessing its sins (which bears no parallel in Christ himself) and relinquishing power and resources via reparations to enact justice and restore relationship. The Minneapolis movement, and those like it, certainly reflects our aforementioned skills of showing up in a God-connected way, noticing as Jesus notices, and responding relationally in concrete ways. Rev. Dr. Curtiss DeYoung, CEO of the Council, noted that when the murder of Floyd occurred where these churches are, "The first thing that we did, of course, like everyone else, was get into the streets and march . . . but there are deep, historic issues that require more than marching."[25] While it is true that these actions speak louder than words, there is still value in the messages of the movement, especially when carried aloft by the body together on the move to launch new efforts or remind of the purpose of ongoing efforts, in much the same way that affirmations of faith in the form of creeds are vital aspects of launching the visible signs of baptism and the Eucharist.

Creeds Reconceived through Flourishing Praxis

As the Nicene-Constantinopolitan Creed, in particular, owes its existence, at least in part, to empire, it may seem contradictory to invoke a reconception of creeds through flourishing praxis as protest signs that speak truth to power. Yet as I sat at my dining room table one January day, carefully crafting easily portable banners with my two traveling companions, creeds were very much on my mind. My research was underway but felt interrupted and, at the same time, urgent. Only

---

[24]   Farnoush Amiri, "Ohio Police Officer Fired in Fatal Shooting of Black Man," Associated Press, December 28, 2020, https://apnews.com/article/ohio -columbus-shootings-police-44e8d192397dbde3346bbf2a962f3d23. "A white Ohio police officer was fired Monday after bodycam footage showed him fatally shooting 47-year-old Andre Hill—a Black man who was holding a cellphone— and failing to administer first aid for several minutes." Several other officers who responded also failed to render aid.

[25]   Crary, "More U.S. Churches."

nine short weeks before, I had sat watching the 2016 general election returns, sputtering, "When I proposed to do doctoral research that I hoped might help mitigate the bitter invective polluting public discourse, I wasn't hoping for this kind of job security!" The work of the court evangelicals (a term I had yet to hear, because John Fea had yet to coin it) had succeeded, and a man my nine-year-old child could not bear to hear speak, because "he's so cruel, a real bully," was bound for the highest office in the nation.

I mused to my neighbor that, as parents and educators, we should fly to Washington, D.C., on inauguration weekend, park ourselves on the sidewalk outside the White House, and hold up signs to the effect of "I'm a mother, I'm an educator, and I'm watching you!" She took me seriously, and we each reached out to a friend (both of whom were also educators)—mine, one in D.C. with whom we might stay, hers, a local friend who had never visited the nation's capital but taught A.P. human geography and felt much the same way we did. The next week, my neighbor called me while I was attending the annual meeting of the American Academy of Religion to say that, if we were really going, we had better get our airline tickets, because a woman in Hawaii had posted the same basic idea to Facebook, it had gone viral, and now there was an actual march on Washington being planned for the day after the inauguration![26] We booked our tickets and began pondering what sort of messages we should put on our protest signs.

In addition to parents and educators, both my neighbor and I were people of faith, dismayed that our mainline Protestant church had suddenly started posting images of the president-elect onscreen during worship, directing the congregation to pray for him, despite never having done so for the sitting president. My neighbor's friend, a self-described "exvangelical," shared our concern to spread a message of faith working through love, not fear. Soon many of the people mentioned in the previous chapter who had begun calling me in dismay with their questions also expressed their fervent wish that they could go with us and asked us to spread messages of defiant hope. They did not want us to be discouraged if our numbers turned

---

[26]   The leadership of the Women's March that originated with this individual's social media post was quickly handed over to a more diverse and experienced team of organizers, who have since borne various forms of criticism, yet the movement continues.

out to be fewer than we and the march organizers hoped, just as we wanted to represent them well.

We finally settled on an idea for our main banner, simply the word "TOGETHER," spelled out in giant block letters comprising the names of the people we were representing, those who could not be bodily present but joined with us in spirit. In the end, the banner contained 250 names. On January 21, 2017, the National Mall (really Independence Avenue) could not contain the half-million marchers gathered. We enjoyed an object lesson in what it is like to be incorporated in another's members all together, as the physical crush of humanity literally carried us in the direction it was going. The movement was so involuntary for our little group that we had to cling tightly to one another's hands, as if glued together, to keep from losing one another in the crowd.

Once the actual marching began, we were able to spread out enough to unfurl our banners. In addition to our TOGETHER banner, we also carried signs that bore messages such as "PROTECT EACH OTHER" and "FEAR BUILDS WALLS/HOPE BUILDS BRIDGES." These messages were statements about the One into whom we believe, to the one who seems to think he wields so much more power. These messages were ones we wished we learned more in the church, heard resounding from the pulpit, or read responsively in a litany.

Creeds reconceived through flourishing praxis are transformed affirmations in the weekly worship service that become marching orders for service. Turning our chanted psalms into protest chants has a long heritage in the civil rights movement and before. "Movement" is key to this flourishing praxis. The Women's March was never about one action of protest and solidarity, but about the movement it would inspire, a fuel of sorts for an active fire of love, to be reinvigorated with every ensuing march but lived out every day in between, through phone calls, letters, donations, campaigns waged, witnesses shared, meals delivered, refugees housed, and relationships forged. In some churches, every weekly worship service serves as an opportunity for creeds reconceived as marching orders to be carried out into the streets after the benediction, spoken by clergy unafraid to speak the truth. Such churches may be so active in the streets that they need to be reminded to return weekly to worship the One whose love they bear into the world. In other churches, the mere thought of what I'm describing seems foolish. After all, plenty of fellow Christians were among our detractors who wondered loudly on social media as we returned home and our images splashed across the news, "If there's so much to protest, why is everyone smiling?!" Our response was simply that the joy and relief of knowing that we were not alone in the work of spreading a message of love and speaking truth to power were not things we could (or should) conceal. The final clause of each classical creed focuses on the fact that we are all *together*, much as the heart of this book has focused on the flourishing made possible when we understand ourselves each to be believers into Christ, and all to be together incorporated in his members, fused inseparably to him, and thus to one another, by Holy Spirit Glue.

The reconception I describe here may seem to take the *corpus permixtum* to the extreme, but unfurling ourselves from our own inward turn to be incorporated in Christ's members requires that we not try to unglue ourselves whenever we think we know better or encounter someone with whom we would rather not share this incorporation. Rather, the challenge from Augustine's day until our own is to remain turned outward with Christ and moving in the directions Christ's limbs are shown to be stretching throughout the New Testament, which by default is never anything that looks like the norm most expect.

Believing-into means moving not along a path of least resistance or greatest dominance, but rather defaulting (which means everyday action and weekly worship, keeping the health and flexibility of the body in balance) to those individuals and groups whom the dominant structures most often deprive of material and relational means of flourishing. Then the default directions in which we move become the path of greatest accessibility for all bodies, where Black is beautiful, queerness is celebrated, neurodivergence is embraced, trauma-sensitivity is exercised with compassion, children are centered and set free from developing implicit bias, the elderly are respected instead of treated as a burden, poor people are a primary priority, unjust criminalization and incarceration are eliminated, addiction is a treatable brain disease (not a moral failing), and diversity of languages and cultures is appreciated as evidence of divine creativity. Of course, if our flourishing praxis, through which we have reconceived catechesis, sacraments, and creeds, is effective, these directions in which we move will change, because the relationship with God, one another, and everyone we meet there will be so deifying for all that deprivation of the means of flourishing will no longer be the reality there. Then it will be time to discern new directions, all of us, together.

CONCLUSION

The narrative arc of this book charted a journey that began with an explanation and exploration of believing-into as the key component of the Christian life, part of a formula exegeted and preached by Augustine. The path then led along the historical trajectory of the formula's loss in translation, in order to arrive at the constructive place where we considered how we might restore believing-into and give rise to greater human flourishing.

Though boldly surrendering in relationship with Christ involves individuals' believing into Christ and by believing to love, cherish, go into him, and be incorporated in his members, the contribution of Christianity to flourishing cannot be merely a personal relationship between individual human and divine that benefits no one else. Therefore, through this same believing-into, the Holy Spirit Glue that binds believers-into with Christ also binds them together with one another. It causes them to see all other bodies as extensions of their own and care profoundly about all others and their flourishing. Thus the doctrinal disputes and demands for dominance that have divided Christians throughout history and driven many of them to inflict harms in the name of Christ all arise from misplaced aims. As Christ demonstrates in the Gospels, all of our conversation—whether inward or outward—should have as its aim a clearer understanding of one another's relationships, communal and divine alike. As the world's religions aid in this flourishing by helping us to see these life-giving relationships as sourced in something inexhaustible, something beyond ourselves yet fully available, strengthening our connections, there remains a challenge for Christianity in this regard: In order to contribute to the flourishing of all, this relational sense of belief and its bold surrender has to be foundational to the most basic practice of Christian faith by every believer, not just a nice aspiration for the upper echelon of super saints and deepest disciples. Chapters 4 and 5, in dialogue with theological interlocutors and practitioners, offered original, concrete suggestions to live into this reality and experience a democratic deification (in the sense that it is available to *everyone* who believes into Christ).

Thus, to return to the question of what can be done in contemporary theology with this curious phrase, this *credere in Deum* that literally is believing into God, possible next steps include exploring the effects of training this lens on various Christian doctrines. This approach offers opportunity for engagement with interlocutors across the theological spectrum. Additionally, exploring case studies in bold surrender by those who have understood the doctrines of Christianity through the relational lens would contribute to the effort of connecting believing into God with contemporary theology. The stories abound of saints, both heralded and lesser known, who have demonstrated the *credendo* crescendo of believing into Christ, even if they did so without articulating their particular practice of faith-working-through-love as "believing into Christ." The hope is that, as more interlocutors join this theological adventure—training the lens on the doctrines most relevant to their work, seeing the relational sense of belief active in everyday life and its contributions to flourishing—more readers will find a role in the restoration of the relational sense of belief and join the journey.

APPENDIX

In the chart, each English translation is as it appears in the NRSV, with modifications (such as words adapted parenthetically or strike-through text) as needed to indicate where the NRSV deviates from the literal Latin. The Latin text is as it appears in the Vulgate (Vatican version). The Greek text is as it appears in the GNT-28 (Nestle-Aland).

The following collection of pericopes is not exhaustive, but is, instead, a representative list of major passages that contain an aspect of the *credere* formula. It is important to note that there are no instances of *credere* + accusative without the preposition *in* (the formula's equivalent of "believe in God"). The only pericopes approximating the concept are that of John 8:24, John 11:27, Hebrews 11:6, and James 2:19. *Credere in* + accusative, on the other hand, appears in abundance across the biblical canon. Also present is a plethora of pericopes with the object of *credere* in the dative form. Please note three instances in which the Koine Greek (from which the NRSV was translated) and Latin Vulgate do not agree: (1) The Jonah passage has the unusual appearance of *credere in* + ablative, which chapter 2 explains had been overtaken by *credere in* + accusative in frequency. As its usage was so rare (and was possibly a copy error, as the Koine Greek lacks any preposition at all), it has been presented as translated for the NRSV. (2) In John 3:15, the Latin text actually reads (as its punctuation suggests) "all who believe, have eternal life in himself," which seems nonsensical. (3) Finally, Acts 16:31 contains two different odd constructions in the Koine Greek and in the Latin Vulgate, the former mentioned in chapter 3 with regard to the possible reasoning behind the odd choice of the earliest known translations of *Tract. Ev. Jo.* into English, "believe on."

A significant contribution to the enlivening of the formula in the church and the world would be the rendering of the biblical passages to reflect the formula. This change would allow the use of the phrase "believe into God/Christ/me/the Father" to seem less awkward as it becomes part of everyday quotation of Scripture. This adjustment would also allow hearers/readers to understand the ways in which Jesus implored those around him to believe into him while connecting to the Jewish people, for whom the language of believing into God resonates as well. Although this is only a sampling from the swath of passages that discuss various forms of believing that God exists, believing what God says is true, and believing into God, it is clear that restoring this language can make a significant difference in how the text is received.

The theological implications of restoring the intended meaning to the text are not minimal, especially regarding soteriology. While "believing into" Christ or God is always put in salvific terms, "believing" Christ or God is only occasionally used thus.

> **Gen 15:6** And he believed the LORD; and the LORD reckoned it to him as righteousness.
>
> καὶ ἐπίστευσεν Αβραμ τῷ θεῷ, καὶ ἐλογίσθη αὐτῷ εἰς δικαιοσύνην.
>
> *Credidit Domino, et reputatum est ei ad iustitiam.*
>
> **Exod 14:31** Israel saw the great work that the LORD did against the Egyptians. So the people feared the LORD and believed ~~in~~ the LORD and ~~in~~ his servant Moses.
>
> εἶδεν δὲ Ισραηλ τὴν χεῖρα τὴν μεγάλην, ἃ ἐποίησεν κύριος τοῖς Αἰγυπτίοις· ἐφοβήθη δὲ ὁ λαὸς τὸν κύριον καὶ ἐπίστευσαν τῷ θεῷ καὶ Μωυσῇ τῷ θεράποντι αὐτοῦ.
>
> *Et viderunt Aegyptios mortuos super litus maris et manum magnam, quam exercuerat Dominus contra eos; timuitque populus Dominum et crediderunt Domino et Moysi servo eius.*
>
> **2 Kgs 17:14** They would not listen but were stubborn, as their ancestors had been, who did not believe in (into) the LORD their God.
>
> καὶ οὐκ ἤκουσαν καὶ ἐσκλήρυναν τὸν νῶτον αὐτῶν ὑπὲρ τὸν νῶτον τῶν πατέρων αὐτῶν (The LXX lacks the phrase referring to belief altogether, ending with the phrase that the NRSV translates "as their ancestors had been.")

Qui non audierunt, sed induraverunt cervicem suam iuxta cervicem patrum suorum, qui noluerunt credere in Dominum Deum suum.

Jonah 3:5 And the people of Nineveh believed God; they proclaimed a fast, and everyone, great and small, put on sackcloth.

καὶ ἐνεπίστευσαν οἱ ἄνδρες Νινευη τῷ θεῷ καὶ ἐκήρυξαν νηστείαν καὶ ἐνεδύσαντο σάκκους ἀπὸ μεγάλου αὐτῶν ἕως μικροῦ αὐτῶν.

Et crediderunt viri Ninevitae in Deo; et praedicaverunt ieiunium et vestiti sunt saccis a maiore usque ad minorem.

Jdt 14:10 When Achior saw all that the God of Israel had done, he believed firmly in God. So he was circumcised, and joined the house of Israel, remaining so to this day.

ἰδὼν δὲ Αχιωρ πάντα, ὅσα ἐποίησεν ὁ θεὸς τοῦ Ισραηλ, ἐπίστευσεν τῷ θεῷ σφόδρα καὶ περιετέμετο τὴν σάρκα τῆς ἀκροβυστίας αὐτοῦ καὶ προσετέθη εἰς τὸν οἶκον Ισραηλ ἕως τῆς ἡμέρας ταύτης.

Videns autem Achior omnia, quaecumque fecit Deus Israel, credidit Deo valde et circumcidit carnem praeputii sui, et appositus est ad domum Israel usque in diem hanc.

Matt 18:6 "If any of you put a stumbling block before one of these little ones who believe in (into) me, it would be better for you if a great millstone were fastened around your neck and you were drowned in the depth of the sea."

ὃς δ' ἂν σκανδαλίσῃ ἕνα τῶν μικρῶν τούτων τῶν πιστευόντων εἰς ἐμέ, συμφέρει αὐτῷ ἵνα κρεμασθῇ μύλος ὀνικὸς ἐπὶ τὸν τράχηλον αὐτοῦ, καὶ καταποντισθῇ ἐν τῷ πελάγει τῆς θαλάσσης.

Qui autem scandalizaverit unum de pusillis istis, qui in me credunt, expedit ei, ut suspendatur mola asinaria in collo eius et demergatur in profundum maris.

Matt 27:42 "He saved others; he cannot save himself. He is the King of Israel; let him come down from the cross now, and we will believe in (into) him."

Ἄλλους ἔσωσεν, ἑαυτὸν οὐ δύναται σῶσαι. εἰ βασιλεὺς Ἰσραὴλ ἐστι καταβάτω νῦν ἀπὸ τοῦ σταυροῦ, καὶ πιστεύσομεν αὐτῷ.

Alios salvos fecit, seipsum non potest salvum facere. Rex Israel est; descendat nunc de cruce, et credemus in eum.

Mark 9:42 "If any of you put a stumbling block before one of these little ones who believe in (into) me, it would be better for you if a great millstone were hung around your neck and you were thrown into the sea."

καὶ ὃς ἂν σκανδαλίσῃ ἕνα τῶν μικρῶν τούτων τῶν πιστευόντων εἰς ἐμέ, καλόν ἐστιν αὐτῷ μᾶλλον εἰ περίκειται λίθος μυλικὸς περὶ τὸν τράχηλον αὐτοῦ, καὶ βέβληται εἰς τὴν θάλασσαν.

Et quisquis scandalizaverit unum ex his pusillis credentibus in me, bonum est ei magis, ut circumdetur mola asinaria collo eius, et in mare mittatur.

John 2:11 Jesus did this, the first of his signs, in Cana of Galilee, and revealed his glory; and his disciples believed in (into) him.

ταύτην ἐποίησε τὴν ἀρχὴν τῶν σημείων ὁ Ἰησοῦς ἐν Κανᾷ τῆς Γαλιλαίας, καὶ ἐφανέρωσε τὴν δόξαν αὐτοῦ, καὶ ἐπίστευσαν εἰς αὐτὸν οἱ μαθηταὶ αὐτοῦ.

Hoc fecit initium signorum Iesus in Cana Galilaeae et manifestavit gloriam suam, et crediderunt in eum discipuli eius.

John 3:15-18 ". . . that whoever believes ~~in him~~ may have eternal life (in himself). For God so loved the world that he gave his only Son, so that everyone who believes in (into) him may not perish but may have eternal life. Indeed, God did not send the Son into the world to condemn the world, but in order that the world might be saved through him. Those who believe in (into) him are not condemned; but those who do not believe are condemned already, because they have not believed in (into) the name of the only Son of God."

. . . ἵνα πᾶς ὁ πιστεύων ἐν αὐτῷ ἔχῃ ζωὴν αἰώνιον. τω γὰρ ἠγάπησεν ὁ Θεὸς τὸν κόσμον, ὥστε τὸν υἱὸν αὐτοῦ τὸν μονογενῆ ἔδωκεν, ἵνα πᾶς ὁ πιστεύων εἰς αὐτὸν μὴ ἀπόληται, ἀλλ᾽ ἔχῃ ζωὴν αἰώνιον. οὐ γὰρ ἀπέστειλεν ὁ Θεὸς τὸν υἱὸν αὐτοῦ εἰς τὸν κόσμον, ἵνα κρίνῃ τὸν κόσμον ἀλλ ἵνα σωθῇ ὁ κόσμος δἰ αὐτοῦ. ὁ πιστεύων εἰς αὐτὸν οὐ κρίνεται· ὁ δὲ μὴ πιστεύων ἤδη κέκριται, ὅτι μὴ πεπίστευκεν εἰς τὸ ὄνομα τοῦ μονογενοῦς υἱοῦ τοῦ Θεοῦ.

. . . ut omnis, qui credit, in ipso habeat vitam aeternam. Sic enim dilexit Deus mundum, ut Filium suum unigenitum daret, ut omnis, qui credit in eum, non pereat, sed habeat vitam aeternam. Non enim misit Deus Filium in mundum, ut iudicet mundum, sed ut salvetur mundus per ipsum. Qui credit in eum, non iudicatur; qui autem non credit, iam iudicatus est, quia non credidit in nomen Unigeniti Filii Dei.

John 5:24 "Very truly, I tell you, anyone who hears my word and believes him who sent me has eternal life, and does not come under judgment, but has passed from death to life."

ἀμὴν ἀμὴν λέγω ὑμῖν ὅτι ὁ τὸν λόγον μου ἀκούων, καὶ πιστεύων τῷ πέμψαντί με, ἔχει ζωὴν αἰώνιον· καὶ εἰς κρίσιν οὐκ ἔρχεται, ἀλλὰ μεταβέβηκεν ἐκ τοῦ θανάτου εἰς τὴν ζωήν.

Amen, amen dico vobis: Qui verbum meum audit et credit ei, qui misit me, habet vitam aeternam et in iudicium non venit, sed transiit a morte in vitam.

John 5:38 ". . . and you do not have his word abiding in you, because you do not believe him whom he has sent."

καὶ τὸν λόγον αὐτοῦ οὐκ ἔχετε μένοντα ἐν ὑμῖν, ὅτι ὃν ἀπέστειλεν ἐκεῖνος, τούτῳ ὑμεῖς οὐ πιστεύετε.

. . . et verbum eius non habetis in vobis manens, quia, quem misit ille, huic vos non creditis.

John 5:46 "If you believed Moses, you would believe me, for he wrote about me."

εἰ γὰρ ἐπιστεύετε Μωσῇ, ἐπιστεύετε ἂν ἐμοί· περὶ γὰρ ἐμοῦ ἐκεῖνος ἔγραψεν.

Si enim crederetis Moysi, crederetis forsitan et mihi; de me enim ille scripsit.

John 6:29 Jesus answered them, "This is the work of God, that you believe in (into) him whom he has sent."

ἀπεκρίθη ὁ Ἰησοῦς καὶ εἶπεν αὐτοῖς, Τοῦτό ἐστι τὸ ἔργον τοῦ Θεοῦ, ἵνα πιστεύσητε εἰς ὃν ἀπέστειλεν ἐκεῖνος.

Respondit Iesus et dixit eis: Hoc est opus Dei, ut credatis in eum, quem misit ille.

John 6:35 Jesus said to them, "I am the bread of life. Whoever comes to me will never be hungry, and whoever believes in (into) me will never be thirsty."

εἶπε δὲ αὐτοῖς ὁ Ἰησοῦς, Ἐγώ εἰμι ὁ ἄρτος τῆς ζωῆς· ὁ ἐρχόμενος πρός με οὐ μὴ πεινάσῃ, καὶ ὁ πιστεύων εἰς ἐμὲ οὐ μὴ διψήσῃ πώποτε.

Dixit eis Iesus: "Ego sum panis vitae. Qui venit ad me, non esuriet; et, qui credit in me, non sitiet umquam."

John 7:5 (For not even his brothers believed in [into] him.)

οὐδὲ γὰρ οἱ ἀδελφοὶ αὐτοῦ ἐπίστευον εἰς αὐτόν.

Neque enim fratres eius credebant in eum.

John 8:24 "I told you that you would die in your sins, for you will die in your sins unless you believe that I am he."

εἶπον οὖν ὑμῖν ὅτι ἀποθανεῖσθε ἐν ταῖς ἁμαρτίαις ὑμῶν· ἐὰν γὰρ μὴ πιστεύσητε ὅτι ἐγώ εἰμι, ἀποθανεῖσθε ἐν ταῖς ἁμαρτίαις ὑμῶν.

Dixi ergo vobis quia moriemini in peccatis vestris; si enim non credideritis quia ego sum, moriemini in peccatis vestris.

John 9:35-36 Jesus heard that they had driven him out, and when he found him, he said, "Do you believe in (into) the Son of Man?" He answered, "And who is he, sir? Tell me, so that I may believe in (into) him."

Ηκουσεν ὁ Ἰησοῦς ὅτι ἐξέβαλον αὐτὸν ἔξω καὶ εὑρὼν αὐτόν, εἶπεν αὐτῷ, Σὺ πιστεύεις εἰς τὸν υἱὸν τοῦ Θεοῦ; ἀπεκρίθη ἐκεῖνος καὶ εἶπε, Τίς ἐστι, Κύριε, ἵνα πιστεύσω εἰς αὐτόν;

Audivit Iesus quia eiecerunt eum foras et, cum invenisset eum, dixit ei: "Tu credis in Filium hominis?" Respondit ille et dixit: "Et quis est, Domine, ut credam in eum?"

John 11:25 Jesus said to her, "I am the resurrection and the life. Those who believe in (into) me, even though they die, will live,"

εἶπεν αὐτῇ ὁ Ἰησοῦς, Ἐγώ εἰμι ἡ ἀνάστασις καὶ ἡ ζωή· ὁ πιστεύων εἰς ἐμέ, κἂν ἀποθάνῃ ζήσεται,

Dixit ei Iesus: Ego sum resurrectio et vita. Qui credit in me, etsi mortuus fuerit, vivet;

John 11:27 She said to him, "Yes, Lord, I believe that you are the Messiah, the Son of God, the one coming into the world."

λέγει αὐτῷ Ναί, Κύριε· ἐγὼ πεπίστευκα ὅτι σὺ εἶ ὁ Χριστὸς ὁ υἱὸς τοῦ Θεοῦ ὁ εἰς τὸν κόσμον ἐρχόμενος.

Ait illi: Utique, Domine; ego credidi quia tu es Christus Filius Dei, qui in mundum venisti.

John 14:1 "Do not let your hearts be troubled. Believe in (into) God, believe also in (into) me."

Μὴ ταρασσέσθω ὑμῶν ἡ καρδία· πιστεύετε εἰς τὸν Θεόν, καὶ εἰς ἐμὲ πιστεύετε.

Non turbetur cor vestrum. Creditis in Deum et in me credite.

Acts 16:31 They answered, "Believe on (upon) the Lord Jesus, and you will be saved, you and your household."

οἱ δὲ εἶπον, Πίστευσον ἐπὶ τὸν Κύριον Ἰησοῦν Χριστόν, καὶ σωθήσῃ σὺ καὶ ὁ οἶκός σου.

At illi dixerunt: Crede in Domino Iesu et salvus eris tu et domus tua.

Acts 16:34 He brought them up into the house and set food before them; and he and his entire household rejoiced that he had become a believer in God (literally "believing God").

ἀναγαγών τε αὐτοὺς εἰς τὸν οἶκον αὐτοῦ παρέθηκε τράπεζαν, καὶ ἠγαλλιάσατο πανοικὶ πεπιστευκὼς τῷ Θεῷ.

cumque perduxisset eos in domum, apposuit mensam et laetatus est cum omni domo sua credens Deo.

Acts 19:4 Paul said, "John baptized with the baptism of repentance, telling the people to believe in (into) the one who was to come after him, that is, in (into) Jesus."

εἶπε δὲ Παῦλος, Ἰωάννης μὲν ἐβάπτισε βάπτισμα μετανοίας, τῷ λαῷ λέγων εἰς τὸν ἐρχόμενον μετ αὐτὸν ἵνα πιστεύσωσιν τοῦτ ἔστιν εἰς τὸν Χριστὸν Ἰησοῦν.

Dixit autem Paulus: Ioannes baptizavit baptisma paenitentiae, populo dicens in eum, qui venturus esset post ipsum ut crederent, hoc est in Iesum.

Acts 22:19 "And I said, 'Lord, they themselves know that in every synagogue I imprisoned and beat those who believed in (into) you.'"

κἀγὼ εἶπον, Κύριε, αὐτοὶ ἐπίστανται ὅτι ἐγὼ ἤμην φυλακίζων καὶ δέρων κατὰ τὰς συναγωγὰς τοὺς πιστεύοντας ἐπὶ σέ,

Et ego dixi: Domine, ipsi sciunt quia ego eram concludens in carcerem et caedens per synagogas eos, qui credebant in te;

Rom 10:14 But how are they to call on one in (into) whom they have not believed? And how are they to believe in one of whom they have never heard? And how are they to hear without someone to proclaim him?

Πῶς οὖν ἐπικαλέσονται εἰς ὃν οὐκ ἐπίστευσαν; πῶς δὲ πιστεύσουσιν οὗ οὐκ ἤκουσαν; πῶς δὲ ἀκούσουσι χωρὶς κηρύσσοντος;

Quomodo ergo invocabunt, in quem non crediderunt? Aut quomodo credent ei, quem non audierunt? Quomodo autem audient sine praedicante?

Gal 2:16 yet we know that a person is justified not by the works of the law but through faith in Jesus Christ. And we have come to believe in (into) Christ Jesus, so that we might be justified by faith in Christ, and not by doing the works of the law, because no one will be justified by the works of the law.

εἰδότες [δε] ὅτι οὐ δικαιοῦται ἄνθρωπος ἐξ ἔργων νόμου ἐὰν μὴ διὰ πίστεως Χριστοῦ Ἰησοῦ, καὶ ἡμεῖς εἰς Χριστὸν Ἰησοῦν ἐπιστεύσαμεν, ἵνα δικαιωθῶμεν ἐκ πίστεως Χριστοῦ καὶ οὐκ ἐξ ἔργων νόμου, ὅτι ἐξ ἔργων νόμου οὐ δικαιωθήσεται πᾶσα σάρξ.

scientes autem quod non iustificatur homo ex operibus legis, nisi per fidem Iesu Christi, et nos in Christum Iesum credidimus, ut iustificemur ex fide Christi et non ex operibus legis, quoniam ex operibus legis non iustificabitur omnis caro.

Phil 1:29 For he has graciously granted you the privilege not only of believing in (into) Christ, but of suffering for him as well—

ὅτι ὑμῖν ἐχαρίσθη τὸ ὑπὲρ Χριστοῦ, οὐ μόνον τὸ εἰς αὐτὸν πιστεύειν ἀλλὰ καὶ τὸ ὑπὲρ αὐτοῦ πάσχειν,

quia vobis hoc donatum est pro Christo, non solum ut in eum credatis, sed ut etiam pro illo patiamini

Titus 3:8 The saying is sure. I desire that you insist on these things, so that those who have come to believe in God may be careful to devote themselves to good works; these things are excellent and profitable to everyone.

Πιστὸς ὁ λόγος· καὶ περὶ τούτων βούλομαί σε διαβεβαιοῦσθαι, ἵνα φροντίζωσιν καλῶν ἔργων προΐστασθαι οἱ πεπιστευκότες Θεῷ. ταῦτά ἐστι καλὰ καὶ ὠφέλιμα τοῖς ἀνθρώποις.

Fidelis sermo, et volo te de his confirmare, ut curent bonis operibus praeesse, qui crediderunt Deo. Haec sunt bona et utilia hominibus;

Heb 11:6 And without faith it is impossible to please God, for whoever would approach him must believe that he exists and that he rewards those who seek him.

χωρὶς δὲ πίστεως ἀδύνατον εὐαρεστῆσαι· πιστεῦσαι γὰρ δεῖ τὸν προσερχόμενον [τῷ] Θεῷ ὅτι ἔστιν καὶ τοῖς ἐκζητοῦσιν αὐτὸν μισθαποδότης γίνεται.

Sine fide autem impossibile placere; credere enim oportet accedentem ad Deum quia est et inquirentibus se remunerator fit.

Jas 2:19 You believe that God is one; you do well. Even the demons believe—and shudder.

σὺ πιστεύεις ὅτι εἷς Θεὸς ἐστίν; καλῶς ποιεῖς· καὶ τὰ δαιμόνια πιστεύουσιν, καὶ φρίσσουσιν.

*Tu credis quoniam unus est Deus? Bene facis; et daemones cre-
dunt et contremescunt!*

1 John 5:10 Those who believe in (into) the Son of God have the
testimony in their hearts. Those who do not believe ~~in~~ God have
made him a liar by not believing in (into) the testimony that
God has given concerning his Son.

ὁ πιστεύων εἰς τὸν υἱὸν τοῦ Θεοῦ ἔχει τὴν μαρτυρίαν ἐν ἑαυτῷ,
ὁ μὴ πιστεύων τῷ Θεῷ ψεύστην πεποίηκεν αὐτόν, ὅτι οὐ
πεπίστευκεν εἰς τὴν μαρτυρίαν, ἣν μεμαρτύρηκεν ὁ Θεὸς περὶ
τοῦ υἱοῦ αὐτοῦ.

*Qui credit in Filium Dei, habet testimonium in se. Qui non credit
Deo, mendacem facit eum, quoniam non credidit in testimonium,
quod testificatus est Deus de Filio suo.*

BIBLIOGRAPHY

Latin texts for the works of Thomas Aquinas are from *Opera omnia S. Thomae*, part of the online Corpus Thomisticum project of the University of Navarre. Available at http://www.corpusthomisticum.org/.

Abraham, William J. *Crossing the Threshold of Divine Revelation*. Grand Rapids: Eerdmans, 2006.

Aland, Barbara, Kurt Aland, Johannes Karavidopoulos, Carlo M. Martini, and Bruce M. Metzger, eds. *The Greek New Testament*. 4th rev. ed. Stuttgart: Deutsche Bibelgesellschaft, 1998.

Allison, Emily Joy. *#ChurchToo: How Purity Culture Upholds Abuse and How to Find Healing*. Minneapolis: Fortress, 2021.

Amiri, Farnoush. "Ohio Police Officer Fired in Fatal Shooting of Black Man." Associated Press, December 28, 2020. https://apnews.com/article/ohio-columbus-shootings-police-44e8d192397dbde3346bbf2a962f3d23.

Audi, Robert. *Rationality and Religious Commitment*. New York: Oxford University Press, 2011.

Augustine. *The City of God XI–XXII*. Edited by Boniface Ramsey. Translated by William S. Babcock. The Works of Saint Augustine: A Translation for the 21st Century 1/7. Hyde Park, N.Y.: New City Press, 2013.

———. *The Confessions*. Translated by Maria Boulding. The Works of Saint Augustine: A Translation for the 21st Century 1/1. Hyde Park, N.Y.: New City Press, 1997.

———. *Confessions*. Translated by J. G. Pilkington. In *A Select Library of the Nicene and Post-Nicene Fathers*, First Series, 1, edited by Philip Schaff. Buffalo, N.Y.: Christian Literature, 1887.

———. *De Civitate Dei*. Edited by B. Dombart and A. Kalb. CCSL 48. Turnhout: Brepols, 1955.

———. *Enarrationes in Psalmos CI–CL*. Edited by E. Dekkers and J. Fraipont. CCSL 40. Turnhout: Brepols, 1956.

———. *De Trinitate*. Edited by W. J. Mountain and F. Glorie. CCSL 50/50A. Turnhout: Brepols, 1968.

———. *Expositions of the Psalms* (73–98). Edited by John E. Rotelle. Translated by Maria Boulding. The Works of Saint Augustine: A Translation for the 21st Century 3/18. Hyde Park, N.Y.: New City Press, 2009.

———. *Expositions of the Psalms* (121–150). Edited by Boniface Ramsey. Translated by Maria Boulding. The Works of Saint Augustine: A Translation for the 21st Century 3/20. Hyde Park, N.Y.: New City Press, 2004.

———. *Homilies on the Gospel of John* (1–40). Edited by Allan D. Fitzgerald. Translated by Edmund Hill. The Works of Saint Augustine: A Translation for the 21st Century 3/12. Hyde Park, N.Y.: New City Press, 2009.

———. *Instructing Beginners in the Faith*. Translated by Raymond Canning. The Works of Saint Augustine: A Translation for the 21st Century 1/8. Hyde Park, N.Y.: New City Press, 2006.

———. *Lectures or Tractates on the Gospel According to St. John*. Translated by John Gibb and James Innes. In *A Select Library of the Nicene and Post-Nicene Fathers* 7, edited by Philip Schaff. New York: Christian Literature, 1888.

———. *Letters*, vol. 6 (1*–29*). Translated by Robert B. Eno. The Fathers of the Church 81. Washington, D.C.: Catholic University of America Press, 1989.

———. *Letters (Epistulae)* (156–210). Edited by Boniface Ramsey. Translated by Roland Teske. The Works of Saint Augustine: A Translation for the 21st Century 2/3. Hyde Park, N.Y.: New City Press, 2004.

———. *Newly Discovered Sermons*. Edited by John E. Rotelle. Translated by Edmund Hill. The Works of Saint Augustine: A Translation for the 21st Century 3/11. Brooklyn, N.Y.: New City Press, 1997.

———. *S. Aurelii Augustini Opera Omnia*. Edited by J.-P. Migne. PL 38. Paris: 1844.

———. *Sancti Aurelii Augustini In Iohannis Evangelium tractatus CXXIV*. Edited by Radbodus Willems. CCSL 36. Turnhout: Brepols, 1954.

———. "Sermons Inédits de Saint Augustin Préchs en 397 (5ème série)." Edited by François Dolbeau. *Revue Benedictine* 104, 1–2 (1994): 34–72.

———. *Sermons on the New Testament* (94A–147A). Edited by John E. Rotelle. Translated by Edmund Hill. The Works of Saint Augustine: A Translation for the 21st Century 3/4. Brooklyn, N.Y.: New City Press, 1992.

———. *Sermons on the Liturgical Seasons* (184–229Z). Edited by John E. Rotelle. Translated by Edmund Hill. The Works of Saint Augustine: A Translation for the 21st Century 3/6. Brooklyn, N.Y.: New City Press, 1993.

———. *Sermons on the Saints* (273–305A). Edited by John E. Rotelle. Translated by Edmund Hill. The Works of Saint Augustine: A Translation for the 21st Century 3/18. Hyde Park, N.Y.: New City Press, 1994.

———. *Teaching Christianity.* Translated by Edmund Hill. The Works of Saint Augustine: A Translation for the 21st Century 1/11. Hyde Park, N.Y.: New City Press, 1996.

———. *The Trinity.* 2nd ed. Translated by Edmund Hill. The Works of Saint Augustine: A Translation for the 21st Century 1/5. Brooklyn, N.Y.: New City Press, 1996.

Avery, Richard K., and Donald S. Marsh. *We Are the Church.* Carol Stream, Ill.: Hope, 1972.

Barrett-Fox, Rebecca. *God Hates: Westboro Baptist Church, American Nationalism, and the Religious Right.* Lawrence: University Press of Kansas, 2016.

Barth, Karl. *Dogmatics in Outline.* Translated by G. T. Thomson. New York: Harper & Row, 1959.

Bede. *The Commentary on the Seven Catholic Epistles of Bede the Venerable.* Translated by David Hurst. Cistercian Studies 82. Kalamazoo, Mich.: Cistercian Publications, 1985.

———. *De Orthographia.* Edited by Charles Williams Jones. In *Opera Didascalia*, edited by Charles Williams Jones, C. B. Kendall, M. H. King, and F. Lipp. CCSL 123A. Turnhout: Brepols, 1975.

———. *In Epistolas Septem Catholicas.* Edited by David Hurst. In *Opera Exegetica*, edited by M. L. W. Laistner and David Hurst. CCSL 121. Turnhout: Brepols, 1955.

Bedford, Nancy. "Theology, Violence, and White Spaces." In *Envisioning the Good Life*, edited by Matthew Croasmun, Zoran Grozdanov, and Ryan McAnnally-Linz. Eugene, Ore.: Cascade, 2017.

Bennett, Charles E. *New Latin Grammar.* Boston: Allyn and Bacon, 1918.

Berrien, Jenny, and Christopher Winship. "Should We Have Faith in the Churches? The Ten-Point Coalition's Effect on Boston's Youth Violence." In *Guns, Crime, and Punishment in America*, edited by Bernard E. Harcourt, 222–48. New York: New York University Press, 2003.

Blair, Peter Hunter. *The World of Bede.* London: Secker and Warburg, 1970.

Bloom, Matthew. *Flourishing in Ministry: How to Cultivate Clergy Wellbeing.* Lanham, Md.: Rowman & Littlefield, 2019.

Brown, Michelle P. "Bede's Life in Context." In DeGregorio, *Cambridge Companion to Bede*, 3–24.

Brown, Peter. *Augustine of Hippo: A Biography.* Rev. ed. Berkeley: University of California Press, 2000.

———. *Religion and Society in the Age of St. Augustine.* New York: Harper & Row, 1972.

Bullivant, Stephen. *Faith and Unbelief.* Mahwah, N.J.: Paulist Press, 2013.

———. *Salvation of Atheists and Catholic Dogmatic Theology*. New York: Oxford University Press, 2012.

Burns, J. Patout. "The Atmosphere of Election: Augustinianism as Common Sense." *Journal of Early Christian Studies* 2, no. 3 (1994): 325–39.

———. "Augustine on the Origin and Progress of Evil." *Journal of Religious Ethics* 16, no. 1 (1988): 9–27.

Burns, J. Patout, and Robin M. Jensen. *Christianity in Roman Africa: The Development of Its Practices and Beliefs*. Grand Rapids: Eerdmans, 2014.

Butler Bass, Diana. *Christianity after Religion: The End of Church and the Birth of a New Spiritual Awakening*. New York: HarperOne, 2012.

Camelot, Thomas. "*Credere Deo, Credere Deum, Credere in Deum*: Pour l'histoire d'une formule traditionnelle." *Revue des Sciences Philosophiques et Théologiques* 30, no. 1 (1941–1942): 149–55.

Cameron, Michael. *Christ Meets Me Everywhere: Augustine's Early Figurative Exegesis*. New York: Oxford University Press, 2012.

Cheng, Patrick S. *Radical Love: An Introduction to Queer Theology*. New York: Seabury, 2011.

Coakley, Sarah. *God, Sexuality, and the Self: An Essay "On the Trinity."* New York: Cambridge University Press, 2013.

———. *The New Asceticism: Sexuality, Gender and the Quest for God*. London: Bloomsbury, 2015.

Congar, Yves. "Reception as an Ecclesiological Reality." Translated by John Griffiths. In *Election and Consensus in the Church*, edited by G. Alberigo and A. Weiler. New York: Herder & Herder, 1972.

Crary, David. "More U.S. Churches Are Committing to Racism-Linked Reparations." Associated Press, December 13, 2020. https://apnews .com/article/race-and-ethnicity-new-york-slavery-minnesota-native -americans-4c7dbcae990bd11dee5a5710c63ece25.

Cross, J. E. "Bede's Influence at Home and Abroad: An Introduction." In *Beda Venerabilis: Historian, Monk and Northumbrian*, edited by L. A. J. R. Houwen and A. A. MacDonald, 17–29. Groningen: E. Forsten, 1996.

Darity, William A., Jr., and A. Kirsten Mullen. *From Here to Equality: Reparations for Black Americans in the Twenty-First Century*. Chapel Hill: University of North Carolina Press, 2020.

DeGregorio, Scott. "Bede and the Old Testament." In DeGregorio, *Cambridge Companion to Bede*, 127–41.

———, ed. *The Cambridge Companion to Bede*. Cambridge Companions to Literature. New York: Cambridge University Press, 2010.

DeTemple, Jill, and John Sarrouf. "Disruption, Dialogue, and Swerve: Reflective Structured Dialogue in Religious Studies Classrooms." *Teaching Theology and Religion* 20, no. 3 (2017): 283–92.

DeTemple, Jill, Eugene V. Gallagher, Kwok Pui Lan, and Thomas Pearson. "Reflective Structured Dialogue: A Conversation with 2018 American Academy of Religion Excellence in Teaching Award

Winner Jill DeTemple." *Teaching Theology and Religion* 22, no. 3 (2019): 223–34.

Eiesland, Nancy. *The Disabled God: Toward a Liberatory Theology of Disability*. Nashville: Abingdon, 1994.

Enos, Richard Leo, and Roger Thompson, eds. *The Rhetoric of St. Augustine of Hippo*: De Doctrina Christiana *and the Search for a Distinctly Christian Rhetoric*. Studies in Rhetoric and Religion. Waco: Baylor University Press, 2008.

Ericksen, Robert P. *Christian Complicity? Changing Views on German Churches and the Holocaust*. Joseph and Rebecca Meyerhoff Annual Lecture, November 8, 2007. Washington, D.C.: United States Holocaust Memorial Museum, 2009.

Fea, John. *Believe Me: The Evangelical Road to Donald Trump*. Grand Rapids: Eerdmans, 2018.

———. *Was America Founded as a Christian Nation? A Historical Introduction*. Louisville: Westminster John Knox, 2011.

Fiedrowicz, Michael. *Psalmus vox totius Christi: Studien zu Augustins "Enarrationes in Psalmos."* Freiburg: Herder, 1997.

Fitzgerald, Allan, and John C. Cavadini, eds. *Augustine through the Ages: An Encyclopedia*. Grand Rapids: Eerdmans, 1999.

Friberg, Timothy, Barbara Friberg, and Neva F. Miller. *Analytical Lexicon of the Greek New Testament*. Grand Rapids: Baker, 2000.

Friedman, Russell L. "The *Sentences* Commentary, 1250–1320 General Trends, the Impact of the Religious Orders, and the Test Case of Predestination." In *Mediaeval Commentaries on the Sentences of Peter Lombard*, vol. 1, *Current Research*, edited by G. R. Evans, 41–128. Leiden: Brill, 2002.

Gaither, Linda L. *To Receive a Text: Literary Reception Theory as a Key to Ecumenical Reception*. New York: Peter Lang, 1997.

Gower, Katherine, Llewellyn Cornelius, Raye Rawls, and Brandy B. Walker. "Reflective Structured Dialogue: A Qualitative Thematic Analysis." *Conflict Resolution Quarterly* 37, no. 3 (2020): 207–21.

Haerpfer, C., R. Inglehart, A. Moreno, C. Welzel, K. Kizilova, J. Diez-Medrano, M. Lagos, P. Norris, E. Ponarin, and B. Puranen et al., eds. World Values Survey: Round Seven—Country-Pooled Datafile. Madrid and Vienna: JD Systems Institute & WVSA Secretariat, 2020. http://www.worldvaluessurvey.org/WVSDocumentationWV7.jsp.

Hahn, Heather. "First Church in Africa Becomes Reconciling." United Methodist News Service, September 9, 2019. https://www.umnews.org/en/news/first-church-in-africa-becomes-reconciling.

Harding, Jennifer Riddle. "Reader Response Criticism and Stylistics." In *The Routledge Handbook of Stylistics*, edited by Michael Burke, 68–84. New York: Routledge, 2014.

Hermanson, Amy K., Drew M. Loewe, Kristi Schwertfeger Serrano, Lisa Michelle Thomas, and Sarah L. Yoder. "Saint Augustine and the Creation of a Distinctly Christian Rhetoric." In Enos and Thompson, *Rhetoric of St. Augustine of Hippo*, 1–10.

Hunter, David G. "Augustine on the Body." In *The Blackwell Companion to Augustine*, edited by Mark Vessey, 353–64. Oxford: Blackwell, 2012.

Kseniya, Melnikova, and Guslyakova Alla. "Linguistic Features of a Politically Correct English Language Discourse." *SHS Web of Conferences* 88 (2020). https://www.shs-conferences.org/articles/shsconf/abs/2020/16/shsconf_lltforum2020_01034/shsconf_lltforum2020_01034.html.

Inglehart, R., C. Haerpfer, A. Moreno, C. Welzel, K. Kizilova, J. Diez-Medrano, M. Lagos, P. Norris, E. Ponarin, and B. Puranen et al., eds. World Values Survey: Round Six—Country-Pooled Datafile. Madrid: JD Systems Institute, 2014. https://www.worldvaluessurvey.org/WVSDocumentationWV6.jsp. Madrid: JD Systems Institute.

Kishi, Katayoun. "Christians Faced Widespread Harassment in 2015, but Mostly in Christian-Majority Countries." Pew Research Center, June 9, 2017. http://www.pewresearch.org/fact-tank/2017/06/09/christians-faced-widespread-harassment-in-2015-but-mostly-in-christian-majority-countries/.

Koch, Anton. *A Handbook of Moral Theology*. Vol. 4, *Man's Duties to God*. Edited by Arthur Pruess. St. Louis: B. Herder, 1921.

Kretzmann, Norman. "Philosophy of Mind." In *The Cambridge Companion to Aquinas*, edited by Norman Kretzmann and Eleonore Stump, 128–59. Cambridge Companions to Philosophy. New York: Cambridge University Press, 1993.

La Bonnadiere, Anne-Marie. *Biblia Augustiniana*. Paris: Études Augustiniennes, 1965–1970.

———. *Saint Augustin et la Bible*. Paris: Beauchesne, 1986.

Laistner, M. L. W., and H. H. King. *A Hand-List of Bede Manuscripts*. Ithaca, N.Y.: Cornell University Press, 1943.

Lee, James K. *Augustine and the Mystery of the Church*. Minneapolis: Fortress, 2017.

Leinhard, Joseph. "Creed." In Fitzgerald and Cavadini, *Augustine through the Ages*, 254–55.

Lombard, Peter. *Magistri Petri Lombardi Parisiensis episcopi Sententiae in IV libris distinctae, Tomus II*. Grottaferrata: Editiones Collegii S. Bonaventurae ad Claras Aquas, 1981.

Luther, Martin. *Lectures on Romans*. Edited and translated by Wilhelm Pauck. Philadelphia: Westminster, 1977.

———. *Römervorlesung*. Martin Luthers Werke Kritische Gesamtausgabe 56. Weimar: Hermann Böhlaus Nachfolger, 1938.

Lutheran World Federation and the Pontifical Council for Promoting Christian Unity. *Joint Declaration on the Doctrine of Justification.* Grand Rapids: Eerdmans, 2000.

McClure, Barbara J. *Emotions: Problems and Promise for Human Flourishing.* Waco: Baylor University Press, 2019.

McCord Adams, Marilyn. "And Finally . . . Really Present Relationship!" *Expository Times* 126, no. 5 (2015): 260.

———. *Christ and Horrors: The Coherence of Christology.* New York: Cambridge University Press, 2006.

———. "Horrors in Theological Context." *Scottish Journal of Theology* 55, no. 4 (2002): 468–79.

———. "Truth and Reconciliation." In *Theologians in Their Own Words,* edited by Derek Nelson, Joshua M. Moritz, and Ted Peters, 15–33. Minneapolis: Fortress, 2013.

McFague, Sallie. *Blessed Are the Consumers: Climate Change and the Practice of Restraint.* Minneapolis: Fortress, 2013.

———. *The Body of God: An Ecological Theology.* Minneapolis: Fortress, 1993.

———. "Falling in Love with God and the World: Some Reflections on the Doctrine of God." *Ecumenical Review* 65, no. 1 (2013): 17–34.

———. *Life Abundant: Rethinking Theology for a Planet in Peril.* Minneapolis: Fortress, 2001.

———. *Models of God: Theology for an Ecological, Nuclear Age.* Philadelphia: Fortress, 1987.

McKeever, Paul. "Seventy-five Years of Moral Theology in America." In *The Historical Development of Fundamental Moral Theology in the United States,* edited by Charles E. Curran and Richard A. McCormick, 5–21. Readings in Moral Theology 11. Mahwah, N.J.: Paulist Press, 1999.

Meconi, David Vincent. *The One Christ: St. Augustine's Theology of Deification.* Washington, D.C.: Catholic University of America Press, 2013.

Miles, Margaret R. *Augustine on the Body.* Missoula, Mont.: Scholars Press, 1979.

Mitchell, Basil. *The Justification of Religious Belief.* Philosophy of Religion Series. New York: Seabury, 1974.

Mohrmann, Christine. "Credere in Deum: Sur l'interpretation theologique d'un fait de langue." In *Mélanges Joseph de Ghellinck, S.J.,* 277–85. Gembloux: J. Duculot, 1951.

———. "Le latin comun et le latin des Chretiens." *Vigiliae Christianae* 1, no. 1 (1947): 1–12.

Morwood, James, ed. *Oxford Latin Desk Dictionary.* New York: Oxford University Press, 2005.

Mounk, Yascha. "Americans Strongly Dislike PC Culture." *Atlantic*, October 10, 2018. https://www.theatlantic.com/ideas/archive/2018/10/large-majorities-dislike-political-correctness/572581/.

Murphy, Francesca Aran, Balázs M. Mezei, and Kenneth Oakes. *Illuminating Faith: An Invitation to Theology*. Illuminating Modernity. New York: Bloomsbury, 2015.

Murphy, James J. "The Debate about Augustine and a Distinctly Christian Rhetoric." In Enos and Thompson, *Rhetoric of St. Augustine of Hippo*, 205–18.

Murphy, Kate. *You're Not Listening: What You're Missing and Why It Matters*. New York: Celadon Books, 2020.

O'Donnell, James J. *Augustine: A New Biography*. New York: Harper Perennial, 2006.

———. "Bible." In Fitzgerald and Cavadini, *Augustine through the Ages*, 99–103.

Pelikan, Jaroslav. *The Christian Tradition: A History of the Development of Doctrine*. Vol. 1, *The Emergence of the Catholic Tradition (100–600)*. Chicago: University of Chicago Press, 1971.

Perschbacher, Wesley J., ed. *The New Analytical Greek Lexicon*. Peabody, Mass.: Hendrickson, 1990.

Ployd, Adam. *Augustine, the Trinity, and the Church: A Reading of the Anti-Donatist Sermons*. New York: Oxford University Press, 2015.

Pojman, Louis P. *Religious Belief and the Will*. London: Routledge & Kegan Paul, 1986.

Price, H. H. *Belief*. New York: Humanities Press, 1969.

Rosemann, Philipp W. *Peter Lombard*. New York: Oxford University Press, 2004.

Rusch, William G. *Ecumenical Reception: Its Challenge and Opportunity*. Grand Rapids: Eerdmans, 2007.

———. *The Trinitarian Controversy*. Philadelphia: Fortress, 1980.

Saarinen, Risto. "Salvation in the Lutheran-Orthodox Dialogue: A Comparative Perspective." *Pro Ecclesia* 5, no. 2 (1996): 202–13.

Sanders, E. P. *Paul: A Very Short Introduction*. New York: Oxford University Press, 1991.

Schiller, Isabella, Dorothea Weber, and Clemens Weidmann. "Sechs neue Augustinuspredigten: Teil 1 mit Edition dreier Sermones." *Wiener Studien* 121 (2008): 227–84.

Six-Means, Horace. "Saints and Teachers: Canons of Persons." In *Canonical Theism: A Proposal for Theology and the Church*, edited by William J. Abraham, Jason E. Vickers, and Natalie B. Van Kirk, 97–118. Grand Rapids: Eerdmans, 2008.

Smith, Lesley Janette. *The "Glossa Ordinaria": The Making of a Medieval Bible Commentary*. Leiden: Brill, 2009.

Smith, Wilfred Cantwell. *Faith and Belief*. Princeton, N.J.: Princeton University Press, 1979.

Soulen, R. Kendall. *The Divine Name(s) and the Holy Trinity*. Vol. 1, *Distinguishing the Voices*. Louisville: Westminster John Knox, 2011.

———. *The God of Israel and Christian Theology*. Minneapolis: Fortress, 1993.

Stookey, Lawrence Hull. *Baptism: Christ's Act in the Church*. Nashville: Abingdon, 1982.

———. *Eucharist: Christ's Feast with the Church*. Nashville: Abingdon, 1993.

Streed, Carl G., J. Seth Anderson, Chris Babits, and Michael A. Ferguson. "Changing Medical Practice, Not Patients—Putting an End to Conversion Therapy." *New England Journal of Medicine* 381, no. 6 (2019): 500–502.

Stump, Eleonore. *Aquinas*. London: Routledge, 2003.

Sugden, Edward H. *The Standard Sermons of John Wesley*. 2 vols. London: Epworth, 1921.

TeSelle, Eugene. "Faith." In Fitzgerald and Cavadini, *Augustine through the Ages*, 347–50.

Thomas Aquinas. *On Love and Charity: Readings from the Commentary on the Sentences of Peter Lombard*. Translated by Peter A. Kwasniewski, Thomas Bolin, OSB, and Joseph Bolin. Thomas Aquinas in Translation. Washington, D.C.: Catholic University of America Press, 2008.

———. *Scriptum super libros sententiarum magistri Petri Lombardi Episcopi Parisiensis*. 4 vols. Vols. 1–2. Edited by P. Mandonnet. Vols. 3–4. Edited by M. F. Moos. Paris: P. Lethielleux, 1929–1947.

———. *Summa Theologica. Complete English Edition*. 5 vols. Translated by The Fathers of the English Dominican Province. Westminster, Md.: Christian Classics, 1981.

Turman, Eboni Marshall. "Black Women's Wisdom." *Christian Century* 136, no. 6 (March 13, 2019): 30–31, 33–34.

United Methodist Church. "By Water and the Spirit: A United Methodist Understanding of Baptism." Baptism Study Committee Report. Nashville: United Methodist Board of Discipleship, 2016.

Volf, Miroslav. *Flourishing: Why We Need Religion in a Globalized World*. New Haven, Conn.: Yale University Press, 2015.

Von Nolcken, Christina. "Notes on Lollard Citation of John Wyclif's Writings." *The Journal of Theological Studies*, 39, no. 2 (1988): 411–37.

Wainwright, Geoffrey. *Methodists in Dialogue*. Nashville: Kingswood Books, 1995.

Ward, Benedicta, SLG. *The Venerable Bede*. Kalamazoo, Mich.: Cistercian Publications, 1998.

Wilhite, David E. *Ancient African Christianity: An Introduction to a Unique Context and Tradition*. New York: Routledge, 2017.

Williams, Delores S. "Black Women's Surrogacy Experience and the Christian Notion of Redemption." In *Cross Examinations: Readings on the Meaning of the Cross Today*, edited by Marit Trelstad, 19–32. Minneapolis: Fortress, 2006.

———. *Sisters in the Wilderness: The Challenge of Womanist God-Talk*. Maryknoll, N.Y.: Orbis Books, 1993.

Wolterstorff, Nicholas. *Justice: Rights and Wrongs*. Princeton, N.J.: Princeton University Press, 2008.

Wood, Sarah. *Conscience and the Composition of Piers Plowman*. New York: Oxford University Press, 2012.

World Council of Churches. *Baptism, Eucharist and Ministry*. Geneva: WCC Publications, 1982.

———. *Confessing the One Faith: An Ecumenical Explication of the Apostolic Faith as It Is Confessed in the Nicene-Constantinopolitan Creed (381)*. Geneva: WCC Publications, 1991.

INDEX